CHICAGO PUBLIC LIBRARY
VISUAL AND PERFORMING ARTS
400 S. STATE ST.

W9-COS-332

The Existential Joss Whedon

The Existential Joss Whedon

Evil and Human Freedom in
Buffy the Vampire Slayer,
Angel, Firefly and *Serenity*

J. MICHAEL RICHARDSON
and J. DOUGLAS RABB

CHICAGO PUBLIC LIBRARY
VISUAL AND PERFORMING ARTS
400 S. STATE ST.   60605

McFarland & Company, Inc., Publishers
Jefferson, North Carolina, and London

LIBRARY OF CONGRESS CATALOGUING-IN-PUBLICATION DATA

Richardson, J. Michael.
    The existential Joss Whedon : evil and human freedom in Buffy
the vampire slayer, Angel, Firefly and Serenity / J. Michael
Richardson and J. Douglas Rabb.
        p.   cm.
    Includes bibliographical references and index.

    ISBN-13: 978-0-7864-2781-9
    ISBN-10: 0-7864-2781-7
    (softcover : 50# alkaline paper) ∞

    1. Whedon, Joss, 1964– — Criticism and interpretation.
I. Rabb, J. Douglas.   II. Title.
PN1992.4.W49R53   2007
791.4302'33092 — dc22   2006034777
    [B]

British Library cataloguing data are available

©2007 J. Michael Richardson and J. Douglas Rabb. All rights reserved

*No part of this book may be reproduced or transmitted in any form
or by any means, electronic or mechanical, including photocopying
or recording, or by any information storage and retrieval system,
without permission in writing from the publisher.*

On the cover: Joss Whedon on the set of *Buffy the Vampire Slayer*,
1997 *(WB Television/Photofest)*

Manufactured in the United States of America

McFarland & Company, Inc., Publishers
    Box 611, Jefferson, North Carolina 28640
    www.mcfarlandpub.com

R0410368519

CHICAGO PUBLIC LIBRARY
VISUAL AND PERFORMING ARTS
400 S. STATE ST.   60605

Contents

CHICAGO PUBLIC LIBRARY
VISUAL AND PERFORMING ARTS
400 S. STATE ST.

Introduction

"Well, it sure ain't no philosophy class, now, is it?"
Buffy the Vampire Slayer 3.5, "Homecoming"

In this study we examine the major works of contemporary American television and screen writer Joss Whedon, including *Buffy the Vampire Slayer, Angel, Firefly,* and *Serenity.* We argue that these works are part of an existentialist tradition which stretches back from the French atheistic existentialist Jean-Paul Sartre (1905–1980), through the Danish Christian existentialist Søren Kierkegaard (1813–1855), to the Russian novelist and existentialist Fyodor Dostoevsky (1821–1881). Both Whedon and Dostoevsky, for example, seem preoccupied with the problem of evil and human freedom. Both argue that in each and every one of us "a demon lies hidden" (*The Brothers Karamazov,* 124). Whedon personifies these demons and has them literally wandering about and causing havoc in the fictional Southern California town of Sunnydale. He also introduces a "Slayer" to fight and subdue these personifications of evil: "In every generation there is a Chosen One. She alone will stand against the vampires, the demons, and the Forces of Darkness. She is the Slayer..." (*Buffy the Vampire Slayer,* opening). Given that the setting of *Buffy* is Southern California, it should not come as a great surprise that the Slayer turns out to be an athletic, fashion-conscious, blonde high school girl, called Buffy, who insists on referring to her sacred calling as "slayage" (the term can also denote the successful results of such activity). Dostoevsky, we contend, treats the subject only slightly more seriously. He does not personify our hidden demons in quite the same way. Rather, he refers to them as "the demon of rage, the demon of lustful heat at the screams of the tortured victim, the demon of lawlessness let off the chain, the demon of diseases that follow on vice" (124).

We thought that Whedon and Dostoevsky's somewhat similar treatments of evil and human freedom just might be worth some serious study,

1

particularly by scholars with our different but complementary academic training: a professor of philosophy and a professor of literature. As we got into this study, we suddenly found ourselves rewarded beyond our wildest expectations. During our research, we made a most extraordinary discovery. The popular philosophy of contemporary America and that of pre–Marxist Russia, represented in Dostoevsky's writings, are so strikingly similar that it is possible to argue that they are in actual fact one and the same. Pre–Marxist Russia and contemporary America actually share the same philosophy, the same values and the same world views.

We fully realize that some may dismiss our claims about contemporary American philosophy because they are based in part on pop culture, on Joss Whedon's popular television series, rather than on what goes on in the philosophy departments of American universities. For this reason, we should point out that the philosophy undeniably found in the novels and short stories of Fyodor Dostoevsky (arguably part of the popular culture of his day) was in striking opposition to the philosophy found in Russian universities of the time. In fact, from 1826 to 1889, philosophy instruction was either strictly forbidden or severely curtailed in Russian universities. For this reason, the Russian literature of the time is "more than usually concerned with recurrent philosophical and quasi-philosophical problems" (Kline, 258). In all his work Dostoevsky is particularly concerned with defending existential freedom and with rejecting the scientific determinism implicit in studies such as N. G. Chernyshevski's *The Anthropological Principle in Philosophy* (1860). We would certainly argue that the immense popularity of Dostoevsky's writings at the time strongly suggests that he was able to strike a chord with his readers, and that he was saying something important, providing philosophical nourishment unavailable to them in their universities. This we take as evidence that the philosophy contained in these popular writings may be regarded as *the* popular philosophy, or at the very least, as *a* popular philosophy of his Russian readers. In a similar way, we argue that the immense popularity of Joss Whedon's television series *Buffy the Vampire Slayer* as well as of the spinoff series *Angel* and the space westerns *Firefly* and *Serenity* suggests that Whedon, like Dostoevsky, has said something of importance to his generation, something not readily available in the educational establishment. This, we contend, is the popular philosophy of contemporary America. We will, of course, explain it in some detail as we develop our argument, looking briefly at other relevant writers and philosophers.

Despite the title of James South's book, *Buffy the Vampire Slayer and Philosophy*, comparatively little has been written explicitly about the philosophy embedded in the series. In fact, despite the subtitle of South's book, *Fear and Trembling in Sunnydale*, it contains not a word on either Kierkegaard or existentialism. Kierkegaard is perhaps best known for his book *Fear and Trembling*. There are, of course, a growing number of useful academic studies of Whedon's work. For example, a number of essays published in South's book and elsewhere look at *Buffy* through the eyes of a particular philosopher and seem to try to impose that philosophy on the Buffyverse, as the world of *Buffy* and *Angel* has come to be known. We argue, on the contrary, that the philosophy to be found there must be drawn from the text itself. In allowing the Buffyverse to speak for itself, we do make critical use of recent studies such as Gregory Stevenson's *Televised Morality: The Case of Buffy the Vampire Slayer*, Rhonda Wilcox's *Why Buffy Matters: The Art of "Buffy the Vampire Slayer,"* and Jana Riess's *What Would Buffy Do?: The Vampire Slayer as Spiritual Guide*, as well as numerous articles published in, for example, *Slayage: The Online International Journal of Buffy Studies*.

Compared to commentaries on the Whedonverse, very much more has been written about Sartre's and Dostoevsky's existential philosophies. Their work has, after all, been subjected to extensive critical scholarship — in Dostoevsky's case, for something like 125 years. Explaining their existentialism is made somewhat less difficult because we have had so many studies to draw upon. We would point out that readers need not have read either Sartre or Dostoevsky, or any of the many commentaries on their work, in order to follow our argument here. The entire existentialist tradition culminating in Jean-Paul Sartre and, we contend, Joss Whedon can be traced back to Dostoevsky. As a foundation for our study we present and discuss a reading of Dostoevsky's existentialism, by Russian philosopher Lev Shestov, which we argue has the interesting parallels to Joss Whedon's work mentioned above. We begin, therefore, by attempting to do for Whedon what Shestov has done for Dostoevsky.

It should also be noted at the outset that readers need not have seen, enjoyed, or even heard of the television series *Buffy the Vampire Slayer*, or Whedon's other works for that matter, in order to follow the argument in this book. Needless to say, true fans of this extremely successful seven-year television series (1997–2003) will find much here to confirm their commitment to the show. They already know, for example, that most people in Sunnydale do not believe in the existence of such things as vampires, demons and so forth, and tend to rationalize the abnormally high murder rate in Sunnydale and environs, providing more plausible, more "reasonable," explanations. We contend that this is in fact a metaphorical representation and implicit criticism of society's unwillingness to look at the root causes, or even to recognize the existence of, real suffering and evil.

The Slayer, of course, fights evil alone and in secrecy, usually governed and guided by what is called a Watchers' Council, which assigns an individual "Watcher" to train and mentor the Slayer. A few of Buffy's closest friends discover her secret identity and help her in her fight with evil, at times allowing her to succeed where she would obviously have failed on her own. The life of the Slayer is a hazardous one and often short. In the Whedon mythology, when one Slayer dies another is always chosen to take her place. Buffy breaks with the Slayer tradition by not working alone, by accepting help from her closest friends, who come to call themselves the Scooby Gang. Though previous Slayers have fought and died alone, Buffy is able to live more fully, fight longer, and, arguably, accomplish more than Slayers of the past by accepting more communitarian values. We will argue that the popular philosophy of contemporary America is captured in Whedon's postmodern mythology and that the vampires and demons and so forth which the Slayer must fight merely put a metaphorical face on the evil that most of us ignore but that some of us attempt to deal with every day of our lives.

We also examine in some detail Whedon's space westerns, *Firefly* and *Serenity*, arguing that the ideal communitarian existential love ethics we find in *Buffy* and *Angel*, though largely absent from *Firefly*, reappear near the end of the movie *Serenity*. We regard Whedon's entire corpus as a single moral argument which represents and examines ethical thinking as narrative and metaphor rather than as grounded in axioms, moral principles, or rules of behavior. Rules themselves, after all, require some form of justification. Rules cannot tell us what to do. At best, they help us draw a line which must not be crossed without some justification, a justification which, for obvious reasons, cannot itself be based on rules.

Whedon was a principal writer of the children's movie *Toy Story*. Though we do not discuss *Toy Story*, it is worth noting that it seems to treat rules in the same way as the rest of Whedon's narratives. The toys' fundamental rule, or principal principle, is not to move about and talk to each other in front of humans. However, the movie teaches that the toys must break even this basic rule in order to do the right thing. In all his works, Whedon is defending a radical existential ethics which goes well beyond anything Dostoevsky and Sartre envisaged. Nothing can tell you what to do — not rules, not reason, not society, not church, not even divine authority. And nothing relieves you of the responsibility for your choices. Such is the nature of existential freedom. Though this kind of existentialist ethics is often criticized as relativistic, Whedon's treatment of morality as metaphor avoids the charge of ethical relativism, because, as we will show, his moral metaphors themselves are grounded in Sartrean corporeal consciousness, in shared experiences as embodied beings.

Throughout our study, we refer to *Buffy the Vampire Slayer* episodes by season and episode number, giving the episode's title for at least the first reference to the episode (e.g., 1.1, "Welcome to the Hellmouth"). We likewise refer to *Angel* episodes by season number, episode number, and title, but preface them with the word *"Angel"* when necessary for clarity (e.g., *Angel* 1.8, "I Will Remember You"). For episodes of *Firefly* we use the DVD release, which includes a number of unaired episodes, and refer to the episodes by title.

Though we explain plot contexts and characters as required, we have made every effort not to introduce too many spoilers. We should warn those readers who have not yet viewed these series that the further you read the more you will learn about plot and character. We certainly hope that our study encourages such readers to watch the episodes or seek out the DVDs, as we do not attempt to deal with every episode, nor do we claim that ours is the only possible interpretation. Our basic claim is that our interpretation of the Whedonverse is consistent with, and can therefore be tested against, the narratives taken as a whole.

Chapter One

Russian Existentialism and Vampire Slayage: A Shestovian Key to the Power and Popularity of *Buffy the Vampire Slayer*

*"Freedom consists in the force and power
not to admit evil into the world"*
(Shestov, *Athens and Jerusalem*, 256)

In this study, we demonstrate that the existentialist tradition starting with the Russian existentialist Lev Shestov drawing, interestingly enough, on Dostoevsky's *Notes from Underground* provides a key to understanding Joss Whedon's exploration of the moral universe of modern America through Slayer and Vampire stories *Buffy* and *Angel,* as well as through the space westerns *Firefly* and *Serenity.* In this chapter we will concentrate on *Buffy the Vampire Slayer,* showing how our Shestovian key helps to explain not only Buffy's power to vanquish vampires, but also the immense popularity of the television series itself. We also show why we regard the Buffyverse as a mytho-narrative for our time which cannot be easily dismissed, as for example in the superficial analysis provided by Michael P. Levine and Steven Jay Schneider's "Feeling for Buffy: The Girl Next Door," which claims that "crucifixes, wooden stakes, and holy water are merely props and jokes that serve functional purposes in the forwarding of the serial narrative" (297).

As Claude Levi-Strauss has argued in *The Raw and the Cooked*, one way to penetrate to the heart of a culture is to examine the way it feeds itself. Since North Americans of Buffy's generation subsist on fast foods, as is explored, for example, in Morgan Spurlock's 2004 documentary film *Super Size Me* and Eric Schlosser's book *Fast Food Nation: The Dark Side of the All-American Meal*, we take seriously Episode 6.12, "Doublemeat Palace." We note in passing that this has not always been done. In fact, even ardent defenders of Season Six have actually dismissed this particular episode. For example, Christopher Wisniewski, in his online article, "The (Un)Bearable Darkness of Buffy," argues

> I need to make an admission here: I take *Buffy the Vampire Slayer* very seriously; there are times when it seems like the one thing pure and good in the cold dark world of network television. And so I take exception to the criticism leveled against Season Six. While it did suffer from a few poorly-timed stumbles that disrupted its flow (see "Doublemeat Palace," in which Buffy gets a job at a fast-food joint only to fall victim to a giant phallic monster growing out of an old woman's head), it also soared [to] dizzying heights [http://www.poppolitics.com/articles/2003-05-20-buffydark.shtml].

We not only take *Buffy the Vampire Slayer* very seriously, but also regard the "Doublemeat Palace" episode as central to understanding the existential import of the entire series. There, after having been fired, Buffy doesn't simply ask for her job back; rather she more perplexingly says, "I'd really like to not be fired anymore." We take this as a significant clue, not just linguistic perversity. Though it is logically impossible both to be fired and not fired at one and the same time, such difficulties do not faze the Slayer. We contend that she is knowingly asking for the logically impossible, which she often has within her grasp. Interestingly enough, Lorraine, the new manager of the Doublemeat Palace, ignoring the logical impossibility of the request, happily complies with it and, smiling, replies, "I think you can not be fired."

According to our Russian existentialist, Lev Shestov, if you have sufficient power and its creative freedom, the law of non-contradiction, sometimes called the law of contradiction [written in logical symbols as: $\sim(p \cdot \sim p)$, and read as "it is not the case that both p and not p"], can, with some difficulty, be overcome by choosing unreason over reason. So for example, although at time t_1 Buffy was definitely fired (for doing a "Soylent Green" in the restaurant), her new boss, Lorraine, at time t_2 (a later time), by uttering the words "I think you can not be fired" makes it that at time t_1 Buffy was never fired. The result is that at the same time she was both fired and not fired, a clear violation of the law of non-contradiction. This is, by the way, very much better than just getting your old job back! Vampire slayers often choose unreason when reason does not please them. This, of course, is a fundamental existential choice, because reason, for obvious reasons, cannot make it for you; it is an authentic leap of faith in the Kierkegaardian sense. Kierkegaard argued that the major decisions in our lives, things like getting married or even going away to university, for example, must be made by each of us individually on our own without help. Of course we can seek out advice from others and attempt to make a rational choice considering all the options, long term consequences and so forth. But Kierkegaard's point is that this is in reality of no help at all, and merely our way of attempting to avoid the anxiety, the extreme angst of existential choice, the fear of the unknown accompanying fateful decisions. Take marriage, for example. Rational guidance is hard to come by. Others can tell you about their own experiences, but no one can tell you what your particular experience will be like. The only way to know is to make the choice, to take the plunge as they say, and then it will be too late. Yet you and only you will be responsible for the consequences of your decision, no matter how disastrous. Such is the nature of existential angst.

Shestov argues that choosing to ignore the law of non-contradiction on some occasions is actually the rational, or at least the preferable, choice. Following Dostoevsky, he asks, "What do the laws of nature and of arithmetic matter to me when, for some reason or another, they do not please me?" (Shestov 1968a, 359; cf. Dostoevsky 1972, 23). In other words, why should we accept reason if unreason is, on occasion, say, more useful? Or, as Dostoevsky himself also puts it, "I agree that two and two make four is an excellent thing; but to give everything its due, two and two make five is also a very fine thing" (Dostoevsky 1972, 23). Shestov is fond of quoting the irrational babbling of Dostoevsky's underground man: "Let the whole world perish so long as I get my cup of tea" (Shestov 1975, 46; Dostoevsky 1972, 116). In *Buffy the Vampire Slayer* Episode 1.12 ("Prophecy Girl") Buffy's friend, Xander, during a pending apocalypse, comes up with a logically similar though not so self-serving utterance: on hearing "Once the Master gets free, the Hellmouth opens, the demons come to party, and everybody dies," Xander responds, "Uh, uh, I don't care. I'm sorry, I don't. Right now I gotta help Buffy." It is, of course, logically impossible to help Buffy, or to have a cup of tea, if the whole world is destroyed.

The *Angel* episode "I Will Remember You" (1.8) illustrates that at least The Oracles, emissaries of the Powers That Be, know they have the power and creative freedom to do the logically impossible. The episode also provides an answer to the classical criticism of Shestov's position. That criticism appears in James C. S. Wernham's *Two Russian Thinkers: Berdyaev and Shestov*. Wernham, like most professional philosophers, cannot even imagine the logically impossible. He can imagine doing the technologically impossible. It was once impossible to travel to the moon or to Mars, for example, but that is no longer impossible. Wernham argues that the logically impossible is not like this, it is not something that is just more difficult to do, it is an impossibility that can never be overcome. It cannot even be conceived; hence, he argues, if we show a position to involve a contradiction we have "refuted it and done so conclusively" (Wernham 1968, 109). But anyone who has seen the *Angel* episode "I Will Remember You" (1.8) has conceived the logically impossible and, in actual fact, imagined it in some detail. The Oracles, by swallowing the day that the ensouled vampire, Angel, is made human again by the blood of the Mohra demon, make it that this day, which has happened, has never happened. Angel alone carries the memory of the day and thus has the ability to slay the Mohra demon when it (re)turns up (again). The first scene of this episode and the last are almost identical: the Mohra demon comes crashing into Angel's office, interrupting his conversation with Buffy. In the first scene Angel and Buffy fight the demon and both find it impossible to kill. It flees back out the window. The rest of the episode involves hunting the Mohra demon, during which Angel is turned back into a human by contact with some of its life-giving blood, losing his vampire strength and thus leaving Buffy alone and helpless against the demon. In the last scene of the episode, the Mohra demon comes crashing through the window, but this time Angel kills it by smashing the jewel in the center of its face with a heavy clock. In answer to Buffy's query "That was unreal — how did you know how to kill it?" Angel replies, "It's a Mohra demon. I — I had a lot of time to catch up on my reading" (1.8). In actual fact, Angel both had and did not have "time to catch up on his reading," the Oracles swallowed the day, making it that the events with the Mohra demon never happened. However, if they had never happened, Angel would not have known how to slay it in the last scene.

Like Buffy and her friends, i.e., the Scooby Gang, Shestov seeks guidance through the interpretation of ancient texts and venerated sages. He notes, for example, "that there lived in the middle ages a certain Peter Damian who declared that it is possible for God to make that which has already been not to be." He adds significantly, "I think that it is not a bad idea to throw this stick into the wheels of philosophy's swift-moving chariot" (Shestov 1968b, 74–75). Shestov sees the story of the Fall recounted in Genesis as the loss of existential freedom through partaking of the fruits of the tree of knowledge (i.e., reason). This, Shestov argues, cuts us off from a God for whom all things are possible, cuts us off from an omnipotent God who can do the logically impossible. Shestov, a Russian Jew, converted to Christianity because he understood that in Christian redemption a truly omnipotent God would not be bound by the law of non-contradiction and hence could make it that he, Shestov, who had sinned, had never sinned. This is much better than a less powerful God's not holding your sins against you! But such an etiolated form of forgiveness would never have tempted Shestov to convert to Christianity. Citing Martin Luther, once regarded by some sects of Christianity as the antichrist (Quinn 1996, 7), Shestov argues that although the principle of non-contradiction is usually regarded as "the most unshakable of principles," Luther was more than willing to believe both this principle and the rational truth that follows from it, "what has been cannot not have been," to be subject to the will of God and thus "to retreat before the divine omnipotence" (Shestov 1968a, 359). According to Shestov, it is only if God is in complete control of reason, rather than being controlled by it (and thus not really omnipotent), that "one can destroy to the root the evil which entered the world along with sin" and thus regain "that freedom which is not the freedom of choosing between good and evil ... but that freedom to create the good as He who made man in His own image creates it (Shestov 1968a, 359).

The Genesis story of the Fall is essential for understanding Shestov, and hence, we would argue, the Buffyverse. But Shestov's interpretation of Genesis is unique because, as he rightly argues, the more standard interpretations have all been written by and for those of us who have already accepted the fruits of reason. Shestov argues that it was this original sin, accepting the fruits of reason, which permitted evil to enter the world and deprived us of a God for whom literally all things are possible. It also deprived us of true existential freedom. We are all constantly confronted with the existential choice between Athens (reason derived from the ancient Greek philosophers) and Jerusalem (the God of ancient Hebrew texts). "For the Greeks the fruits of the tree of knowledge were the source of philosophy for all time, and by this very fact brought men freedom. For the Bible, on the contrary, they were the beginning of enslavement and signified the fall of man" (Shestov 1968a, 325). In his major book, aptly titled, *Athens and Jerusalem,* Shestov confronts us with this primordial existential choice in the context of the story of the Fall, the temptation of Adam and Eve. Do we choose reason? Can we choose otherwise? "The Serpent, craftiest of the animals created by God" offers Eve the fruits of reason, the fruits of the Tree of Knowledge. When Eve at first refuses, saying that God had forbidden them the fruits of that particular tree "that they might not die," the Serpent tells her "You shall not die, but God knows that the day you eat of these fruits your eyes will be opened and you will be like God, knowing good and evil" (Shestov 1968a, 280). This Genesis story of the Fall is at the very root of Western Civilization. It raises the fundamental question: Will accepting the fruits of reason from the Tree of Knowledge make us like God or lead to our death? The Serpent tells us, "Your eyes will be opened." God proclaims, "You shall die." As Shestov puts it, "If God has spoken truly, knowledge leads to death; if the serpent has spoken truly, knowledge makes man like God. This was the question posed before the first man, and the one posed before us now" (Shestov 1968a, 280).

Since most of us have followed the Greeks and accepted the fruits of reason we are no longer free, but are bound by its necessary laws. According to Shestov this also means, whether we realize it or not, that deep down in our souls we must believe "it was not the serpent but God who had deceived man" (Shestov 1968a, 256). Nor can we truly understand God's advice to Adam: "As for the tree of knowledge of good and evil, you shall not eat, for on the day you eat thereof you shall surely die" (Shestov 1968a, 255). We refer to God's words here as "advice" advisedly. They do not constitute a commandment. Nor are they a threat of any kind. Rejecting these mundane interpretations, Shestov argues, "God's words do not mean that man will be punished for having disobeyed, but that knowledge hides in itself death" (Shestov 1968a, 279). Those of us who live solely by reason, those of us who seek knowledge, will find it impossible to accept that in God's warning, "A relationship is thus established between the fruits of the tree of knowledge and death" (Shestov 1968a, 279). Nor can we easily comprehend how accepting the laws of reason can somehow limit our freedom and bring evil into the world. Yet, this is precisely what Shestov is arguing. "Adam before the fall, participated in the divine omnipotence. It was only after the fall that he fell under the power of knowledge and at the same moment lost the most precious of God's gifts — freedom" (Shestov 1968a, 256). Because we have accepted the fruits of reason, we are today condemned to believe that our only freedom is merely the freedom to choose between good and evil. But Shestov argues, "God, the freest being, does not choose between good and evil. And the man whom He had created did not choose either, for there was nothing there to choose: evil did not exist in paradise" (Shestov 1968a, 256). Since there was no evil in paradise the freedom lost in the Fall could not have been the freedom to choose between good and evil. Shestov offers us a much more profound understanding of freedom, an understanding which goes far beyond anything that could be discovered by reason alone. According to Shestov, we find in the ancient Hebraic texts, "Freedom consists in the force and power not to admit evil into the world" (Shestov 1968a, 256).

Shestov credits Dostoevsky with the insight that reason and evil are inseparable. "The violence and frenzy of Dostoevsky's speech when he talks of the self-evident truths sufficiently shows that he felt the deep, indissoluble bond that exists ... between knowledge and the evil that rules the world" (Shestov 1968a, 331). If there were no evil in paradise and if evil now rules the world, from whence did this evil come? Perhaps a more telling question might be where and how did this evil enter the world. In the parlance of the Buffyverse, what was the first Hellmouth and how was it opened? The first Mouth of Hell was in actual fact the tree of knowledge, and it was and still is opened by ravenously devouring the fruits of reason, allowing evil to enter the world, thus making saviors of souls and slayers of vampires necessary to the present day. It is no coincidence that a Hellmouth is located under Sunnydale High School, a knowledge-dispensing institution. Joss Whedon, creator of this mythology, in discussing the first episode, notes, "Sunnydale High School is based on every high school in America because so many kids believe their school is built on a Hellmouth" (Whedon Season One DVD interview). He also explains where the idea of the Hellmouth came from, saying, "We needed a reason why every monster in ... history would come to Sunnydale and so the Hellmouth became sort of the central concept for us, because it allows us to get away with anything" (Whedon Season One DVD interview). We note in passing that if you reject the law of non-contradiction anything is possible. In logic, from contradictory premises any conclusion and its opposite may be derived. The main point here is that at the very root of knowledge lies the Hellmouth. In Season Seven, the non-demon nerd-villain Andrew confesses that he was tempted to open the Hellmouth, in the basement of the rebuilt high school, by the promise that he and his friends would be like gods. He imagines the three of them wearing togas dancing in a cliché version of the Elysian Fields singing, "We are as gods! We are as gods!" (7.16, "Storyteller"). This is certainly reminiscent of the serpent's promise, "You will be like God" (Genesis 3:5). The entire scene in fact looks not unlike a parody of the scene with the Oracles in *Angel* Episode 1.8, discussed above.

At the end of Seasons Three and Seven, we see Buffy and her friends taking the extreme measures of blowing up the entire high school or destroying all of Sunnydale in an effort to close the Hellmouth and thus prevent evil from entering the world. But of course there already is evil in the world, and much of *Buffy the Vampire Slayer* is concerned with fighting evil demons and stopping them from opening the Hellmouth (again).

Still, most of what comes out of the Hellmouth is simply the personification of evil. But vampires are very much more than this. That is why a Slayer is needed to deal with them. What then is the secret of Buffy's power over them? We have promised a Shestovian key to that power. In order to get at this key, it is necessary to answer briefly another obvious criticism of Shestov's position.

As we have seen, Shestov presents rational arguments for his position. But why should we accept his reasons if his conclusion is that we should choose unreason over reason? There seems to be something contradictory about presenting rational arguments to reject reason, not that a contradiction would faze Shestov. Shestov's answer to this kind of criticism would be to point out that he is not completely rejecting reason; rather, he is merely recommending that we not allow it, or anything else, to dominate us: "To discard logic as an instrument, a means or aid for acquiring knowledge, would be extravagant. Why should we?" He sees no reason to reject reason entirely. However "logic, as an aim in itself, or even as the *only* means to knowledge, is a different matter" (Shestov 1977, 55). The Greek philosophers, according to Shestov, fell into accepting this one-sided method of searching for knowledge, and he certainly rejects any such an approach, "even if he has against him all the authorities of thought — beginning with Aristotle" (Shestov 1977, 55).

Shestov would certainly agree with Dostoevsky, "two and two make four is an excellent thing." But he would also concur, "to give everything its due, two and two make five is also a very fine thing" (Dostoevsky 1972, 23). Shestov cannot accept the so-called eternal immutable truths of reason because to accept their necessity would be to admit that God too would be ruled and hence limited by the laws of logic. Shestov will not deny the omnipotence of God: "Immutability does not rule God, it serves Him, as do all the other truths which, insofar as they were created, possess only an executive power and only for so long as they are of some use" (Shestov 1968a, 345). In other words, Shestov does not deny or reject reason altogether. He uses it as a tool rather than falling victim to the necessity of its laws. Buffy, too, in her battle with evil uses reason when it suits her. In fact we argue that her wooden stake is an instantiation of the law of non-contradiction, a symbol of reason, a chip off the tree of knowledge, so to speak. It is a tool which she uses most effectively to confront the logical impossibility of vampires, the undead. They are both dead and not dead are they not? As Milly Williamson observes in *The Lure of the Vampire: Gender, Fiction and Fandom from Bram Stoker to Buffy*, "Being undead, the vampire signifies a lack of signification — it does not have meaning in the cold light of day. But the vampire presents us with a dilemma because it continues to exist despite a lack of meaning" (44). That the stake functions mythologically as the law of non-contradiction explains why a wooden stick is "more effective than it sounds" (4.12, "A New Man") and why vampires simply "go poof" when the point of their own logical absurdity is driven home. We are arguing that Buffy's secret weapon is the law of non-contradiction. Why do vampires succumb to a weapon made of wood? Some say that it invokes the wooden crucifix since vampires, as personifications of evil, also fear the sign of the cross. But we argue, rather, that it recalls the Tree of Knowledge, which, as is the case with all trees, is not merely made of wood but is in actual fact wood itself. The Tree of Knowledge is also symbolic of the law of non-contradiction. Thus, having the law of non-contradiction firmly in hand is the key to the Slayer's power.

Even Dracula himself succumbs briefly to Buffy's penetrating logic (5.1, "Buffy vs. Dracula"). He keeps coming back after being staked, which suggests, or perhaps confirms, that he is a much more sophisticated vampire than most. This is no mere gypsy trick; rather, it suggests that he has chosen a very Shestovian approach to logic. Like Buffy he seems to be able to choose when to accept the dictates of reason, and in particular, the law of non-contradiction. This should not really be surprising, as Shestov is much more widely read in places like Dracula's Romanian homeland than he is in North America. In fact some of the work on Shestov we published in English was so well received over there that it has since been translated into Romanian and is available on the Net (Rabb, 1983; *www.geocities.com/ aga_10/religiesiratiune.htm*). Whether or not Dracula is actually familiar with Shestov, we do have it on the authority of Elizabeth Kostova's *The Historian* that he was an avid reader and kept such an extensive library that he was in the habit of kidnapping and turning prominent historians to help him with his cataloguing and research.

Buffy's power and that of Dracula come from the same place, which, we contend, is the ability to choose either reason or unreason whenever it suits. Dracula knows this. When Buffy asks him, before she realizes who he is, "Do you understand what a Slayer is?" he replies knowingly, "Do You?" Later on, he responds to her assertion that she comes from a long line of good guys by saying, "But your power is rooted in darkness. You must feel it" (5.1). Both Buffy and Dracula have the dark freedom of existential choice. This kind of choice is truly existential, is disturbingly authentic, because reason cannot tell you how to choose or even when to choose. As Buffy herself says, "There's no mystical guidebook, no all-knowing council — human rules don't apply.... There's only me. I am the Law" (7.5, "Selfless").

The popularity of the series itself is found in the way it not only embodies existential choice, but also privileges ancient texts over the more sterile aspects of the high school curriculum at Sunnydale. The high school itself, being built on the Hellmouth, is in effect the Tree of Knowledge transplanted. Its motto engraved in Latin above the front door is translated as "Enter all ye who seek knowledge" (2.17, "Passion"). The language is an ironic echo of Dante's description of Hell, "Abandon hope all ye who enter here" (*Inferno* 3.9). Angelus obviously takes the school motto as an invitation to enter "Hell," while giggling the words, "What can I say? I'm a knowledge seeker" as he enters and kills Jenny Calendar, Giles's girlfriend, fellow teacher, and self-described techno-pagan (2.17). Throughout the first three seasons, the "high school seasons," the knowledge contained in the formal curriculum is seen by the students as largely irrelevant. The Scooby Gang retreats to Giles's library to consult his ancient tomes when it comes to important things like fighting evil. Even when Buffy's friend, Willow, and Jenny Calendar, for example, use their computer skills to aid in the battle against evil, the use of this kind of knowledge and technology is always subordinated to the guiding wisdom of ancient authors and texts. The Scooby Gang never use reason, the logos (logic), as "an aim in itself, or ... the only means to knowledge" (Shestov 1977, 55). Today's teens relate, also finding high school alienating and irrelevant because it doesn't tell you who you are, doesn't answer the existential questions teenagers feel the need to ask. The Buffy mythos fills this spiritual and intellectual void felt by many teens and adults too; as Joss Whedon points out, the damage done by institutionalization in high school is often irreparable. Indeed, a central myth of the Buffyverse is that high school is horrific. Whedon, referring to the popularity of the series among adults, notes that, "People out of high school respond because people never get over high school" (Whedon Season One DVD interview). We might mention in passing that institutional Christianity seems to preach that people never get over the first opening of the Hellmouth either. Whedon seems to see high school as perpetuating original sin. The Buffyverse is a reminder that high schools merely perpetuate the limiting logos introduced into the world by acceptance of the Tree of Knowledge and hence they continue the thralldom introduced by the original opening of the Hellmouth.

The Buffyverse encourages viewers to ask questions about the problem of evil in the world which they may find too difficult or painful to deal with in more direct ways. It raises questions about whether the magico-mythico religious or the logo-ratio secular is better equipped to deal with evil. Do we fight the axis of evil by sending in troops equipped with the latest in military technology or by reading and by understanding the ancient sacred texts of our enemies? As the episodes about the secret Government paramilitary operation called the Initiative clearly show, the logo-ratio technology used by the military leaves much to be desired. Again the problem is relying exclusively on the logos, ignoring completely the magico-mythico. Indeed, at the very root of the Initiative is evil in the persona of the significantly-named Adam, the robo-demon the Initiative builds ostensibly to fight evil. Adam turns out, instead, to be evil incarnate, a perfect combination of the evils of technology and demonhood which seem naturally to work well together. It takes the magical cooperation of the whole Scooby Gang to defeat it.

There are of course many reasons for the immense popularity of *Buffy the Vampire Slayer* (cf. Anderson, 2003; Bieszk, 2005; Bloustien, 2002; Buttsworth, 2003; Campbell and Campbell, 2001; Cover, 2004b; Fudge, 1999; Hastie 2005; Heinecken, 2004; Jarvis, 2001; Kaveny, 2003; Postrel, 2003). What we are exploring here is one of the deeper reasons the youth of America have almost unconsciously been drawn to the Buffyverse. It provides teens raised in secular homes with a much needed mythos which surreptitiously includes the Biblical story of the genesis of evil through partaking of the Tree of Knowledge. It encourages us to smell the rat in the logo-ratio secular, the rat in the *rati*onal (cf. 2.16, "Bewitched, Bothered, and Bewildered"). Youth raised in more fundamentalist religious households also find the Buffyverse strangely compelling, for it allows them to rebel against the narratives their parents find sacred without rejecting the values and mythos found in those texts. In other words, they too have the existential freedom both to rebel and not to rebel at one and the same time.

We will show in the following chapters that this ideal form of freedom, which is not even restricted by the law of non-contradiction, by reason itself, is explored throughout *Buffy the Vampire Slayer* and *Angel.* Its full ethical implications are brought out by contrasting it with the much more restrictive form of freedom portrayed in *Firefly* and most of *Serenity.*

Chapter Two

Moral Choice in
Buffy, Angel and *Firefly*:
Ethics in the Whedonverse

Attention has often been drawn to the martial arts in *Buffy*. After all, if demons, vampires and so forth are personifications of evil, then you need some form of disciplined martial arts if you are going to fight evil, as Buffy and the Scooby Gang seem intent on doing. However, until now it has not been noted that the martial arts in *Buffy* are also used to develop an important distinction between the moral discipline of the two Slayers, Faith and Buffy. For example in Episode 3.7 "Revelations," we see Gwendolyn Post, Faith's renegade Watcher, asking her if she would like to do some training. Faith's reply is significant. She says, "As in kicking and punching and stabbing?" Gwendolyn smiles and replies, "Yes, that's the idea," and Faith says, "I'm your girl." Earlier in this same episode, we see Giles, Buffy's Watcher, asking her if she would like "to do a spot of training." Interestingly enough, this fades immediately to Buffy and her vampire "boyfriend" Angel doing taiji together in Angel's mansion. This, as might be expected, ends in an embrace. Buffy pulls away in an exercise of extreme self-discipline. In the ensuing conversation, Angel asks, "What are we doing?" and Buffy replies, "Training" and then adds, apologetically, "and almost kissing."

Two important lessons can be drawn from this scene. First, that the slow, harmonious, meditative movements of taiji, an acknowledged internal martial art, serve as a foundation in training for the more vigorous fighting forms, an insight to which Faith and her Watcher are completely oblivious. Faith's "kicking, punching, stabbing" conception of training merely turns her into a fighting machine, not unlike the buffybot of Season Six. In fact to emphasize this, in an amusing scene in 6.1, "Bargaining Part One," we find Giles trying in vain to impart Eastern meditative philosophy, complete with the esoteric discipline of qigong, to an increasingly baffled buffybot. He even instructs this machine to concentrate on its breathing, pointlessly asking it to "think of the breath as chi [qi]. Air as a, a life source." Of course the only life source of the buffybot is a battery. We leave unexplained for the moment how Angel, a non-respiring vampire, can possibly do taiji and qigong, circulating the qi (usually considered the life force) throughout his body.

The second lesson embodied in this taiji scene with Angel is that the self-discipline Buffy shows here goes well beyond the martial arts, and is in fact a manifestation of the moral virtue at the root of moral choice itself as portrayed in the entire Whedonverse, as the worlds created by Joss Whedon have come to be called.

In Chapter One, we argued that moral choice in the Buffyverse is portrayed as a form of radical existential choice in which true "[f]reedom consists in the force and power not to admit evil into the world" (Shestov, *Athens and Jerusalem,* 256). This is symbolized by various attempts to close the Hellmouth or prevent it from being opened. Our grounds for using the concept of existential choice here come from the episode "Lovers Walk" (3.8), in which we find that a scene in which Buffy and her mother are discussing going away to university, ostensibly to meet boys more her own age, fades into a shot of Buffy's 250 year old boyfriend, Angel, reading Jean-Paul Sartre's *Nausea* in the original French.

Whedon, in the DVD commentary on the *Firefly* episode entitled "Objects in Space," claims that Sartre's *Nausea* is the most important book he has ever encountered and also admits that Sartre and Camus are the only two existentialist philosophers he has ever read. The *Buffy the Vampire Slayer* episode "Lovers Walk" (3.8) gives us a somewhat amusing example of Sartrean nihilistic existential choice, a choice so restricted as to seem almost meaningless, or at the very least pointless. Alfred Stern points out in his study *Sartre: His Philosophy and Existential Psychoanalysis,* "Sartre says that a slave in his chains [and who is destined to die in those chains] is as free as his master, adding: 'The life of the slave who revolts and dies in the course of the uprising is a free life'" (241). It might better be said that the master shares the same fearful freedom as his slave. According to Sartre, we define ourselves only through our choices, and we are responsible for the consequences of those choices no matter how disastrous they may be.

Sartre gained his insight into the meaning of existential choice through personal experience during the Nazi occupation of France during the early 1940s. There choice was often between being shot or collaboration with the enemy. Yet Sartre writes, "We were never more free than during the

German occupation" (Sartre 1947, 498). The full nature and import of existential choice becomes most apparent when one is face to face with death. This is an authentic choice because as Sartre says, "it could always have been expressed in concrete terms: 'Rather death than...'" (Sartre 1947, 499). This starkest of choices is exactly what confronts Willow and Xander when imprisoned by the vampire Spike, who wishes to compel Willow to use her developing Wiccan powers to perform a love spell to reunite him with his former sire and girlfriend, Drusilla. Xander wants to know what options face them in captivity. Willow's answer is an almost perfect parody of Sartrean atheistic existentialism: "Well, I figure either ... I refuse to do the spell and he kills us, or I do the spell and he kills us." Whedon ups Sartre's binary choice by letting Willow posit a third option: "He's so drunk he forgets about us, and we starve to death. That's sort of the best one" (3.8). The ironic tone here suggests an implicit critique of Sartrean nihilism. Willow and Xander are saved by their friends and thus their fate does not reflect any of the nihilistic options considered. Hence, they are not as isolated and alone as the Sartrean philosophy would have it. The world is both more complex and more communal than Sartre allows. In the Buffyverse, it sometimes seems as if Hell is everything but other people. This is in direct contrast to Sartre's famous claim, "Hell is — other people!" (*No Exit*, 45).

In fact, the kind of moral choices made by Buffy and the Scooby Gang seem considerably closer to a much more optimistic Christian existentialism than to the nihilism of Sartre's atheistic existentialism. Whedon actually admits, "the Christian mythos has a powerful fascination to me, and it bleeds into my storytelling" (cited in Anderson 2003, 213). We submit this bleeding of the Christian mythos is, quite literally, the salvation of the Buffyverse in that it saves it from Sartre's extreme nihilism. We might even say that Whedon inadvertently reinvents Christian existentialism, but for the fact that the philosophy of moral choice depicted in the Buffyverse is equally compatible with a Buddhist perspective, as is shown in Jana Riess's *What Would Buffy Do?: The Vampire Slayer as Spiritual Guide*. Gregory Stevenson notes in *Televised Morality: The Case of Buffy the Vampire Slayer*, "Joss Whedon is neither a devotee of neopaganism nor of Christianity, yet the worldview of *Buffy* reflects both" (61). Although we are arguing that Whedon, in effect, reinvents the kind of Christian existentialism found in Shestov and Dostoevsky, there is certainly no evidence of direct influence on Whedon from either Christian or Russian existentialism. However, when Shestov discovered the Christian existentialist Soren Kierkegaard rather late in his writing career, he found him most compatible. It is also true that Shestov had an indirect influence on Sartre through Sartre's teachers Husserl and Heidegger. We must of course emphasize that Sartre, like Whedon, is an avowed atheist.

Buffy is certainly faced with existential choice of the most fundamental nature. Right from the very first episode ("Welcome to the Hellmouth"), she is constantly having to choose to be the chosen one. This is an authentic existential choice. No one, not even Giles her Watcher, can make it for her. As Buffy herself says in the episode "Selfless," expressing a good deal of existential angst, "There's no mystical guidebook, no all-knowing council — human rules don't apply.... There's only me. I am the Law" (7.5). Buffy's claim here to be the law is very different from Faith's claim in "Consequences" (3.15) that as Slayers, "we don't need the law. We 'are' the law." As we will show in Chapter Three, Faith is merely fleeing, in Sartrean "bad faith," from the guilt of having mistakenly killed a human bystander. Buffy, on the other hand, has come to the realization that moral choice is ultimately the kind of choice that nothing, not even reason itself, can make for you, that you, and only you, are fully responsible for every choice you make. Further, as almost every episode in the entire series confirms, the wrong choice could have disastrous consequences, usually the end of the world, the final apocalypse. No wonder the angst of moral responsibility hangs heavy on every choice we make.

In the *Angel* episode "Epiphany" (2.16), we are treated to a major insight, at least on Angel's part, about the significance of moral choice. He has just found and revived his only friend on the police force, Kate, in her apartment after her suicide attempt. The attempt was made because she was fired from the police force (primarily for taking seriously Angel's mission to control the vampire and demon population of L. A.). During their ensuing conversation, Angel makes a very Sartrean observation to the effect that in a nihilistic world in which "nothing we do matters," in which there is no grand plan, "no big win," our everyday choices and actions can be seen as existentially significant, "all that matters is what we do. because that's all there is. What we do, now, today." Angel, admitting that he has had a kind of epiphany, concludes, "All I wanna do is help. I wanna help because I don't think people should suffer, as they do. Because, if there is no bigger meaning, then the smallest act of kindness is the greatest thing in the world" (2.16). This insight is perfectly consistent with a Sartrean atheistic existentialism; in fact, it is a fairly good encapsualization of Sartre's existentialism. If there is no God, "no grand plan," then the only meaning in life is the meaning we bring to it through our own decisions and actions. However, Kate, whom Angel has just saved from a suicide attempt, suggests that there is something more to life, that there may well be some higher power looking out for them. Thanking Angel for rescuing her, she says, "I'm very grateful. I never thought you'd come for me, but ... I got cut a huge break and I believe ... I don't know what I believe, but I have faith. I think maybe we're not alone in this" (2.16). When Angel asks her why she thinks so, she points out that she was unconscious when he broke into her apartment to rescue her, that she had never invited him in. Vampires, of course, cannot enter a home unless they are explicitly invited in. Angel's entry into Kate's home to rescue her is made even more significant by the fact that several episodes earlier Angel had to watch Kate's father be killed because Angel could not enter his home to rescue him. Where love is concerned, the Powers That Be seem willing to intervene. The Powers That Be, incidentally, are never fully defined or explained, and are sometimes irreverently referred to as the PTBs.

As we noted in the previous chapter, the *Angel* episode "I Will Remember You" (1.8) illustrates that at least The Powers That Be have the power and creative freedom to suspend the laws of the universe. By swallowing the day in which Angel is made human by the blood of a Mohra demon, Their Oracles make it that this day, which has happened, has never happened. Angel alone carries the memory of the day and thus has the ability to slay the Mohra demon when it turns up (again?). Suspending such laws is certainly something The Powers That Be are most reluctant to do. As the Oracle proclaims, "it is not to be undertaken lightly." They undertake this for Angel on this one occasion only because they have determined, "He is not a lower being" since, for love of Buffy, he was "willing to sacrifice every drop of human happiness and love he has ever known for another [person]." As we will see, this kind of self-sacrifice grounded in love is a common theme in *Buffy the Vampire Slayer*.

Moral choice in the Buffyverse, indeed in the entire Whedonverse, does not always emphasize such momentous self-sacrifice. It is, nevertheless, still existential choice. Nothing, not moral principles, not even reason itself, can make it for us. This is often illustrated in the negative. For example, when Anya, a reformed vengeance demon made human again, wants her boyfriend Xander to leave town with her in order to avoid fighting the mayor's ascension to a gigantic demon snake, he tells her he can't leave because he has friends on the line. Xander then comments critically on Anya's moral stance: "That humanity thing's still a work in progress, isn't it?" (3.21). In *Firefly*, the character Jayne seems to share Anya's moral perversity. For example, in the "Jaynestown" episode, when his former partner, Stitch, accuses Jayne of abandoning him to the enemy, Jayne replies,

"You'd'a done the same." To which Stitch offers the following moral retort, "Not ever! You protect the man you're with. You watch his back! Everybody knows that — 'cept the 'hero of Canton.'" We can see the beginning of moral development in Jayne when a local throws himself in front of Jayne to shield him from Stitch's shotgun blast. The local is killed. Jayne finds this kind of self-sacrifice for another person totally inexplicable, saying over and over, "Don't make no sense." Yet he also wonders, "Don't know why that eats at me so...." He seems not yet to understand why rational self-interest ought not to be a guide to action.

In the Whedonverse, rational self-interest is most certainly not the moral ideal. In fact, what makes us moral beings is not reason, but rather the ability to love and respect one another. We have already seen that it is love, not reason, which makes Angel more than "a lower being" in the eyes of the Powers That Be. Though Giles lets Buffy get away with far more than other Watchers would, the one time he is truly disappointed in her and actually makes her feel guilty is when, in the episode "Revelations" (3.7), she fails to tell him of Angel's return, after losing his soul and briefly reverting to the evil vampire, Angelus. Speaking sternly, Giles rebukes her, saying, "I won't remind you that the fate of the world often lies with the Slayer. What would be the point? Nor shall I remind you that you've jeopardized the lives of all that you hold dear by harboring a known murderer. But sadly, I must remind you that Angel tortured me ... for hours ... for pleasure. You should have told me he was alive. You didn't. You have no respect for me, or the job I perform." Again, this is a lesson in the negative. Buffy has failed to respect Giles not simply as her Watcher but, more importantly, as a person, and that is the source of her shame and guilt. Moral integrity, the integrity of the person, is of the utmost importance. Further, we are responsible through the choices we make for the kind of persons we become. Giles has drawn Buffy's attention to the unethical choice she has made in keeping Angel's return to herself.

Another illustration of the importance placed on personal integrity can be seen in the "Serenity" episode of *Firefly*. Mal, the ship's captain, displays his integrity by ensuring a wary new crew member that he won't kill him in his sleep by saying, "You don't know me, son. So let me explain this to you once: If I ever kill you, you'll be awake, you'll be facing me, and you'll be armed."

A principal difference between *Buffy the Vampire Slayer* and *Firefly* is that Buffy herself respects all human life, whereas Captain Malcolm Reynolds of the Firefly class spaceship Serenity tends to respect only innocent folk. If you come gunning for him, he is going to shoot back. It's a Space

Western after all. Still, Mal is a man of integrity. In the *Firefly* episode "The Train Job," when Mal and his crew discover that the shipment they were hired to heist turns out to be irreplaceable medicine needed by a frontier mining community, they deliver it there rather than to the villain who hired them. They do this at some considerable risk to themselves, as they have already learned that their employer has the reputation of torturing and killing anyone who crosses him, or for that matter even irritates him. We might mention in passing that stealing from the Alliance seems to be fair game, as Mal and his friends were on the losing side of a war with the Alliance, a totalitarian regime made up of China and the United States, judging from the Alliance version of the Stars and Stripes, as well as the fact that practically everybody speaks English with a smattering of Chinese.

Concerning Mal's moral integrity, having learned that many will die without the medicine he has stolen, Mal returns it to the village. In the process of returning the medicine, he is captured at gunpoint by some of the miners and their sheriff, whom he had met earlier while claiming merely to be looking for work in the mines. The following conversation between the Sheriff and Mal is significant. The Sheriff says to him, "You were truthful back in town. These are tough times. Hard to find yourself work. A man can get a job, he might not look too close at what that job is.... But a man learns all the details of a situation like ours, well then he has a choice." Mal's response tells us a lot about his integrity: "I don't believe he does."

This emphasizes something very important about the concept of moral choice. There are some choices we simply cannot permit ourselves to make. Although this may, on the face of it, seem to limit existential freedom, in the final analysis it actually enhances our freedom for, as we have noted at the beginning of this study, true "[f]reedom consists in the force and power not to admit evil into the world." This is illustrated most dramatically in Buffy and the Scooby Gang's sealing of the Hellmouth.

However, there are many less dramatic but equally informative illustrations of this important insight. As is often noted in the Buffyverse, we all have our own demons to slay. There is a sense in which each one of us is a potential Hellmouth, since, as Wolfram and Hart, the evil law firm in the *Angel* series, are only too aware, we are all capable of evil. But, it is also the case that we are all capable of love and respect as well. The choice is ours. We need not admit evil into the world. In this power lies true freedom. An excellent, if somewhat exaggerated, example of this is the case of Willow's werewolf boyfriend Oz. In "New Moon Rising" (4.19), when Oz recognizes that he must learn to control the wolf within him if he is ever to have a loving, not lethal, relationship with Willow, he goes off to Tibet "to the monks there to learn some meditation techniques. Very intense [he says]. All about keeping your inner cool" (4.19). When he returns, it appears that he has acquired the moral strength to control his inner wolf with the help of "some herbs and stuff. Some chanting. A couple of charms" (4.19). Mastering these kinds of Eastern, i.e. Tibetan, meditation techniques has given Oz the inner power of self-control. He can even wander about under a full moon without transforming into a werewolf. There are obvious parallels here with the Eastern disciplines of taiji and qigong, which as we have seen, Buffy and Giles use as a foundation for martial arts training. They all encourage inner discipline.

Unfortunately for Oz, not to mention Willow and her new friend and romantic partner, Tara, the self-discipline he acquires is not quite powerful enough to deal with the intense anger and jealously which overcome him when he learns of Willow's affection for Tara. Even in the throes of such extreme emotions, he still attempts to do the right thing. In an effort to save Tara, he tells her to run when he starts to lose control and realizes he can no longer keep the wolf from breaking out. Ultimately, he chooses to leave Sunnydale, since in Willow's presence he can never be sure that his Tibetan meditative techniques will be enough to control the evil beast within. Still, whether through Eastern meditation or painfully tearing himself from the company of the one he loves, Oz as an individual has, through inner resolve, acquired the force and power to prevent evil from entering the world. This, in less dramatic ways, is the existential choice open to all of us. It is no less painful, and no less difficult than the choices portrayed in the Whedonverse. Further, there is no guarantee that we can always save ourselves, much less the world. But then as Giles says as he and the Scooby Gang mystically fuse with Buffy in battle against Adam, the Initiative's evil robo-demon, "Just because this is never going to work is no reason to be negative" (4.21, "Primeval"). Such is the ethics of the Whedonverse and, like it or not, of real life as well.

It is our contention that the ideal of existential freedom depicted in the Buffyverse, though largely absent from *Firefly*, is achieved and endorsed at the end of the movie *Serenity*. In order to establish our thesis, it is necessary to begin with a much more detailed analysis of existential choice and the ideal of freedom found in *Buffy the Vampire Slayer* and *Angel*. We reserve full discussion of *Firefly* and the movie *Serenity* until the penultimate chapter.

Chapter Three

Buffy, Faith and Bad Faith: Choosing to Be the Chosen One

In this chapter and the next we compare the two slayers, Buffy and Faith, in terms of their existential freedom and moral character. But wait. How can there be *two* slayers when the Slayer is the chosen *one* and is meant to fight evil alone? As the opening of each of the early episodes forcefully reminds us, "In every generation there is a Chosen One. She alone will stand against the vampires, the demons, and the Forces of Darkness. She is the Slayer" (*Buffy the Vampire Slayer* opening). Well it turns out that in the Whedon mythology, when one Slayer dies another is chosen. In the finale to Season One (1.12, "Prophecy Girl"), the Season's Big Bad, the Master, succeeds in killing Buffy in accordance with an ancient prophecy, leaving her to drown in a pool of water. Fortunately, she is immediately found and revived by her friend Xander and thus was clinically dead only for a matter of moments (her boyfriend Angel, being a non-respiring vampire, was unable to give her the kiss of life). Thus the prophecy was both fulfilled and not fulfilled at one and the same time. This confuses even the evil Master. When Buffy shows up for their final confrontation, the Master can hardly believe she is still alive and, referring to the prophecy about the death of the Slayer, says in disbelief, "You were destined to die! It was written!" Buffy, true to character, replies, "What can I say? I flunked the written" (1.12, "Prophecy Girl"). The brief period of Buffy's technical death is sufficient to allow the activation of a successor Slayer by the name of Kendra. It is important to note that Buffy is not the "official" Slayer from this moment on. Kendra is killed at the end of Season Two and is in turn replaced by Faith. Buffy, however, while not being the official Slayer, still has Slayer power and, more importantly, chooses to use it for the good of humanity: in short, she behaves as though she were still *the* Slayer, not "merely" *a* slayer. Later, when Faith lies in a coma for eight months and afterwards is incarcerated for a number of years, the Watchers' Council likewise treats Buffy as though she were still *the* Slayer and thus under its command, though Buffy, as usual, chooses to follow only those "commands" she herself judges worthy. As we will see, she is not one to be ordered about. Unlike Faith, however, she does know where her duty lies.

It is useful to use the character of Kendra to facilitate our discussion of Buffy and Faith. In "Choosing Your Own Mother: Mother-Daughter Conflicts in *Buffy*," J.P. Williams has argued that from the perspective of the Watchers' Council, Kendra is the perfect Slayer, "solemn, respectful, and efficient ... possesses more information about slaying than Buffy ... [and] employs that knowledge exactly as her superiors instruct" (63). In fact, when Buffy discovers that Kendra has actually studied the Slayers' Handbook, Buffy's response is, "Handbook? What handbook? How come I don't have a handbook?" (2.10, "What's My Line, Part 2"). Giles reveals a lot about Buffy's character by telling her that the handbook "would be of no use in your case." As Williams notes, Buffy develops and utilizes experiential knowledge; on the other hand, Kendra, lacking field experience, has an essentially static approach to slaying entirely dependent upon knowledge derived from what others have told her or from what she has learned from print sources such as the Slayer's Handbook (Williams 63). One result of this difference is that Buffy is willing to question orders, whereas Kendra clearly is not. As Jana Riess argues in *What Would Buffy Do?: The Vampire Slayer as Spiritual Guide*, Kendra makes some progress under Buffy's guidance and begins to emerge from the restraints of her "by-the-book slaying," becoming educated rather than merely trained. Ultimately however, falling victim to the vampire Drusilla's hypnotic gaze, "Kendra is killed because," according to Jana Riess, "she has always obeyed without question and has not strengthened her mind and spirit by discovering her own unique path" (70). As Jessica Prata Miller confirms, "Kendra lacks moral autonomy not because she memorized the handbook and follows the rules, but because she does so unquestioningly" (46). Insofar as moral integrity is concerned, Kendra's moral authority is imposed from the outside, and is therefore not autonomous.

The character of Faith clearly exhibits the important ethical distinction between mere freedom and moral autonomy. If Kendra is hampered by following external discipline originating from the Watchers' Council, then Faith is handicapped by the total lack of any discipline whatsoever. Whereas Kendra has been trained to control and never show her emotions, Faith indulges and revels in hers at almost every opportunity. She enjoys the activity of slaying, happily admitting that it makes her "hungry and horny" (3.3, "Faith, Hope, and Trick"). When she first arrives in Sunnydale, Faith regales the Scooby Gang with stories of her previous slayage exploits, including wrestling alligators and nude slaying. Xander in particular is enthralled by her titillating tale of naked slayage, saying, "Wow. They should film that story and show it every Christmas" (3.3). Faith's lack of restraint may be refreshing at first, but it soon reveals its darker sides. Faith, after all, is the Slayer who goes bad.

Now, given that Joss Whedon is using the series to explore the concepts of "freedom" and "evil" in the context of changing moral values, and given that Whedon claims that Jean-Paul Sartre's book *Nausea* is the most important book he has ever read (DVD commentary on *Firefly* "Objects in Space"), it is surely more than mere coincidence that the Slayer who misuses her freedom and goes bad is called Faith, especially since Sartre is best known for using the concept of "Bad Faith" (*Mauvaise Foi*, *L'Être et le Néant*, 85ff) to analyze the flight from freedom by which he characterizes the human condition. At any rate, we find Sartre's notion of Bad Faith most useful in helping us get at what we believe the series is suggesting about freedom and evil, not just in the fictional town of Sunnydale, but in America today. Like most existentialist philosophers, going back at least as far as Dostoevsky (1821–1881), Sartre prefers to do philosophy by writing novels and short stories or plays rather than by producing abstract logical arguments. Existentialists claim that our actual existence is particular, concrete, unique and cannot really be captured in language, which tends to be abstract, general, universal and far too logical and linear to deal with the chaos of being human. Sartre has written a number of long philosophical essays as well, but these too are filled with concrete examples which bring out the emotional impact central to his position. This is a good thing, because Sartre can be rather obtuse in his purely philosophical exposition, as for example in *Being and Nothingness* when he describes the human condition, or the "being" of human being, as that "being which is what it is not and which is not what it is" (100). This is, in part, just a convoluted way of saying that we all have future plans and projects and that what we are depends entirely on what we choose to become through the choices that we make. But this implies a fearful freedom, since we really are nothing but what we choose to become in the future. This is in fact the "Nothing" in the title of Sartre's book *Being and Nothingness*. We are "nothing" apart from the free existential choices that we make and we are, further, entirely responsible for those choices and thus for whatever it is that we become. This is an awesome responsibility and is necessarily accompanied by extreme anxiety, or what is often called existential angst.

To avoid these very strong unpleasant emotions, we will do almost anything to conceal from ourselves the kind of existential freedom which Sartre claims human beings exercise in creating themselves through the choices that they make. It is this attempt to hide from our own freedom which Sartre calls living in Bad Faith. One example he gives in *Being and Nothingness* is that of a woman on a first date with a young man she has only recently met, or at least with whom she is not all that familiar. At one level, she knows only too well the man's sexually charged hopes for the evening, or at least for the relationship. However, as Sartre puts it, "she does not want to see possibilities of temporal development which his conduct presents" (96). He obviously finds her attractive and tells her so. She accepts the compliment as a mere objective description of the present moment, dismissing from her consciousness any future intentions on the part of her companion. She thinks of him as "sincere and respectful" in exactly the same way as say "the table is round or square, as the wall coloring is blue or gray" (97). The table and the wall are mere things in the present; they neither have nor can have any future intentions toward her. She would like to think of her companion in much the same way, as just another unthreatening object, but one which admires her, yes even desires her. Yet, as Sartre puts it, "the desire cruel and naked would humiliate and horrify her" (97). She therefore refuses to recognize the desire as a desire, thus refusing to recognize the fearful freedom of choice in either herself or her date. But, Sartre asks, what if he holds her hand? Now, surely, she must make a decision. To continue holding hands is, in a sense, to consent to flirt. But as Sartre puts it, "To withdraw it is to break the troubled and unstable harmony which gives the hour its charm" (97). The whole point of Bad Faith is to ignore our freedom of choice, essentially to pretend for as long as possible that a decision is not required, or even possible. One strategy here to accomplish this would be for her to leave her hand in his, but somehow not notice that it is there. At the same time she will speak of other things, her life, her plans and goals, and thus, indirectly, her freedom, herself as conscious subject. Sartre concludes, "during this time the divorce of the body from the soul is accomplished; the hand rests inert between the warm hands of her companion — neither consenting nor resisting — a thing" (97). But all of this of course is Bad Faith.

For Sartre there is no distinction between body and soul. Though we are not things, our only consciousness of the world is a bodily consciousness. We experience the world from the point of view of the body we are, and we exercise our freedom by moving bodily through the world and bodily moving objects in that world. Some of the objects we encounter may be obstacles to our plans and projects, and some we may force to function as means to accomplish our ends, a shovel for example to help us plant a garden or a body. We also encounter other people. Unlike mere physical objects, they too have freedom, plans and projects which may, Sartre would say must, conflict with our own. To reduce this conflict we do what we can, always in Bad Faith, to negate their freedom or to deny our own freedom. At some level, we also want to be recognized by these other persons, but recognized as free conscious beings, not the mere things or objects to which they, also in Bad Faith, would like to reduce us in order to preserve their own precious freedom. Sometimes, however, we welcome the flight from freedom under the Look of the Other, for without freedom comes relief from responsibility. Whatever we have done, no matter how reprehensible, if we believe we did not do it freely, then we can convince ourselves that we are not to blame. The denial of freedom is, thus, also the denial of responsibility.

All this will become clearer as we apply it to Faith, the Slayer who goes bad. We first meet her, as do Buffy and the Scooby Gang, at the Bronze, where she is dancing in very sexy attire, frantically and provocatively. Cordelia even remarks with her typical sarcasm, "Check out Slut-O-Rama and her Disco Dave." All eyes are upon this spectacle. Faith certainly knows how to capture attention. The Scoobies see her leave with someone they recognize as a vampire. Vampires often pick up meals (take out?) at the Bronze. Buffy and the Scoobies follow Faith outside to rescue her, only to find that there is "a new Slayer in town" who not only holds her own in fighting the vampire by herself, but also easily dispatches him with a stake she borrows from Buffy (3.3, "Faith, Hope, and Trick"). The scene then switches back to the interior of the Bronze with Faith the center of attention, bragging about her Slayer activities to the Scooby Gang. Buffy sits quietly by, unable to get a word in. She keeps trying, but is constantly cut off as Xander, totally enthralled, encourages Faith to tell them more, particularly about naked slayage. We think it might be revealing to ask, "Why does Faith so obviously want to be the center of attention? Is this just her, or is there a deeper meaning here?"

As we noted above, Sartre argues that we all naturally seek recognition from others. But it is actually more than mere recognition which we require from others. Indeed, Sartre would agree that it is others who in fact teach us who we are (Sartre 1972, 366). He goes on to argue that "the perception of my body is placed chronologically after the perception of the Other" (469–470). There are in fact many important descriptions of the self or person which require what Sartre would call "the Look" of the Other.

These descriptions have been characterized as "outside view predicates" by Phyllis Sutton Morris in her book *Sartre's Concept of a Person: An Analytic Approach*. Such predicates or descriptions are, she argues, "those which, when applied to ourselves, imply an 'outside view' in either a literal or figurative sense" (Morris 1976, 136). Examples of outside view predicates can be either positive or negative judgments, including such descriptors as "desirable," and "beautiful," or "ugly," and "embarrassed," for example. This explains why Sartre claims that the awareness of our own body is chronologically after we become aware of the Look of the Other. It is only by being a body that we can perceive the world, but we cannot perceive our own body in the way we perceive other objects, just as for example, the eye cannot see that it is seeing. We therefore require the Look of the Other for a more complete understanding of ourselves, even though the Other may try to restrict our existential freedom.

Faith's attention-getting behavior, we soon learn, is connected with the fact that her Watcher has been killed, and that she feels guilty about being unable to prevent it. She has actually fled to Sunnydale to escape an ancient vampire called Kakistos (from the Greek "the worst of the worst"), whom she and her Watcher were unable to defeat. This casts an entirely new light on Faith's bragging to the Scooby Gang about her slaying exploits. She is trying desperately to maintain (at least in their eyes) the image she has of herself as a Slayer. Slayers, it will be remembered, traditionally work alone, and as a result the Watchers' Council seems to have been developed as a way of controlling and directing the Slayer's power, containing it in effect, as well as providing support for the individual Slayer active in any given generation. Lacking the Look of her Watcher to reinforce her self-image as the Slayer, Faith seems to be desperately reaching out to the Scooby Gang (including Buffy and Giles) for such validation. She is in effect saying, "Look at me! See what a great Slayer I am!" This, of course, makes the concept of Slayer an outside view predicate for Faith.

"Slayer" is, arguably, an outside view predicate for Kendra as well. She is portrayed as completely under the control of the Watchers' Council, and constantly seeking their approbation. For example, we see her seeking Giles' approval by stressing how diligent she has been in her studies, ostentatiously referring to books, such as *Dramius* Volume 6, of which Buffy has never heard (2.10, "What's My Line," Part 2). Kendra has no real life outside the Slaying. Having learned to rely on the Look of her Watcher, Kendra, in fighting the clairvoyant vampire Drusilla, easily succumbs to Drusilla's hypnotic look and is killed by her. It is significant that Drusilla, in hypnotizing Kendra, says, "Look at me, Dearie.... Be ... in my eyes. Be

... in me" (2.21, "Becoming, Part 1"). Drusilla, in effect, possesses Kendra's freedom. We noted above that Jana Riess and Jessica Prata Miller argue that Kendra is killed because she obeyed her Watcher without question rather than discovering her own way. We would add that Kendra's death is the result of her passive acceptance of the role of Slayer in Bad Faith, in the manner that we have called an outside view predicate. She is thus controlled by the Look of the Other, the very Look she has in fact courted all her life.

Superficially, Faith's case looks different in that she is wild and freewheeling compared to the staid and mechanical Kendra. Nonetheless, Faith is every bit as much a slave to the Look. She does, however, try to control the attack on her freedom which the Look of the Other necessarily entails. As we have seen, she cultivates Xander's gaze in particular. Faith, however, very forcefully negates any hold Xander's Look might have on her freedom. She accomplishes this by actually taking Xander's freedom from him. Faith seduces him, or rather, has violent sex with him, obviously in complete control. It's poor Xander's first time. He's never been "up with people before." The scene ends with Xander's being pushed out of her motel room, holding his clothes in a bundle in front of him, as she slams the door saying, "That was great. I gotta shower" (3.13, "The Zeppo"). A short time later, when Xander unwisely returns to her motel room, Faith, kissing him roughly a number of times, ends up choking him, and, in fact, would probably have killed him, if he had not been rescued by Angel (3.15, "Consequences").

Faith's even more violent approach to Xander on the occasion of his second visit is not unexpected, since she has, in the intervening episode, "Bad Girls" (3.14), accidentally killed a human bystander while helping Buffy slay vampires. Faith, as usual fighting with enthusiastic abandon, is enjoying the battle so much that she is unable to pull back in time to avoid staking the bystander in spite of Buffy's warning, "FAITH, NO!" (3.14). It is important that Buffy, in spite of the heat of battle, is able to distinguish human from vampire. Buffy, unlike Faith, has not yet completely abandoned herself to the exciting violence of her calling. Faith enjoys it too much, and we are shown the consequences. Despite Faith's visceral response to the manslaughter, her own immediate and visible shock at what she has done, she goes into denial, tries to cover up the crime by disposing of the body, and attempts to convince herself that this killing doesn't really matter. She pretends that she "doesn't care," and contends that Slayers do so much good for humankind that, in the balance, the death of one innocent bystander hardly matters. Faith's attitude here is not unlike that of Raskolnikov in Dostoevsky's *Crime and Punishment,* a novel originally published in serial form in 1866 and therefore part of the popular culture of the time, just as *Buffy the Vampire Slayer* is today. Although Raskolnikov's act of killing his victim was premeditated murder, still he thinks such acts are justified given the big picture, providing that there is some benefit to humanity. In fact, before the murder, he had published an article arguing that some people are superior, and therefore they have justification for committing cold-blooded murder, even on a massive scale like Napoleon's or Caesar's, providing that a balance of good over evil results. He happily discusses his article with the police officer investigating the crime, pointing out that, in his view, the world is divided into two classes of people — the ordinary run of human beings who constitute the bulk of humanity, and a much smaller class of "extraordinary" people to whom the rules, laws, and restrictions that regulate the lives of ordinary persons do not rigidly apply. Though at this point he denies that he himself is a member of the "extraordinary" class, in that he does not want to admit to the crime, he does say to the police officer with whom he is debating, "I simply intimate that the 'extraordinary' man has the right ... I don't mean a formal, official right, but he has the right in himself, to permit his conscience to overstep ... certain obstacles, but only in the event that his ideas (which may sometimes be salutary for all mankind) require it for their fulfilment" (219–220).

Though Faith is unwilling to discuss her crime with the police, and in fact weights the body and disposes of it in the river in order to conceal the event, she does present Buffy with very similar arguments in order to justify her actions to her fellow Slayer. Faith first points out that she and Buffy are "extraordinary" in that they help people by being warriors built to kill. In response to Buffy's admonition that that fact does "*not* mean that we get to pass judgment on people like we're better than everybody else!," and have the right to kill human beings, Faith responds, "We *are* better!... That's right, better. People need us to survive" (3.15, "Consequences"). This clearly echoes Raskolnikov's line of argument, the principal difference between the two at this point being that Raskolnikov uses this type of cost-benefit analysis as a pretext for a crime prior to committing it, while Faith introduces the argument after the fact in order to justify the crime, especially to herself. When she then turns to a life of crime by working for the secretly demon Mayor Richard Wilkins III, this line of reasoning is no longer available to her. She has, after all, jettisoned the helping humanity part, which provided the argument with what little utilitarian plausibility it possessed, either for her or for Raskolnikov.

So why does Faith move from this one crime, which is largely acci-dental, and certainly not premeditated in any sense, to a very self-conscious career of crime, which includes the murder of human beings solely on the Mayor's orders? She does not even question these orders or assume that the crimes somehow contribute to the greater good of humankind. When, for example, one of her victims, an apparently harmless vulcanologist, asks "Why?" to Faith's informing him, "Boss wants you dead," she answers while stabbing him, "You know, I never thought to ask" (3.21, "Graduation Day Part 1"). The fact that Faith often and happily calls the Mayor "boss" should tell us something about a fairly fundamental change in her character. When we first meet her, she seems to be a self-motivated Slayer, even more autonomous than Buffy herself. Some commentators have even likened her to the characters played by Sylvester Stallone and Arnold Schwarzenegger (Jessica Prata Miller 47). So why all of a sudden, when she chooses to go evil, does she acquire a boss and lose her autonomy, becoming in effect merely a tool for his manipulation? It certainly looks as though she freely chooses to join the Mayor, walking into his office, informing him that she has dusted his assistant, the vampire Mr. Trick whom the Mayor had sent to kill her, and announcing, "I guess that means you have a job opening" (3.15, "Consequences"). We argue that this demonstrates that not all choices result in expanded freedom or autonomy, and that not all choices are as freely made as they appear to be. In Buffy's eyes, Faith is a criminal. Buffy tells Faith how badly she ought to feel, "Look, I know what you're feeling because I'm feeling it, too.... Dirty. Like something sick creeped inside you and you can't get it out. And you keep hoping that it was just some night-mare, but it wasn't" (3.15, "Consequences"). Buffy is obviously ashamed of what they have done. She herself is actually an accessory after the fact, since she didn't inform the police or even her Watcher Giles. We contend that such concepts as "criminal," "dirty" and "shame" are functioning here as what we have called outside view predicates. We are suggesting that Faith is driven to side with the Mayor by Buffy's Look, in the Sartrean sense of Look, as that which fixes and threatens to define you, limiting your free-dom. It is important to remember that Faith has fled to Sunnydale in search of approval, particularly that of her fellow Slayer, Buffy. She is now finding the exact opposite. Buffy looks upon her as dirty, shameful, a criminal. Having been labeled a criminal, Faith chooses to become the most impor-tant criminal in the Mayor's employ. Faith thus plays the role which Buffy, through her judgmental attitude, has, in effect, unwittingly chosen for her. This is a clear example of Sartre's notion of Bad Faith. Yes, we are argu-ing that Faith is living in Bad Faith (even before she goes bad).

Sartre, in his book *Saint Genet: Actor and Martyr*, argues that the writer Jean Genet led a life of crime due primarily to the fact that as a child he was accused of stealing. Sartre claims that Genet succumbed to the Look, to the outside view predicate "thief," and thus became what he already was in the eyes of others. This is a classic example of the Look. It ossifies the freedom of human beings, turning them into mere things, objects without plans or projects. In the employ of the Mayor, this would appear to be all that Faith can look forward to, being an object that serves to carry out the projects and plans of "the boss." She is no longer an autonomous subject with her own future firmly in hand. In this crucial respect, working for the Mayor is not all that different from working for the Watchers' Council. The Council's role is to control and direct the Slayer's power, and it chooses to do this largely by attempting to limit the Slayer's freedom, giving her orders and expecting them to be followed without question or examination. As we have noted above, Kendra is the ideal Slayer in the Council's view precisely because she is more than willing to regard her Watcher as "boss." At one point, while working with Buffy, Kendra suggests, "We can return to your Watcher for our orders" (2.10, "What's My Line? Part Two"). Of course, Buffy, as might be expected, speaks quite in character when she responds, "I don't take orders. I do things my way." Kendra is likewise every bit in character when she retorts, "No wonder you died" (2.10, "What's My Line? Part Two"). This retort turns out to be sadly ironic since, as we know, it is Kendra who dies because she cannot resist the objectifying Look of Drusilla.

Although Faith is also in flight from freedom, she does not suffer the same fate as Kendra. There is still a future open to her and thus the possibility of regaining her autonomy. Her flight from freedom is an attempt to avoid accepting responsibility for the death she has caused (that of the bystander), or that she was unable to prevent (that of her Watcher).

We are shown that Buffy, in very similar circumstances, immediately accepts responsibility for her actions. In Episode 2.11, she believes that she has killed a human being, Ted, who was dating her mother, Joyce. Buffy catches him in her bedroom reading her diary, and Ted violently slaps her when she attempts to retrieve it. She defends herself, hardly restraining her Slayer strength, which results in Ted's falling down the stairs. He is pronounced dead. Although her mother tells the police that Ted *fell* down the stairs, Buffy interrupts, admitting that she hit him. When the police learn that he attacked her in her bedroom, they do not arrest her, though they continue their investigation, interviewing teachers at Buffy's school, and so forth. Buffy obviously feels very guilty, telling the Scooby Gang that she really doesn't know whether it was an accident or the result of the fact that she did not like Ted's dating her mother. Xander asks her, "What was he? A-a demon? A giant bug? Some kind of dark god with the secrets of nouvelle cuisine? I mean, we are talking creature-feature here, right?" (2.11, "Ted"). None of the Scooby Gang believe that Buffy is capable of deliberately harming a human being. It is just not in her character, and they tell her so. But Buffy recognizes, "I'm the Slayer. I had no right to hit him like that." She really doesn't seem to know why she attacked him as she did. She obviously did not like his dating her mother, and wonders if she were jealous about his monopolizing her mother's attention. But he also threatened her, not just physically, but also psychologically, suggesting that he would tell her mother about the "nonsense" in her diary concerning vampires and slayers. At this point, her mother does not know that Buffy is the Vampire Slayer. In the typical postmodern self-mocking way for which the series has become famous, when Buffy demands the return of her diary, Ted responds, "Or what? You'll slay me? I'm real. I'm not some goblin you made up in your little diary. Psychiatrists have a word for something like this: delusional. So, from now on, you'll do what I say, when I say, or I show this to your mother, and you'll spend your best dating years behind the walls of a mental institution" (2.11). We later learn that before coming to Sunnydale, Buffy actually did spend a short time in a mental institution, until she chose to stop talking about vampires and her slayage activities (6.17, "Normal Again"). This, then, was even more of a threat than viewers of Season Two would realize. However, Buffy clearly cannot determine the real reason that she attacked Ted with the ferocity she did — her loathing of him, his physical and psychological threats, his intrusion into her privacy, his intrusion into her relationship with her mother, or even his winning of the affections of her friends Xander and Willow, using food to tempt the former and free computer software to allure the latter.

Interestingly enough, Sartre, in his play *Dirty Hands* (*Les Mains Sales*), explores the very issue of not knowing one's own motives for action. He suggests that this is something individuals are sometimes unable to determine on their own without the help of an outside observer. Sartre describes a member of the Resistance who has been ordered to commit a political assassination. Interestingly enough, his code name is "Raskolnikov." He gets a job as the intended victim's private secretary and moves both himself and his wife into the victim's home in order to have access to him. However, he finds that he cannot bring himself to kill the intended victim until he finds him embracing and kissing his wife. Unfortunately, our hero, being a Sartrean hero, is unable to say whether this was a political assassination or a crime of passion, even though his life depends upon it. Buffy seems to be faced with exactly the same kind of dilemma. It is clear, however, that she does feel remorse and tremendous guilt, and, unlike Faith, is certainly ready to take responsibility for her actions. This suggests that Buffy is both more autonomous and of better moral character than her fellow Slayer. We can also see that she was speaking from experience when she told Faith, "I know what you're feeling.... Dirty. Like something sick creeped inside you and you can't get it out" (3.15, "Consequences").

Actually, it transpires that Ted was in reality a murderous robot who, after reactivating himself in the morgue, tells Buffy's mother that he was clinically dead for only a few moments and had lain unconscious in the morgue. Meanwhile, the Scoobies have found the bodies of Ted's four former wives in his home, and Buffy is able to save her mother from becoming number five. This is a comedy-horror-drama after all. Still, Buffy, unlike Faith, does not have to learn how to live with the guilt of killing a human being. Angel, the 250-year-old vampire with a soul, gives Faith a chilling description of living with this kind of guilt: "I won't lie to you and tell you that it'll be easy, because it won't be. Just because you've decided to change doesn't mean that the world is ready for you to. The truth is no matter how much you suffer, no matter how many good deeds you do to try to make up for the past, you may never balance out the cosmic scale. The only thing I can promise you is that you'll probably be haunted, and maybe for the rest of your life" (*Angel* 1.19, "Sanctuary").

However, it takes Faith some time to discover that she actually does want to change, that she needs to acknowledge the deeply buried guilt which at best she experiences only semi-consciously. In "Sanctuary," Angel reminds her that going into the darkness of evil was her own choice: "That ... was your choice.... You thought that you could just touch it. That you'd be okay. Five by five, right, Faith? But it swallowed you whole. So tell me — how did you like it?" In the previous episode (*Angel* 1.18, "Five by Five"), we are reminded that Angel knows first-hand about such guilt. We see a number of flashbacks of Angel without his soul, as Angelus, one of the most vicious and murderous vampires in history. This is the episode in which Faith flees Sunnydale for Los Angeles, and after a brief but vigorous crime spree, has a battle with Angel during which both she and the audience learn that she is not trying to kill Angel, but rather she is desperately attempting to get Angel to kill her, because she can no longer live with the pain and anguish of her now fully-conscious guilt. Faith has always felt this guilt on some level since staking the bystander. We see her bending over the body of her unintended victim and touching the wound with her hand, which she pulls away in obvious horror. Shortly after, we see her in her motel room obsessively scrubbing at the blood on her shirt in a fashion that cannot but bring to mind Lady Macbeth's equally futile attempt to wash away guilt by washing away its physical signs (3.14, "Bad Girls"). We note in passing that Joss Whedon and his crew are famous for reading Shakespeare aloud for recreation. Buffy arrives at the motel while Faith is doing her Lady Macbeth, and in the ensuing discussion, reminds Faith, "Faith, you can shut off all the emotions that you want. But eventually, they're gonna find a body." Of course, Buffy is referring to the authorities' finding the victim's body, which Faith admits she has already disposed of. However, the grammar of the sentence suggests literally that it is the emotions that will eventually find a body to wrack with guilt and possibly even illness. Faith's body is the likely candidate. This is quite consistent with Sartre's analysis of the emotions. In *The Emotions: Outline of a Theory*, Sartre argues that our body deals with such emotions as terror, or horror, for example, by either fainting, screaming, or running away, anything that physically, yet magically, blocks the horror that terrifies us. Of course we know rationally that fainting, or screaming, or running away will not really change the actual situation; but then, the emotions are not rational. Sartre argues that the emotions work at the level of the magical, which, we would point out, fits rather well with the Buffyverse.

As we have seen, Faith's way of running away is to leave her friends, Buffy and the Scooby Gang, by joining up with the Mayor and helping him open the Hellmouth through his ascension into a higher being as a giant demon serpent. The Mayor, of course, helps Faith bury her guilt by giving her positive reinforcement for carrying out his orders, which, as we have seen, include further killings, actual premeditated murders. The Mayor's positive reinforcement includes various gifts. Some are employment related, like a dagger that especially gratifies Faith. "This is a thing of beauty, boss" she says as she caresses, licks, and sniffs it (3.19, "Choices"). Others are more domestic items such as an innocent country-girl style of dress, very different from the provocative style Faith generally favors; an apartment; a video game system; informal lessons in etiquette; and so forth. In short, he treats her not only as a favorite employee, but also as a daughter. He tells her, in fact, that "no father could be prouder" after she has killed the vulcanologist for him (3.21, "Graduation Day, Part One"). Paternal approbation via the approving Look of a father figure is even more valuable to someone like Faith than a mere employer's approval. It gives her her first true sense of belonging to something like a family. The Mayor and Faith have become the evil equivalent of the Giles-Buffy relationship. We note, for example, that Quentin Travers, the head of the Watchers' Council, says when firing Giles as Buffy's official Watcher, "Your affection for your charge has rendered you incapable of clear and impartial judgment. You have a father's love for the child, and that is useless to the cause" (3.12, "Helpless"). It is perhaps more than a little ironic that Quentin Travers considers normal enough human emotions to be damaging to the cause of good, since it is those very normal human emotions that prove to be the undoing of the demonic Mayor. In effect, he is defeated in large part because Buffy is able to exploit his paternal affection for Faith. In the events leading up to the climactic battle in 3.22, "Graduation Day, Part Two," Buffy has put Faith in a coma by stabbing her with the very dagger that Faith had gratefully received from the Mayor. In order to lead the Mayor, now ascended to a gigantic serpent demon, towards the cache of explosives she and the Scooby Gang have hidden in the high school, Buffy taunts him with the dagger, reminding him of what she did to Faith with it: "You remember this? I took it from Faith. Stuck it in her gut. Just slid in her like she was butter" (3.22). The Mayor/serpent pursues Buffy through the hallways until he is right where he needs to be in order to be blown to bits and buried in the sealing of the Hellmouth by the blast that destroys the entire school. What a fitting climax to any high school graduation! This is a great example of how the show works on so many levels.

From a Sartrean perspective, the dagger and Buffy's stabbing Faith with it turn out to be even more important. The dagger is Faith's possession. As we have seen, upon receiving it, she admires it almost erotically. Sartre would say that she possesses it in the sense of putting her spirit into it. It is as though the dagger thus becomes a part of her, or rather that she has become the dagger. It is the symbol of her warrior nature but also a mere physical object with no freedom to choose projects and plans for the future as humans do. This is one way in which Faith can deny her freedom and thus responsibility for what she has done. She is nothing but a weapon to be wielded by the freedom of the Mayor. She is merely the instrument of the Mayor's will, as Dostoevsky might put it. "*You* murdered him; you are the real murderer, I was only your instrument, your faithful servant" (*The Brothers Karamazov*, 330). Faith herself has no more responsibility than the dagger itself would have. *Daggers* don't kill people, people do. Of course, she is lying to herself in Bad Faith. Daggers don't kill people, *people* do.

Sartre points out that it is in actual fact impossible to lie to yourself, since to lie is to conceal the truth, and in order to conceal the truth, you must know what it is. Some might want to say, with Freud, that a person in Faith's position knows the truth, or feels her guilt, "unconsciously." Interestingly enough, a Freudian interpretation of Dostoevsky's *Crime and Punishment* leads to a reading of that text as a narrative not so much about crime and punishment as about "the internal discord in Raskolnikov's soul" which ultimately forces him to confess to his crime. As the classic 1935 study, "The Problem of Guilt in Dostoevsky's Fiction," by Russian-born scholar A. Bem argues, "The crime ... does not penetrate Raskolnikov's soul and conscious mind, but conceals itself in his subconscious as a potential force of his conscience" (626). Sartre, however, rejects the Freudian solution to the puzzle of lying to yourself, because it involves appealing to this very notion of the subconscious or unconscious mind. Sartre argues in effect that introducing the concept of the unconscious is just cheating, inventing two persons where there is, in actual fact, only one: "I must know the truth very exactly *in order* to conceal it ... and this not at two different moments ... but in the unitary structure of a single project" (*Being and Nothingness*, 89). Instead of saying that Faith, or Raskolnikov, for example, feel their guilt "unconsciously," Sartre would say that they are "pre-reflexively" conscious of it. We become reflexively conscious of ourselves only after we encounter the Look of the Other, when we begin to see ourselves as others see us, and thus apply outside view predicates to ourselves. This is, certainly, one of the meanings of being self-conscious, embarrassed in front of others. Sartre uses the concept of reflexive consciousness quite literally. The single consciousness turns back upon itself and thus becomes conscious of its very consciousness. The term "reflexion" means, quite literally, "to bend back" as, for example, the word "return" means "to turn back." The word "flexible" means "the ability to bend." So "reflexion" literally means "to bend back."

According to Sartre, it is the Look of the Other that forces our consciousness to bend back upon itself, as it attempts to look out upon the world. We have already seen that Faith was fleeing from Buffy's judgmental Look, not wanting to accept responsibility for her guilt. Buffy's Look becomes quite literal when she stabs Faith with the dagger Faith regards as her possession, as the objectification of herself. We regard this moment as the beginning of Faith's reflexive consciousness of her own guilt, her self as object (the dagger) turning back upon itself (quite literally Faith's body). Faith keeps taunting Buffy by claiming that if Buffy kills her, she becomes her, because Buffy would then have deliberately killed a human being (3.17, "Enemies"). When Buffy finally stabs Faith in battle, Faith looks at Buffy and says, "You killed me" (3.21, "Graduation Day, Part One"). This, we contend, is Faith's first recognition (since the accidental staking of a human bystander) that killing a human being is a tremendous crime, and that she has committed it. Buffy has, in a sense, possessed Faith by taking her dagger since the dagger was Faith's possession.

It is important to understand the two different, but related, senses in which Faith herself possesses the dagger and is possessed by it. Certainly she owns it; it is the object of her possession. This is simply a legal property right. The more telling sense of possession is the one in which her spirit, as it were, possesses the object. Sartre gives a number of examples of such possession. A haunted house, for instance, is possessed by the ghost of a former owner or inhabitant, "To say that a house is haunted means that neither money nor effort will efface the metaphysical absolute fact of *its possession* by a former occupant" (*Being and Nothingness* 750).

We have an example of this in the Buffyverse when the character Cordelia Chase moves from *Buffy the Vampire Slayer* to the *Angel* series (when Cordy moves from Sunnydale to Los Angeles). In Los Angeles, she discovers it is very difficult to find a decent apartment she can afford. When she is finally shown a charming old apartment in her price range that is actually vacant, she is delighted and moves in immediately. She soon discovers why such a great apartment has been vacant. It turns out to be haunted by a ghost called Dennis, who has frightened off all previous tenants. Cordelia is not about to let a little thing like phantom Dennis deprive her of an otherwise perfect apartment. As she lies in bed on her first night in the apartment, the glass of water on her bedside table suddenly begins to boil and the bed itself levitates. Her response is, "I just knew this was to good to be true. I just knew it! I'm from Sunnydale, you're not scaring me, you know" (*Angel* 1.5, "Room With A View"). She eventually develops a very cordial relationship with phantom Dennis, as he opens drawers, helps her find things, etc. It turns out that Dennis and his insane mother lived in this apartment many years ago, and that his overly possessive mother had walled him up in an alcove of the apartment, where Cordelia eventually discovers his body during renovations. He is, it seems, very much possessed by the apartment.

The whole notion of objects possessing spirits is more widely believed than one would think in a rational world. Sartre points to the fact that many people are willing to pay a small fortune to buy relics or any objects owned by famous or historical people. The object itself may be worthless, but we somehow think that by buying that object we are possessing something of the previous owner. In a somewhat magical sense, we are possessing the previous owner, actually becoming that famous person to some extent. As Sartre argues, "To possess is to be united with the object possessed in the form of appropriation; to wish to possess is to wish to be united to an object in this relation" (*Being and Nothingness* 751). Sometimes, even just imitating the attributes (i.e., objects, clothes, habits, etc.) of a celebrity will suffice — look, for instance, at the world of Elvis impersonators, as well as the crowds of pilgrims who visit the "shrine" at Graceland every year, many in costume or driving pink cadillacs. For Sartre, it is the possession of another person which is of paramount importance, because the Look of the Other is a form of possessing: "By virtue of consciousness the Other is for me simultaneously the one who has stolen my being from me and the one who causes 'there to be' a being which is my being" (*Being and Nothingness* 475). Buffy, in taking Faith's dagger, a dagger, functioning like a relic, which is possessed by Faith's spirit, is in effect taking Faith herself, possessing Faith. She then makes Faith conscious of herself, and reflexively conscious of her concealed guilt and remorse, by returning the dagger to her in the most forceful way possible, by stabbing her, making it part of her, thus revealing to her the gut-wrenching guilt from which she has been fleeing. The dagger, then, is a symbol of Faith's guilt as well as the objectification of Faith herself in her attempt to hide from that very guilt. The dagger thus functions, in part, like Macbeth's spectral dagger, which, he says, appears before him, "its handle towards my hand." Faith's dagger is rather more revealing, since hers is more than simply a "dagger of the mind" (Shakespeare, *Macbeth* 2.1., 34, 38). And, unfortunately for Faith, the pointy end abruptly moves in her direction. Although she exclaims to Buffy, "You killed me," as the knife slips into her body "like she was butter," she does not in fact die. We see her wounded body falling from her upper-floor apartment and landing in the back of a passing truck, which continues on its way.

We next see the now comatose Faith lying in a hospital bed where she remains for eight months until her awakening in Episode 4.15, after a series of dreams in which Buffy both stalks Faith and stabs the Mayor with Faith's dagger. Thus Buffy's Sartrean Look, and hence Faith's growing consciousness of guilt, pursue Faith relentlessly, even in her dreams. When she awakens, Faith continues to try to negate Buffy's Look. She actually hunts Buffy, intent on what she consciously thinks is "payback." When they finally happen to meet on the crowded campus of UC Sunnydale, Faith's first words to Buffy are, significantly, "You're not me" (4.15, "This Year's Girl"). We see this, at some level, as Faith's attempt to deny her possession by Buffy, implicit in the Look. However, she is beginning to become conscious of her guilt, brought on by this very Look. Before they fight, Buffy expresses her concern that there are too many innocent bystanders around. Faith responds,

"No such animal." If Faith can say that there is no such animal as an innocent person, then Faith must realize at some level that she herself is not innocent, but is in fact guilty of horrendous crimes. Their fight at this point is cut short by the arrival of the police. Faith flees. She later encounters a demon who gives her a package containing a videotape and a mysterious object, which she shortly discovers is a gift from the late Mayor, which allows her to switch bodies with Buffy.

The body-switch episodes, "This Year's Girl" (4.15) and "Who Are You" (4.16), the latter written and directed by Whedon himself, make quite literal the Sartrean outside view predicates necessary for Faith's reflexive consciousness of herself and thus of her own guilt through the Look of the Other. Whether intended or not, the body-switch is a brilliant device for exploring the impact of Sartrean outside view predicates. Faith can see herself as Buffy sees her, since she is seeing herself, or at least her body, from Buffy's point of view, literally from Buffy's body, which she now occupies. Talk about possessing the Other! Buffy, too, is more than shocked to find herself in Faith's body and being pursued by agents of the Watchers' Council. Faith thinks that she finally has the opportunity to take over Buffy's life, a life which at some level she has always wanted. In fact, she gets to sleep with Buffy's current love interest, Riley Finn, but finds herself unready for the genuine love, tenderness, and concern he shows toward her. To keep up the pretense, her cover in effect, of Buffy the Vampire Slayer, she actually saves a young girl from a vampire attack, but again she is unprepared for the Look of genuine gratitude as the girl says, "Thank you. Thank you" (4.16). The Look from Riley establishes Buffy (not Faith in Buffy's body) as someone worthy of love and respect, while the Look from the rescued girl establishes Faith in Buffy's body (and potentially Faith herself) as a hero, a champion, someone worthy of admiration as well as gratitude. At this point, however, Faith is disturbed and confused by these Looks. She is having a kind of moral experience that has not been available to her before, but she is not yet ready to fully appreciate all of its ramifications for her possible future.

Confused and conflicted, Faith attempts to flee Sunnydale and start a new life and identity as Buffy, but at the airport she happens to see a television news report of an ongoing hostage taking situation at a local church. From the report, it is obvious to her that the culprits are vampires since the police seem unable to defeat the ones they have encountered. (Most of Sunnydale do not know that vampires exist and they would certainly not be mentioned in a serious television *news* report.) Faith realizes that she is probably the only one capable of saving the hostages. Having played the role of Buffy the Vampire Slayer, having quite literally lived in Buffy's body, Faith begins to feel the responsibilities of the Slayer and rushes off to save the hostages, instead of turning her back on them and catching her plane. As Karl Schudt argues in "Also Sprach Faith: The Problem of the Happy Rogue Vampire Slayer," Faith finally comes to recognize a basic moral truth: "She has strength and the means to defend the defenseless, and therefore has the duty to do so." He concludes, "Furthermore, she must save the people because the sort of person she will be if she doesn't is unacceptable" (32). We would add that she has already become that unacceptable person, but that she is now beginning to become reflexively conscious of her untenable position. This is a crucial step toward her redemption. Gregory Stevenson, in *Televised Morality: The Case of Buffy the Vampire Slayer*, finds it significant that this step toward redemption occurs in a church, and argues, "It is here that she confesses the truth about herself and begins to experience the weight of moral responsibility" (122).

But an even more significant event occurs. The real Buffy (locked in Faith's body) has managed to escape from and elude the agents from the Watchers' Council and shows up at the church to save the hostages. The vampires having been dispatched, Faith turns her attention to the real Buffy, seeing her own body from the outside. The two Slayers fight. Gregory Stevenson quite rightly points out, "[t]he visual impact of this scene is crucial as Faith (in Buffy's body) repeatedly punches her own face in a fit of self loathing and cries out 'You're nothing! You're disgusting!'"(122). The dialogue, actually Faith's monologue delivered on the verge of tears between violent punches, is even more dramatic than Stevenson reports. It is more like, "You're nothing. Disgusting! Murderous bitch! You're nothing. You're disgusting" (4.16). These are all, of course, outside view predicates. Faith is finally seeing herself as Buffy sees her and is even harder on herself than Buffy has ever been. Faith has suddenly come to realize what kind of person she has become.

We think the repetition of her judgment "You're nothing" could have an even deeper significance. Just as the term "possession" has two different but related meanings, legal ownership and spiritually inhabiting an object, so too the term "nothing" can mean two quite different things. Besides the derogatory "your loss would be no loss" obviously meant in the monologue here, another meaning of "nothing" can be "no thing." This is the Sartrean meaning of "nothing" as it appears in his book *Being and Nothingness* (no-*thing*-ness). It is intended to draw attention to existential freedom, to the fact that human beings *are* freedom as Sartre would put it. Mere physical objects, on the other hand, are only things and cannot make themselves into any thing else. As we explained in more detail above, we human beings can, through the choices we make and the projects we undertake, continue to constantly remake ourselves, and therefore because of these indeterminate potentialities can never say what it is that we are. As Buffy once famously described herself, "I'm cookie dough. I'm not done baking. I'm not finished becoming whoever the hell it is I'm going to turn out to be" (7.22, "Chosen"). We always have the potential for radical conversion. Faith may currently see herself as "a disgusting murderous bitch," but that can be, for her, a step toward redemption because she is not a thing (not even her dagger) and can therefore change. We suggest that the repetition of the reflexive "You're nothing" could be seen as Faith's dimly conscious (pre-relexive) realization of this possibility. We admit, indeed insist, that the extremely negative outside view predicate meaning of "you're nothing" is what is foremost in Faith's consciousness at this moment. She truly sees herself as "a disgusting murderous bitch," and cannot stand what she has become.

Fortunately, for viewers and slayers alike, the real Buffy, thanks to her Wiccan friend Willow, has acquired another magical body-switching device and is able to activate it during their fight. The re-embodied Faith flees to Los Angeles and we next see her in the *Angel* series, engaging in the crime spree we mentioned above. The most significant event in this crime spree is the kidnapping and gruesome torturing of her former Watcher, Wesley Wyndham-Pryce. We contend that the fact that Faith chooses to bind and torture the very Watcher assigned to her after Kakistos killed her original Watcher corroborates our Sartrean reading of Faith's redemption narrative. If, as Gregory Stevenson, Karl Schudt, and we ourselves acknowledge, Faith is already on the path toward redemption, why does she suddenly revert to this especially loathsome criminal activity? She is, after all, threatening to employ all "five basic torture groups. We've done blunt, but that still leaves sharp, cold, hot and loud" (*Angel* 1.18, "Five By Five"). Her behavior makes sense only if she is trying to to negate the freedom of her Watcher while preserving his Sartrean Look, which brands her as the criminal she perceives herself to be. She still requires the Look, but no longer wants the loss of freedom and possibilities the Look implies. She still seems to be trying to take ownership of her crimes in much the way that Jean Genet did.

She still does not fully see the possibility of redemption through radical conversion, and in order to rid herself of the overwhelming guilt closing in upon her, she attempts to get Angel to kill her by picking the fight with him we mentioned earlier: "I'm evil! I'm bad! I'm evil! Do you hear me? I'm bad! Angel, I'm bad! I'm ba-ad. Do you hear me? I'm bad! I'm bad! I'm bad. Please. Angel, please, just do it. Angel please, just do it. Just do it. Just kill me. Just kill me" (*Angel* 1.18, "Five By Five"). This is not as extraordinary an event as it might seem. Criminals often try to goad police officers into a fight to the death, a fight they know the police are bound to win. Police forces are in fact trained to recognize and avoid this sort of situation, colloquially referred to as "suicide by cop" (see, for example, Barr, 2005; Center for Suicide Prevention, 1999; Conner, 2003; Dingsdale, 1998; Gerberth, 1993; Huston, et al., 1998; Kennedy, et al., 1998; Keram and Farrell, 2001; Lindsay and Lester, 2004; Lord, 2004; Parent, 1998, 2004; Pyers, 2001; Stincelli, 2004; Treatment Advocacy Center, 2005; VanZandt, n.d; Wilson et al., 1998; and the "Suicide by Cop Websites" in the bibliography).

Eventually, Faith, with Angel's help, freely chooses to turn herself in to the police and serve time in prison for the crimes she has committed. That this represents her move toward autonomy is confirmed by the fact that no prison can contain a Slayer against her will. When her services as Slayer are once again required by Angel and Wesley, she has no difficulty breaking out of prison, which again confirms our contention that she was freely choosing to accept her punishment (*Angel* 4.13, "Salvage").

Ironically, once out of prison, Faith finds herself working with Wesley. Even more ironically, she has occasion to criticize him for torturing a drug-addled prostitute for information. Wesley retorts defensively, "Oh, you have a problem with torture now? I seem to recall a time when you rather enjoyed it." Faith responds significantly, "Yeah, well, it's not me anymore. You know that" (*Angel* 4.14, "Release"). Wesley replies to this claim by hurling a series of outside view predicates at Faith: "This the part where you tell me you've turned a new leaf, found God, inner peace? We both know that isn't true. You haven't changed. You can't.... Because you're sick. You've always been sick. It goes right down to the roots rotting your soul. That's why your friends turned on you in Sunnydale, why the Watchers' Council tried to kill you. No one trusts you, Faith. You're a rabid dog who should've been put down years ago!" (4.14). Faith obviously has changed, since she is not devastated by these outside view predicates. She also refuses to accept Angelus's similar claim that she is unable to change: "Nothing will ever change who you are, Faith. You're a murderer, ... an animal, ... and you enjoy it.... Just like me." Faith proves that she will no longer be categorized and stultified by the Look of the of the Other, in responding, "No! You're wrong. I'm different now. I'm not like you" (4.14). It is now evident, we contend, that Faith, by once again choosing to be the Slayer, the Chosen One, has achieved the strength of character and level of autonomy necessary for redemption, and is approaching the authenticity and moral integrity which, as we will show, Buffy has possessed all along.

Chapter Four

Slayer Authenticity: Constructing Reality Through Existential Choice

As we explained in the previous chapter, throughout the entire series Buffy continually has to choose her fate, to be the Chosen One. As Gregory Stevenson argues in *Televised Morality: The Case of "Buffy the Vampire Slayer,"* "the role of fate in *Buffy's* world is ultimately tempered by free will" (71). From her very first meeting with her Watcher, Rupert Giles, she is most reluctant to accept the duties of the Slayer, telling him that she didn't think that there would be vampires in Sunnydale and that she doesn't care, and that she has "retired" (1.1, "Welcome to the Hellmouth"). We soon learn that she does in fact care and has not quite retired: when she sees her new friend Willow leaving the high school hangout, the Bronze, with a young man that Buffy recognizes as a vampire, she immediately, almost instinctively, goes to Willow's rescue, thus choosing to continue being the Slayer. Shortly after that, Xander's friend Jesse goes missing, presumed vamped, and Buffy again chooses the role of the Slayer, saying, "Jesse is *my* responsibility. I let him get taken" (1.1). It seems that whenever Buffy sees people in trouble, she remembers the duties of her calling and again chooses to be the Slayer. It is important to note that she always has a choice. One dramatic illustration of this comes at the end of Season Two and the beginning of Season Three, when she flees Sunnydale and her life as Slayer, having experienced the multiple traumas of 1) being expelled from high school; 2) being thrown out of the house by her mother, who has just discovered her daughter's secret world of vampires and slayage; 3) being suspected and sought by the police for the murder of Kendra; and 4) sending her 250-year-old vampire boyfriend, Angel, to Hell in order to save the world (again), her most difficult choice of all thus far in the series. Season Three begins with her seeking anonymity in Los Angeles, living under the name of Anne, and trying to lead a normal life as a waitress in a greasy spoon. She soon meets up with a Sunnydale acquaintance, Chanterelle, now going under the name of Lily, whom she had previously saved (2.7, "Lie to Me"). She finds that she has to help her yet again, as Lily is kidnapped by a missionary from a demonic "religiously oriented" homeless shelter. Lily and other homeless people are forced into slavery in an underground hell-like factory in which extreme anonymity is forced upon all the workers, who are literally deprived of their names and identities. When Buffy infiltrates this dimension, she is told by the demon prison guard, "Whatever you were does not matter. You are no one now. You mean nothing" (3.1, "Anne"). At this crucial point, we can see by the resolve in Buffy's face that she chooses to reject anonymity and once again to embrace the role of Slayer. When asked who she is, instead of saying "no one," as all of the slaves are forced to do, she replies, "I'm Buffy. The Vampire Slayer. And you are...?" (3.1), and then leads the slaves in a revolt, freeing them from this hell dimension by displaying her old martial arts prowess. The entrance to this dimension seals up right after Buffy and the former slaves escape, so that one more evil is thus prevented from entering the world. The episode concludes with Buffy giving her identity of Anne to Lily and returning to Sunnydale to resume her duties as Slayer. Stripped of its demonic metaphorical content, the episode draws attention to our usual uncaring attitude towards the homeless and how we are all capable of making a difference if we so choose. Lily herself, under the name of Anne or Annie, finds meaning and redemption by choosing to run a homeless shelter, as we learn in the *Angel* series (*Angel* 2.12, "Blood Money"; 2.14, "Thin Dead Line"; 5.22, "Not Fade Away").

The whole concept of choice is explored more fully in episode 3.19, "Choices." Near the end of their final year of school, Xander seems to be deciding to follow Kerouac for a life on the open road. The rest of the Scooby Gang are trying to choose among the admission letters they have received from various universities. Although Buffy's mother is very proud that Buffy has been accepted into Northwestern, Buffy herself is concerned that as the Slayer, she does not have the freedom to leave Sunnydale, a concern loudly seconded by the new watcher Wesley Wyndham-Pryce, who in fact explicitly forbids her to go: "You cannot leave Sunnydale. By the power invested in me by the Council, I forbid it." Buffy, of course, does not want to be defined by her "Slayerness," yet she is torn because the Slayer may well be needed in Sunnydale, given that the Hellmouth is about to open with the ascension of the secretly demonic mayor, Richard Wilkins III. (We note with amusement in passing the politician-as-demon portrayal.) In addition to trying to devise a schedule whereby she could both attend Northwestern and return periodically to Sunnydale on school holidays to help out Giles *et al.* in their demon-fighting, she attempts to bring matters with the Mayor to a head by taking the battle to him right away. She devises a scheme to penetrate the Mayor's magically protected room in City Hall in order to learn more details of his ascension, but in the process of carrying out this plan, her friend Willow is taken prisoner by the rogue–Slayer Faith, who is now working for the Mayor. During her captivity, Willow confronts Faith about her choice to join the dark side and the consequences of that choice: "You know, it didn't have to be this way. But you made your choice. I know you had a tough life. I know that some people think you had a lot of bad breaks. Well, boo hoo! Poor you. You know, you had a lot more in your life than some people. I mean, you had friends in your life like Buffy. Now you have no one. You were a Slayer and now you're nothing. You're just a big selfish, worthless waste." As Gregory Stevenson notes, "One message that resonates clearly throughout *Buffy* is that all individuals bear ultimate responsibility for their actions, even though a variety of factors may influence those actions.... Willow's message to Faith clearly enunciates the point that as tragic as a bad childhood may be, it does not excuse one from becoming a bad adult" (156–7).

Wesley and the Scooby Gang wrestle with the problem of whether or not to trade Willow's freedom for an item central to the rituals surrounding the Mayor's ascension, which they had stolen from City Hall. Wesley's priority, as a Watcher, is to prevent at all costs the Mayor's ascension and the opening of the Hellmouth. He argues that they have and must destroy "the key to the Mayor's Ascension. Thousands of lives depend on our getting rid of it. Now I want to help Willow as much as the rest of you, but we will find another way" (3.19). Wesley is clearly willing to sacrifice Willow's life in order to save thousands of others. He represents the rational, utilitarian, or consequentialist, approach to decision-making, choosing the lesser of two evils. But remember our key to understanding the Buffyverse is, "Freedom consists in the force and power not to admit evil into the world" (Shestov *Athens and Jerusalem* 256). Freedom is not simply choosing between right or wrong, good or bad, and it most certainly is never choosing evil, lesser or otherwise.

The Mayor already is convinced that he can get the key to his ascension back by trading Willow because he believes he has an understanding of what motivates and drives Buffy. In a private conversation with Faith, he makes the following uncomplimentary comparison between Buffy and his pet dog, Rusty: "A dog's friendship is stronger than reason, stronger than its own sense of self-preservation. Buffy's like a dog, and hey, before you can say Jack Robinson, you'll get to see me kill her like one."

Buffy clearly believes that reason would require the sacrifice of the one to save the many. During their argument with Wesley, Giles attempts to calm them down by saying, "Alright! Let's deal with this rationally," whereupon Buffy retorts, "Why are you taking his side?" Choosing to trade for Willow, risking the lives of thousands with the Mayor's ascension, is certainly not the rational thing to do, but that is exactly the choice that the Scooby Gang believes to be the only right choice. Wesley thinks that they should find another way to rescue Willow; the Scooby Gang obviously believes they should find a way to stop the Mayor and save Sunnydale that does not involve sacrificing Willow. Ultimately that is exactly what they do.

What we find most interesting here is the portrayal of moral reasoning, or should we say, rather, moral decision-making, since it does not seem to follow the dictates of reason. It is important to note that the Mayor does not really understand Buffy's motivation in making such decisions. Buffy is not like a dog in blindly rejecting reason in favor of friendship. It is true that she is unwilling to sacrifice her friend Willow, but this is not simply because Willow is a friend, that strangers are somehow less important, even thousands of them. That would be truly demonic, and quite in keeping with the Mayor's character, but not with Buffy's.

We get a better insight into the integrity of Buffy's moral character in episode 3.15 "Consequences." As we discussed at length in the previous chapter, Faith goes bad after accidentally killing a human being while chasing vampires. She dismisses the incident with the same kind of impersonal utilitarian cost-benefit analysis we have seen Wesley use to justify sacrificing Willow. Faith feels it necessary to present her rationalization of the accidental killing to Buffy as follows: "I'm sorry about the guy. I really am! But it happens! Anyway how many people do you think we've saved by now, thousands? And didn't you stop the world from ending? Because in my book that puts you and me in the plus column.... In the balance, nobody's gonna cry over some random bystander who got caught in the crossfire" (3.15). Buffy's response to this reveals a lot about her moral character. She lets Faith know that she is wrong in thinking that "nobody's gonna cry over some random bystander," replying to Faith with a grief-stricken "I am." For Buffy, feelings and emotions are relevant to moral judgments. Moral discourse is neither abstract nor impersonal.

In the light of this, Jessica Prata Miller, in "'The I in Team': Buffy and Feminist Ethics," argues that Buffy approaches moral issues from what Miller calls "the care perspective" derived from Carol Gilligan's classic study

In a Different Voice (Miller 2003, 36; Gilligan 1982). We do not disagree. In fact we argue that Buffy is using, and indeed Whedon is developing, what we call a virtue ethics emphasizing moral character in decision-making; and certainly care is seen as one of the more important virtues. In episode 6.8 ("Tabula Rasa"), we get further confirmation of Buffy's moral character and its foundation in the virtue of care: when suffering from amnesia, she still instinctively goes to the aid of both Dawn and Spike, neither of whom she recognizes at the time. Buffy's moral character, her moral virtues, seem to be independent from her role as the Slayer. Not knowing that she is the Slayer, Buffy still protects people, not because it is her duty as the Slayer, but simply because she cares, and because it is the right thing to do. In the process, she does discover, to her surprise, that she is in fact the vampire slayer.

We are proposing that the entire series of *Buffy the Vampire Slayer* can be seen as a sustained moral argument in which theories such as utilitarianism are found wanting, and more acceptable alternatives, such as a virtue ethics grounded in care, are proposed and defended. This kind of moral argument cannot, of course, be a rational argument since, as we have seen, reason itself is often questioned. The series presents, rather, an indirect form of argument in which difficult hypothetical cases are imagined and various ways of dealing with them considered. Television drama is an excellent and entertaining way of presenting such arguments.

We have here a good example of how these arguments work. Regular viewers of *Buffy*, in fact any viewers who have seen the episodes in their original order, will have been prepared to be somewhat suspicious of Wesley's willingness on utilitarian grounds to sacrifice the one, Willow, to save the many (Episode 3.19, discussed above). In episode 3.15, just four episodes earlier, viewers will already have seen Faith use the same type of argument to rationalize her admittedly accidental killing of an "innocent" bystander, and they will have also seen that this kind of thinking is at least part of what leads Faith to the dark side. It leads her at least to claim not to care about killing a fellow human being. As she tells Buffy, who is understandably upset, "You don't get it. I don't care." This is a crucial turning point not just for Faith but also for the viewer. Up to this point most of us have been empathizing with Faith, imagining what it would be like to adopt her attitude toward life. After all, she is almost a paradigm of the American rugged individualist. She is totally self-reliant, needing no one, doesn't let the rules or authority figures get in the way, and receives an almost erotic pleasure out of practically everything she does, particularly what she was chosen, and chooses, to do.

If we are in any doubt that this paradigm of radical individualism is under attack in these episodes, the episodes that follow, particularly in Season Four and when Faith shows up in *Angel*, dispel any such illusion. Faith does not like the person she has chosen to become. As Karl Schudt argues in "Also Sprach Faith: The Problem of the Happy Rogue Vampire Slayer," Faith finally "sees the shape of her own life course, and it disgusts her. She makes an aesthetic evaluation of herself and doesn't like what she sees" (32). Although we do not have here a rational argument proceeding by deduction from proven premises, we have nevertheless a moral argument against not only the American ideal of radical individualism, but also the related utilitarian ethics as well. As Schudt concludes, "Rival moralities may not be able to be resolved rationally, but the results of choices in accordance with them differ greatly. Faith's life has become ugly" (32). From our existentialist perspective, it is also important to remember that this is the life Faith has chosen for herself. This shows that Slayers are free to choose either their duty as Slayer or, as with Faith, a life in support of the dark side, using her gifts as the Chosen One to support rather than to fight evil.

Oddly enough, some commentators write as if Buffy does not have this kind of freedom. Lorna Jowett, for example, in *Sex and the Slayer: A Gender Studies Primer for the 'Buffy' Fan*, asserts, "Buffy is 'chosen' to be Buffy the Vampire Slayer (fairly typical for action heroes or superheroes); she does not have the power to make her own choices. The Watcher's Council controls Buffy's power through Giles, who directs its use and can even remove it" (Jowett 2005, 24). Jowett seems to think that it is not until near the end of Season Three that "Buffy begins to realize her lack of agency, leading to her 'graduation' from the Council" (Jowett 2005, 24). We are, on the other hand, arguing that right from day one Buffy has a very real grasp of her own sense of agency, so much so that Giles sees immediately that he must leave it to her to choose to adopt the duties of the Slayer. Just because she does in fact choose these duties does not mean that she was not free to choose otherwise, just as Faith did, though admittedly with disastrous consequences.

In "Choices" (3.19), Buffy does begin to see that being the Slayer is starting to restrict her choices. As we have seen, she wants to attend Northwestern University, but her Slayer duties seem to keep her in Sunnydale. Wesley, as we have seen, actually orders her to stay there. Giles, who is much more familiar with Buffy's character, comments on Wesley's command by saying sarcastically, "Ah yes, that should settle it." Giles obviously recognizes and respects Buffy's freedom of choice, even if Buffy herself is beginning to question it, regarding Sunnydale as a kind of prison. Near the end of this episode, she confides in Willow, "I'm never getting out of here. I kept thinking if I stopped the Mayor or ... but I was kidding myself. I mean, there is always going to be something. I'm a Sunnydale girl, no other choice." It is Willow who restores Buffy's faith in freedom. Despite having been accepted into Oxford, M.I.T., Harvard, Yale "and every other college on the face of the planet," Willow tells Buffy that she has decided to attend UC Sunnydale (3.19). Buffy responds to this news by saying, "I won't let you," to which Willow retorts, "Of the two people here, which is the boss of me?" Buffy thinks that Willow is choosing to stay because of her, but Willow quickly disabuses Buffy of this, affirming both her own autonomy and her commitment to a care ethics: "Actually, this isn't about you. Although I'm fond, don't get me wrong, of you. The other night, you know, being captured and all, facing off with Faith. Things just, kind of, got clear." It will be remembered that Faith was threatening to kill Willow at this point. Willow is telling Buffy that it was this experience, rather than reason, that helped her choose to stay in Sunnydale and fight evil. Jean-Paul Sartre would regard Willow's choice as an authentic existential choice "because it was made face to face with death" (Sartre 1947, 498). As Willow assures Buffy, "I mean, you've been fighting evil here for three years, and I've helped some, and now we're supposed to decide what we want to do with our lives. And I just realized that that's what I want to do. Fight evil, help people. I mean, I-I think it's worth doing. And I don't think you do it because you have to. It's a good fight, Buffy, and I want in." Buffy is overjoyed with Willow's decision and her reasons for making it; moreover, this conversation leads Buffy to reassess her feeling that Sunnydale is a prison. Instead of seeing Sunnydale as confining, she begins to see staying and doing her duty as an opportunity: "It's weird. You look at something and you think you know exactly what you're seeing, and then you find out it's something else entirely."

The full extent of Buffy's freedom of choice comes out most clearly in episode 6.17, "Normal Again," in which even the viewers have difficulties in knowing exactly what they are seeing. Buffy appears to be under treatment in a psychiatric hospital suffering from the psychotic belief that vampires and demons exist and are threatening the inhabitants of Sunnydale while she is some kind of superhero, the Vampire Slayer, devoted to saving the world. The transition between the world of vampires and slayers, and life in the psychiatric hospital is made seamless so that it really is impossible to tell which is the reality and which is the delusion. The episode begins with Buffy fighting a demon who injects her with a delusion-inducing poison using a spike growing out of his hand. Immediately we find ourselves watching a scene in a psychiatric institution where a hospital-gowned Buffy is being injected with a sedative, in exactly the spot where the demon infected her. A kindly psychiatrist is constantly attempting to cure her of her delusions by asking her to reject what he believes to be her imaginary friends. She is told of her Slayer life that "none of that's real, none of it. You're in a mental institution. You've been with us now for six years." The seamlessness of the transition is enhanced by the fact that we are watching the sixth season of *Buffy*. The question naturally arises: have we been wasting our time watching a psychiatric delusion for the last six years? This was a most disturbing episode for Buffy and viewer alike, and many would say that it never gets resolved. We argue, on the contrary, that Buffy is given the ultimate Either/Or, the ultimate existential freedom to choose either life as the Slayer or the normal life she has always craved. We contend that neither life is a delusion, that both are potential realities, either of which Buffy may choose and thus actualize. In the psychiatric hospital, Buffy's mother tells her, "You're our little girl, Buffy. Our one and only. We've missed you so much. Mom and Dad just want to take you home and take care of you." There is certainly a strong incentive to choose life with Mom and Dad. The Slayer's parents are long divorced. In fact at this point Buffy, who had been living with her mother, is entirely on her own, her mother having died, the absentee father not even attending the funeral.

In the course of his psychoanalysis, Buffy's psychiatrist suggests that "Buffy's delusions are multi-layered" that "She believes she's some type of hero ... but that's only one level. She's also created an intricate latticework to support her primary delusion. In her mind, she's the central figure in a fantastic world beyond imagination." In a postmodern, self-referential descriptive summary of the themes, genres, motifs, and techniques of the series, the Doctor continues, saying, "She's surrounded herself with friends, most with their own superpowers ... who are as real to her as you or me. More so, unfortunately. Together they face ... grand overblown conflicts against an assortment of monsters both imaginary and rooted in actual myth. Every time we think we're getting through to her, more fanciful enemies magically appear." He even describes Buffy's sister, Dawn, as a completely implausible interpolation into Buffy's central delusion, but we, the viewers, have been witnessing the very same thing whilst willingly suspending our disbelief. He describes Dawn as "A magical key. Buffy inserted Dawn into her delusion, actually rewriting the entire history of it to accommodate a need for a familial bond." Again, the Doctor is simply describing what is actually going on in the series as a whole at this point. Dawn really is a mystical key, which would permit unspeakable evil to enter the world. The guardian monks in charge of the key have magically disguised it as Buffy's sister in order to guarantee that she will protect it with her life: "They had to be certain the Slayer would protect it with her life, so they sent the key to her, in the form of a sister" (5.18, "Intervention"). In the process, these monks have created an elaborate series of instant life memories for all the characters, complete with altered family photographs and records, which incorporate Dawn as though she were always present. The result is that Dawn's early childhood both does and does not exist at one and the same time.

Through psychoanalysis, Buffy's psychiatrist attempts to get Buffy to admit the logical inconsistencies in her so-called delusional world, hoping that the recognition of such incongruities will snap her out of it and back into the world of rational reality, "but that created inconsistencies, didn't it? Your sister, your friends, all of those people you created in Sunnydale, they aren't as comforting as they once were. Are they? They're coming apart." The Doctor is partially correct; in Season Four the Scooby Gang are growing up and as a result are also beginning to grow apart. This is facilitated by the vampire Spike who is deliberately sowing dissension among the ranks as he helps the Initiative's robo-demon, Adam, isolate Buffy from her friends (4.20, "The Yoko Factor"). The process of separation begun in Season Four has gathered considerable momentum by Season Six, with Buffy's coldness and remoteness from her friends; Willow's growing addiction to magic for selfish and manipulative purposes and the rift this creates between her and Tara; Dawn's kleptomania arising from her sense of being neglected; the catastrophic cancellation, at the altar, of Xander's and Anya's wedding; and the move of the group's father figure, Giles, back to England; not to mention Buffy's death and unwilling resurrection. Buffy's psychiatrist attempts to exploit all this dissension, all these fissures in the fabric of what he sees as Buffy's delusion, in order to convince her to effect a final separation from her "imaginary" friends. He tells her that it's not going to be easy, that she must rid her mind of everything that supports her hallucinations, including slayage, but most especially, her friends that keep dragging her back into the Sunnydale world. He points out to her that "last summer" she had what he calls a "momentary awakening" until these friends pulled her back in. This "momentary awakening" in the psychiatric hospital corresponds to the period of Buffy's death at the end of Season Five, when she sacrifices herself to save her sister Dawn and prevent the key from opening a portal to evil.

What the psychiatrist sees as her friends pulling her back is in fact Willow and the rest of the Scooby Gang performing a magic ritual to restore Buffy's life, since they believe it is possible to use magic to restore a life that has been taken by magic. If our interpretation is correct, Buffy's description of what it was like when she was dead is, contrary to her own belief, not a description of Heaven, but rather a description of life in the psychiatric hospital: "I was warm ... and I was loved ... and I was finished. Complete. I don't understand about theology or dimensions, or ... any of it, really ... but I think I was in heaven" (6.3, "After Life"). It also means that Willow and company are in a sense correct in their belief that they have brought her back from Hell, if we assume that life in a psychiatric hospital, or the need for it, is a form of Hell.

With the support of her mother, Buffy acts on the psychiatrist's advice to get rid of her Sunnydale friends. "They're not really your friends, Buffy. They're just tricks keeping you from getting healthy" (6.17). We see Buffy actually tie her friends up in the basement of her Sunnydale home. Unable, or at least unwilling, to kill them herself, she releases the same demon that had originally infected her in the hopes that he will kill them for her. The Scooby Gang occasionally keep demons chained up; in this case, to use the demon venom to develop an antidote to what they perceive as Buffy's delusion: "Alternative realities. Where we're all little figments of Buffy's funny-farm delusion." The difficulty that Buffy is having in making a choice between these two alternative realities is emphasized by the fact that she refuses to drink the first antidote developed by Willow, surreptitiously dumping it into a wastebasket. Having released the monster, Buffy cannot stand to see her friends being attacked by it. The scene shifts to the psychiatric hospital where Buffy's mother is attempting to support her very agitated daughter, saying, "Buffy? Buffy! Buffy, fight it. You're too good to give in, you can beat this thing. Be strong, baby, ok? I know you're afraid. I know the world feels like a hard place sometimes, but you've got people who love you. Your dad and I, we have all the faith in the world in you. We'll always be with you.... You've got a world of strength in your heart. I know you do. You just have to find it again. Believe in yourself" (6.17). Ironically, Buffy does find strength in herself, and uses it to slay the demon she has just set upon her friends. Getting her strength from the hospital reality, she nonetheless chooses Sunnydale and her true friends. And not only does she save her friends, but there is a sense in which her very choice actually creates the friends that she saves, since that is the reality she chooses. Not only could she have chosen otherwise, it certainly looks as though she came very close to doing so.

Our interpretation of events is confirmed, we believe, by the parallel story of Cordelia in the *Angel* episode "Birthday" (3.11), which was broadcast only two months before "Normal Again" (January 14, 2002 and March 12, 2002, respectively). In her Sunnydale High School days, Cordelia was the beautiful rich girl who relied for her very obvious popularity on her good looks and her father's money. At the end of "Choices" we discover that her father has lost all his wealth due to problems with the IRS, and although she has been accepted by several universities, she cannot afford to choose any of them. Hence, she leaves Sunnydale for Los Angeles, with dreams of becoming a movie or television star. When these ambitions do not pan out, in *Angel* Season One, she finds herself working with Angel Investigations as part of its efforts to "help the helpless" (*Angel* 2.7, "Darla"). In its early days, Angel Investigations is aided by the demi-demon, Doyle, who receives visions from the Powers-That-Be; these visions guide Angel's efforts at keeping the people of LA safe from sundry forms of evil. When Doyle dies, with a dying kiss he passes the gift of these visions on to Cordelia, who, not having the strength of a demon, suffers immense pain when enduring them. By the time we reach the Third Season of *Angel*, the pain of the visions has become so severe that she can no longer endure them.

Unknown to the rest of Angel's team, Cordelia has been taking numerous painkillers to cope with these visions, and in "Birthday" she is visited by the demon guide Skip, who tells her that the visions will soon result in her death. He offers her an important choice — her life can be magically changed to the life she has always dreamed of, where she is a rich and famous television star. As in the "Normal Again" episode of *Buffy*, we find seamless transitions between her two realities, keeper of visions at Angel Investigations and star of the popular TV sitcom *Cordy!* Skip offers her the choice between these two realities after she has been mystically put into a coma during an especially painful vision. Angel and other members of Angel Investigations, including Charles Gunn, Wesley Wyndham-Pryce, and Fred Burkle, spend their time desperately trying to revive her. She seems to be having an out-of-body experience in which she can see her friends working to resuscitate her prostrate body, but cannot communicate with them or even manipulate objects. Her friends even keep walking straight through her spectral body, much to her consternation. She is most concerned with giving them the information she had just learned from her vision, particularly the address of the young woman about to be attacked by an eyeless, three-mouthed monster. She is able briefly to occupy Angel's sleeping body and through it write the crucial address (171 Oak) on the wall of his room in their headquarters, the old Hyperion Hotel. But it is only the address itself that she has time to write because she is immediately ejected from Angel's body and hears her friends talking about her CAT scans that show that she is dying from the stress of her visions. Then her guiding demon, Skip, materializes. Preliminary to answering her many questions about what is happening to her, he takes her to a place where she will feel most comfortable, which for Cordelia is, of course, a shopping mall, or, rather, what Skip calls, "a construct of a mall. You know, like in the *Matrix*" (*Angel* 3.11). After Skip tells her that she will never awaken from the coma and that when her next vision hits, she is certain to die, she chooses the alternative life the Powers-That-Be have offered through Skip and finds herself the star of a well-known Los Angeles sitcom entitled *Cordy!* But as the star of *Cordy!* she has that "nagging feeling that [she's] supposed to be somewhere, doing something, but ... can't remember what" (*Angel* 3.11). Her instinct leads her to the Hyperion Hotel, which turns out, in this alternative reality, not to be the headquarters of Angel Investigations, but a thriving first-rate hotel. She instinctively goes to what, in the other reality, was Angel's room and tears away the wallpaper to reveal the address, 171 Oak. Not knowing why, she goes to this address, and is invited in by the young female occupant who is thrilled, but somewhat puzzled, to have the famous Cordelia Chase, star of *Cordy!*, visit her. The young woman shows Cordelia the pentagram she has just drawn on the floor as part of her attempt to use a spell to bring back her absent father, but, not surprisingly, what appears is the eyeless, three-mouthed monster of Cordelia's vision from the other reality (OK, it surprised the young woman and Cordelia, but viewers of *Angel* have come to expect such twists). At this moment, Gunn and a one armed Wesley burst in and kill the monster. Both, it will be remembered, are now working as part of Angel Investigations, of which this Cordelia has never heard, having gone smoothly from Sunnydale into stardom. Cordelia recognizes Wesley from Sunnydale and they briefly reminisce about their past (their kiss in 3.21 "Graduation Day, Part I"; Wesley's tendency at that time to faint when facing monsters, etc.). Wesley then tells Cordelia that Angel is no longer the person she knew in Sunnydale. He has "retreated into himself" due to the death of Doyle and has been suffering intensely from the visions which were passed on to him at Doyle's death. As Wesley explains, "The visions have taken a toll, and the isolation. Sometimes he sends us out to save people he killed two hundred years ago" (*Angel* 3.11). Wesley and Gunn then take Cordelia to see Angel, who is shackled in a room, trembling, muttering incoherently, occasionally repeating the address 171 Oak, and writing it on the wall with his finger. Cordelia cannot stand to see Angel suffering like this, and though he does not recognize her, she instinctively places her hands on his face and kisses him gently. The power to have visions immediately passes from Angel to Cordelia in exactly the same way we had seen it pass from Doyle to Cordelia with his dying kiss. She then says, "I remember everything. The visions they're mine." Skip reappears and chastizes Cordelia, saying, "We made a deal. You gave up the visions, not to mention the certain death that goes with them, and you get to live out your dream. Call me crazy, but I thought that was a pretty fair trade." Cordelia responds, significantly, "Sure it's fair. But it wasn't me." She is willing to give up her lifelong dream of stardom, wealth, and popularity, which she had actually been experiencing, for the pain and possible death of helping others through her visions. Skip explains that even the Powers-That-Be cannot make a human being strong enough to withstand the visions. We have seen in Angel's condition that even a vampire is not strong enough to endure them. On Cordelia's insistence, Skip admits that there may be a small loophole — the only way Cordelia can continue having the visions is by becoming part demon herself, a process that is extraordinarily painful and could result in side effects that are "numerous and unpredictable" (*Angel* 3.11). But Cordelia, like Willow in "Choices," has chosen her fundamental project: "I know my purpose in this world and it includes the visions." She is willing to endure anything, to undergo any sacrifice, to fulfill the destiny she has chosen, and she tells Skip, "So demonize me already." The scene seamlessly shifts back to Angel Investigations' headquarters in the ruinous and old Hyperion Hotel and Cordelia awakening from her coma with a painful scream. She has chosen the life of service to others, at considerable cost to herself, a choice that rational self-interest would hardly recommend.

Nikki Stafford, in *Once Bitten: An Unofficial Guide to the World of Angel,* compares the "Birthday" episode (3.11) to *It's a Wonderful Life* and *A Christmas Carol,* as well as two episodes of *Buffy* (3.9, "The Wish" and 3.10, "Amends") but, from our standpoint, incredibly, omits any reference to "Normal Again"(Stafford 2004, 217–220). "Birthday" and "Normal Again" are, we suggest, more like each other than they are like Stafford's so called analogues, in that they both involve moral choices which alter not only the future, but also the past. For example, when Scrooge in *A Christmas Carol* decides to amend his parsimonious ways, that choice will certainly help out Bob Cratchit with the medical bills for Tiny Tim, but will not alter the fact that in the past Tiny Tim became ill in the first place and that in that past his father might have found suitable medical care if Scrooge had paid him enough. There is certainly no sense Scrooge is creating a reality with which he must deal. It is quite different, for example, with Cordelia in "Birthday." As Janet Halfyard notes, "She may have been taken to a reality where none of the events of Seasons One or Two have occurred, but her character's development remained intact. Thus, when she is confronted with what has happened to Angel and Wesley in this version of reality, she is again forced into a moral choice and again does not hesitate: she seeks to be made part demon, takes back her visions and rejects the other life she was offered."

It is important to remember that the two alternate realities in "Birthday" are, though clearly incompatible, both presented as real. Neither of them can be dismissed as a dream sequence or some sort of an illusion. Cordelia must choose between them and thus actualize one of them (but we note in passing that vestiges of the path not chosen can and do remain, in those nagging feelings that one has left something undone, the main link between the two realities in this episode).

Viewers who have seen this episode of *Angel* are thus prepared for the similar two realities Buffy is confronted with in "Normal Again," broadcast only two months after "Birthday" (*Angel* 3.11). They therefore need not dismiss either of the alternative realities in "Normal Again" as delusional. This is especially important since both the viewers and the Slayer's friends, the Scooby Gang, learn something about Buffy's past that they did not know before. She confesses to Willow and her friends that before moving to Sunnydale from Los Angeles, she had in fact spent a short time in a mental institution, and she wonders aloud, "What if I'm still there? What if I never left that clinic?" (6.17). Well, what if she were still there? Then the whole of Sunnydale, vampires, and Slayers and the Scooby Gang would be just part of a psychotic delusion. We contend that when Buffy chooses to save her friends whom she had confined to the basement of her home in Sunnydale, her choice in fact actualizes that reality, thus choosing the ultimate freedom "the force and power not to admit evil into the world" (Shestov, *Athens and Jerusalem*, 256).

Cordelia, too, in giving up the reality of a rich and famous television star, is choosing, through her visions, to have "the force and power not to admit evil into the world." She also saves her friends, Wesley and Angel, for both were maimed in the TV star's reality. Once her final choice is made, that reality no longer exists, but we cannot say that it never existed. There is a very real sense in which Cordelia both was and was never a famous TV star, just as Buffy at one and the same time both left and had never left the psychiatric institution. The only thing preventing us from accepting this seemingly absurd situation is our commitment to the law of non-contradiction, to reason itself. Our Shestovian key to understanding

Buffy, outlined in Chapter One, involves the recognition that the exclusive acceptance of reason is itself an existential choice. The episode "Normal Again" brilliantly characterizes Buffy's so-called delusions as self-contradictory. The psychiatrist is actually trying to cure her of such delusions by forcing her to recognize these contradictions. Her choice is then between the rational and the non-rational, but choosing the psychiatrist's vision of normality would be giving up "the force and power to prevent evil from entering the world." The fact that neither Buffy nor Cordelia is willing to do so speaks well for their moral character, and perhaps puts the rest of us to shame. As Janet Halfyard notes in "The Greatest Love of All: Cordelia's Journey of Self-Discovery," Buffy and Cordelia are "chosen ones, chosen by mystical forces and given a gift with which to serve the world; both have to give up their childish dreams of the lives they expected to lead in order to do this.... Both are also offered an alternative reality that might well be easier to live in than the one they are currently in" (2003). As we have argued, both choose to reject this offer of an alternative life. Further, it is an existential choice which is neither supported by, nor supportive of, reason.

The existential choices presented in these episodes of *Buffy the Vampire Slayer* and *Angel* are specific instances of the primordial existential choice presented mythologically as the serpent's offer of the fruits of reason from the Tree of Knowledge. As we show in the next chapter, the episodes dealing with the Initiative in *Buffy the Vampire Slayer* are a further exploration of this fundamental myth, critiquing reason as it manifests itself in science and technology.

Chapter Five

Riley and the Initiative: Some Limitations of Science and Technology

A major, and obvious, source of the popularity and power of *Buffy the Vampire Slayer* is its use of the myth that high school is Hell. This, of course, rings true for all of us. It should not be surprising, therefore, that Sunnydale High School is built on a Hellmouth. However, in Chapter One we argued that a deeper root for this popularity and power is the fact that the series in fact rests on a more fundamental, though often buried and suppressed, myth in Western culture — that of original sin. This involves the Hellmouth's being opened by partaking of the fruits of reason from the Tree of Knowledge offered by the serpent in Genesis. We made much of the high school as a knowledge-dispensing institution, situated directly above an extraordinarily active Hellmouth. In Season Four of *Buffy the Vampire Slayer*, a number of the Scooby Gang are off to the University of California at Sunnydale, having graduated from high school. We remind you of the giant demon serpent interrupting graduation, which we take as a nod to the Genesis story. However, if our interpretation is at all plausible, shouldn't the Hellmouth really be under the university, the more advanced knowledge-dispensing and knowledge-generating institution? Well, it turns out that there is something even more sinister beneath UC Sunnydale. There is a secret government experimental laboratory and covert military headquarters called the Initiative. Some of UC Sunnydale's professors and teaching assistants actually work there as well; indeed, their university personas might even be regarded as a cover for their covert military operations. Unlike the majority of Sunnydale citizens, these government operatives recognize the existence of vampires and demons. They label them "Hostile Sub-Terrestrials" (HSTs). The role of the Initiative is not only "curtailing the sub-terrestrial menace" (4.11, "Doomed"), but also

capturing various specimens for experimentation in order to discover what
military use can be served by their kind, or parts thereof. This is certainly
applied research with a vengeance! The Initiative episodes could well serve
as a warning to universities against the uncritical acceptance of applied
research funding.

Buffy unknowingly becomes involved with one of the Initiative's operatives, her psychology professor's teaching assistant, Riley Finn. Not only
is there a lesson here about undergraduates dating their tutors, but we also
learn from Riley's example how the Initiative as a whole conceptualizes the
world it works in; that is, how it thinks through problems and implements
"solutions." Riley, at least at the outset, seems to use a fairly limited binary
logic and value system: "Demons bad, people good.... Something wrong
with that theorem?" (4.19, "New Moon Rising"). He has trouble getting
his mind around Buffy's revelation that there just might be some good
demons and vampires. The Initiative is, in some ways, even more horrifying than the Hellmouth, for it is not simply the Tree of Knowledge. It is
an example of what humanity has done with the gift of knowledge. Reason
has been applied to military technology and, as we shall see, to ethically
questionable experimenting and meddling with the very nature of human
beings in order to create more "efficient," more invulnerable, super soldiers. This should not be too surprising, considering that the gift of reason from the Tree of Knowledge is, as we have said, a gift from the serpent,
the embodiment of evil, Satan, at the root of Western civilization.

We can substantiate our interpretation of knowledge as Satan's gift
and the Initiative as scientific knowledge run amuck by examining Riley
Finn's re-education at the hands of Buffy, well actually, in the arms of Buffy.
This is, of course, ironic since he is the teaching assistant in her psychology class, but then they say that a good teacher learns from his or her students, and Riley certainly learns a lot from the Slayer. Riley begins by being
very happy as an operative with the Initiative in that he feels that he is
protecting the general population from an evil they know nothing about
(HSTs, Hostile Sub-Terrestrials). He certainly believes that the Initiative
is doing good work, which is necessary, especially in Sunnydale, a hotspot
for demon activity due to the Hellmouth. However, the Initiative, it seems,
knows nothing about the Hellmouth or of the actual existence of the Slayer.
When Riley and Buffy finally reveal to each other that they are both demon
fighters in their own way, Riley takes Buffy to meet the Initiative's head
scientist, who turns out to be Professor Maggie Walsh, Buffy's psychology
professor. Professor Walsh is most excited to meet the Slayer, as she admits
even the Initiative believed that the Vampire Slayer was mere mythology:

"We thought you were a myth" (4.12, "A New Man"). In fact, Riley's fellow commandos in the Initiative had actually dismissed and derided the whole notion of the Vampire Slayer: "Oh, yeah, I've heard of the Slayer.... Well, the way I got it figured the Slayer is like some kind of boogey man for the Subterrestrials, something they tell their little spawn to make them eat their vegetables and clean up their slime pits. Sorry, sorry, it's a myth, Rye. All part of that medieval folklore garbage kooks dream up to explain things we deal with every day" (4.11, "Doomed"). This highlights one of the major differences between the Initiative's approach to research and that of the Slayer. Giles and the Scooby Gang, as we have seen, do much of their research by consulting medieval texts, sources which, unlike the weighing and measuring done by the Initiative's scientific team, actually indicate the motives and objectives of various kinds of demons. Since the Initiative regards demons as simply generic non-thinking animals for whom motives and objectives beyond the merely destructive are inconceivable, it misses the big picture entirely and really has no idea how to deal with demons in all their individual manifestations. When Riley asks one of his fellow commandos how he explains the "things [they] deal with," his colleague puts him down by telling him, "They're just animals, man, plain and simple. Granted they're a little rarer than the ones you grew up with on that little farm in Smallville" (4.11, "Doomed"). Maggie Walsh describes the target of one of their hunts as "Sub-T: 67119. Demon class: Polgara species" (4.13, "The 'I' in Team"), and the vampire, Spike, despite having a name and a very distinctive personality, is referred to merely as "Hostile 17." Buffy, on the other hand, when she is finally accepted into the Initiative, tends to ask what they consider to be inappropriate questions about monsters and demons, such as, "What do they want?" (4.13, "The 'I' in Team"). She is told in response, "They're not sentient. Just destructive." She is also told by the Initiative scientists that they "study the physiology of every subterrestrial's natural defenses" (4.13, "The 'I' in Team"). She is not, however, told why they wish to study these natural defense mechanisms. Even Riley and his fellow commandos are not aware of the kind of applied research that is being carried on in the Initiative.

Buffy and the Scooby Gang learn from their contacts in the demon world about the Initiative's current secret projects, particularly the sinister project in room 314. Rupert Giles, Buffy's Watcher, learns from an old friend who has since gone to the dark side as a worshipper of Chaos that the demon world, which is far from being a mere aggregate of non-sentient animals incapable of forming intentions relevant to humans, is aware of and concerned about the Initiative's activities: "It's always been rumors out there but only one thing's coming through clear. That something's harming demons and it's not the Slayer.... There's something called '314' that's got them scared most of all. The kind of scared that turns to angry. I know we're not particularly fond of each other, Rupert. But we are a couple of old mystics. This new outfit, it's blundering into new places it doesn't belong. It's throwing the worlds out of balance. And that's way beyond Chaos, mate" (4.12, "A New Man," cited in more detail in Breton and McMaster, 12). Buffy herself learns from the vampire, Spike, that the Initiative is capturing and experimenting on demons and vampires. Spike (aka Hostile 17) tells her that he has escaped from the Initiative, but not exactly unscathed. They have experimented upon him, and as part of their "xenomorphic behavior modification" (4.13) program, have implanted a microchip that neurologically neuters him as a vampire, making it impossible for him to physically harm a human being without suffering intense pain. He is in fact reduced to telling the Scooby Gang that he hates them and having to remind them that he is evil. However, since he can still harm demons without activating his chip, he finds himself, somewhat reluctantly, helping the Scooby Gang and the Slayer more and more in their fight against demons and evil.

The question now becomes whether or not the Initiative itself is evil. Giles and the Scooby Gang are certainly concerned when Buffy joins the Initiative, so much so that Buffy feels it necessary to reassure them, saying, "It just means that when I patrol I'll have a heavily armed team backing me up. Plus, boyfriend going to work with me: big extra perk" (4.13, "The 'I' in Team"). It turns out that Buffy is, in fact, blinded by the possibility of working with her boyfriend. The Initiative's "xenomorphic behavior modification" program is part of a larger project to create the perfect soldier by combining robotics with demon and human parts. Room 314 contains the prototype, the first such invincible soldier, appropriately called Adam by his Dr. Frankenstein–like creator, Maggie Walsh. As Anita Rose points out in "Of Creatures and Creators: Buffy Does Frankenstein," Walsh is like Victor Frankenstein, not only because she is building a monster out of "spare" parts, but also because she is doing it surreptitiously (135–138). Room 314 is a secret within a secret. The Initiative is a covert operation, and even the Initiative's commandos, including Riley Finn, have no idea what Walsh and the few scientists in the know are doing there. Maggie Walsh, although working in relative independence, is in fact carrying on the kind of research begun by the Initiative as early as 1943, when it was called the "Demon Research Initiative" (*Angel* 5.13, "Why We Fight"). In the *Angel* episode, we also learn during a flashback that this kind of research was actually begun by the Nazis: "Intra-Gehirn Anregung und Macht ueber Sub-Damonen. Genauer: Vampire" (5.13). We learn that the Nazis have been cutting into vampires' brains, working on "stimulation and control" in order to create an invincible army. Our vampire, Spike, is seen working both sides, wearing a Nazi uniform. Ironically, on his way to the United States with a captured prototype German U-boat, Spike expresses concern that the Americans might get a hold of the German research, because he certainly wouldn't want the Americans experimenting on him. With reference to the submarine crew, Spike says, "But if the Yanks are after this stuff, too, I'm eatin' the lot of them." And, most ironically, with reference to an American commander, he says, "And I'm not getting experimented on by his government" (5.13). Of course, that is exactly what happens. Some sixty years later, Maggie Walsh and her scientists insert the vampire neutering chip into Spike's brain.

Riley's greatest disillusionment with the Initiative and its covert experimentation comes in confrontation with Maggie Walsh's creation, Adam, the "kinematically redundant, biomechanical demonoid" (4.14, "Goodbye Iowa"). Riley is horrified when it calls him "brother" and suggests that Maggie Walsh is their mother, in that they have both been programmed by her: "She was the one who shaped your basic operating system. She taught you how to think, how to feel. She fed you chemicals to make you stronger — your mind and body. She said that you and I were her favorite children. Her art. That makes us brothers. Family" (4.14). Riley indignantly protests to Adam, "I cannot be programmed! I'm a man!" (4.14). He just cannot believe that the vitamins he has been taking and the food the Initiative has been feeding him contain drugs to enhance his strength and so forth, that he is part of Maggie Walsh's experimentation. He later learns that she has had a microchip implanted in him, and that Adam can activate it and thus control his will (4.21, "Primeval"). Riley is as much a victim of the Initiative's unethical Nazi-like modes of experimentation as is Spike.

This is the final step in Riley's disillusionment with the Initiative. Prior to this, Buffy has discovered that he has been going through withdrawal from the chemicals the Initiative has been feeding him. In fact, it is Buffy who first discovers that the Initiative has been experimenting on its troops when she sneaks into their headquarters and overhears some scientists, with rather German-sounding names, worrying that since Maggie Walsh's death at the hands of Adam, the drugging schedule for the soldiers has been disrupted, sending them into dangerous withdrawal: "These guys don't know they've been getting meds in their food so we better get them in here stat" (4.14, "Goodbye Iowa").

This certainly explains Riley's erratic behavior, at least to some extent. The fact that he suspects (rightly) his hero, Maggie Walsh, of attempting to murder his girlfriend, Buffy, and that he also suspects (wrongly) that Buffy has murdered Maggie, has also contributed to his confused state and disillusionment. He can't believe that Maggie Walsh would attempt to have anyone killed, not to mention someone he loves. But Maggie Walsh does want to get rid of the Slayer. She has seen her influence on Riley, whom she found trying to look through the window of room 314, a room in which he had taken no interest at all before meeting Buffy. In essence, Buffy and her inquisitiveness introduce an element of unpredictability into Walsh's world, something Walsh cannot control, and this makes Walsh feel threatened and fearful about the future of her pet project: "I've worked too long. Too long ... to let some little bitch threaten this project. Threaten me. She has no idea who she's dealing with. Once she's gone, Riley will come around. He'll understand. It's for the greater good. He'll see that. And if he doesn't.... Well, first things first. Remove the complication and when she least expects it..." (4.13, "The 'I' in Team").

Walsh's reasoning here is just another example of using the ends to justify the means. We have already seen this kind of thinking in Faith's rationalization of her action when she accidentally kills a human bystander. She mistakenly thinks that the good that Slayers do far outweighs the death of a single individual, innocent or otherwise. As we have already noted, this kind of reasoning leads Faith to the dark side, working with the human form of a giant demon serpent in attempting to open the Hellmouth.

If there is any doubt that this kind of utilitarian reasoning leads to evil, a character called the Operative in Joss Whedon's movie *Serenity* should give pause for thought. The Operative, like members of the Initiative, is a covert government agent who firmly believes that he is working for a better world, though unlike the members of the Initiative, he is clear-sighted enough to know that he himself can never be a part of this "brave new world," and even calls himself a "monster," acknowledging that he is a "thing of darkness." He is certainly willing to sacrifice thousands of lives to accomplish his objectives. And, like Riley, he finds himself completely disillusioned when he discovers the true nature of the government for which he is working.

Maggie Walsh is, in fact, killed by Adam as soon as he is brought to life. He stabs her with the retractable bony skewer in his forearm transplanted from the captured Polgara demon. The wound looks not unlike that which might be produced by a wooden stake and immediately members of the Initiative, including a reluctant Riley, suspect the Slayer. Riley has in fact seen a live video communication from Buffy to Professor Walsh, a communication that makes it clear that Walsh has attempted to have Buffy killed, but which also could be read as a plausible threat against Walsh's life on Buffy's part, "Professor Walsh. That simple little recon you sent me on ... wasn't a raccoon. Turns out it was me trapped in the sewers with a faulty weapon and two of your pet demons. If you think that's enough to kill me, you really don't know what a Slayer is.... Trust me when I say you're gonna find out" (4.13). Riley doesn't really know what to make of this video evidence. While he watches it, Professor Walsh tells him, "two of our hostiles broke free and escaped into the tunnels. She ... went after them on her own. She's dead, Riley." So what his trusted superior and mentor tells him and what he is seeing with his own eyes at the same time are mutually contradictory. Not knowing what to make of this confusing and emotionally disturbing situation, he simply walks out, though ordered to stop by Walsh. This is the first time he has disobeyed a direct order, but it won't be the last.

Some time later (six episodes actually), Riley discovers that the Initiative has captured a werewolf and is beginning to experiment upon it, allowing it to change into human form and then forcing the wolf back out again through painful negative stimulation. Riley recognizes this victim as Willow's boyfriend, Oz, a student at UC Sunnydale: "Come on, the guy's a student, I know him" (4.19, "New Moon Rising"). This is someone Riley knows personally, one of Buffy's friends, and thus someone whom it is rather difficult to see simply as an HST. Oz is certainly not a non-sentient animal. Buffy, Willow, and their friends have learned to cope with Oz's lycanthropy and at this point Oz has himself learned, within limits, to master and subdue the wolf within. Riley is, unfortunately, unable to get his colleagues in the Initiative to see or to care about the essential humanity in Oz.

In fact, Riley tries to help Oz escape. Unfortunately, the attempt is thwarted, and Riley too finds himself locked in a cell. He is rescued by Buffy and her friends when they sneak into the Initiative to rescue Oz and they are surprised to find that Riley, too, is locked up. Buffy exclaims in surprise when she learns why he is incarcerated, "Riley tried to help Oz escape?" Earlier, Riley had expressed shock upon hearing that Willow was dating a werewolf, "I'm just saying it's a little weird to date someone who tries to eat you once a month" (4.19). Riley's thinking has come a long way under Buffy's influence.

The end of the episode makes it clear just how far Riley has progressed. After Buffy and her friends rescue Oz and after Riley has left the

Initiative for good ("I leave now, I can't ever come back"), Riley and Buffy hide out in the ruins of the old high school. We contend that it is highly significant that their hideout is the high school, which was blown up at the end of the previous season in order to prevent the Mayor's ascension to the giant demon serpent. The destruction of the high school, it will be remembered, was, in fact, the killing of the serpent in order to prevent the opening of the Hellmouth, in a sense, rectifying the Genesis story in which the serpent's gift of knowledge was accepted. Buffy, in effect, is the anti–Eve. Hiding out in the remains of the old high school, the knowledge-dispensing institution, Buffy and Riley are now, in effect, sitting among the ruins of reason. This serves to emphasize Riley's recent choice to reject the Initiative, humanity's militarization of reason and scientific knowledge.

In a thoughtful moment, Riley repudiates the binary "demons bad, people good" world view of the Initiative that has motivated him thus far: "I was in a totally black and white space, people versus monsters, and it ain't like that." He then adds a crucial phrase — "especially when it comes to love" — that echoes Buffy's earlier comment about dating werewolves, "love isn't logical, Riley. It's not like you can be Mister Joe Sensible about it all the time" (4.19). Riley no longer sees the world in black and white; it is now, we should like to say, seen in living color rather than shades of gray. When his commanding officer threatens Riley that he is a dead man if he leaves the Initiative with Oz and Buffy, Riley replies, "No, sir. I'm an anarchist" (4.19). He is on a high here. He knows what he has to do, even though it involves self-sacrifice, giving up his entire military career, which gave meaning to his life until now. Doing the right thing often involves self-sacrifice in the Buffyverse. Even though ethical decisions are not always clear cut, black and white, it is still often the case that the right course of action is obvious. The point is that you cannot be told by others or by rules what you ought to do. You must choose for yourself, even if it involves changing who you have been in the past. Riley now has access to personal knowledge, to the subjective. He realizes that the so-called objectivity of the Initiative leads to an unacceptable way of looking at and dealing with the world. Not only had he seen them treating someone he knew person-ally, Oz, as a mere object of scientific investigation, but he had also expe-rienced becoming such an object himself, as the Initiative scientists, including Maggie Walsh, had altered his thinking through drugs and social programming, all without his consent, and even without discussing it with him. He also now realizes that all of his fellow commandos, his friends, were objectified in exactly the same way by the Initiative scientists. They have all been treated with the same lack of respect as they and the scientists had been treating the captured demons such as Spike. Just as the chip inserted into Spike's brain altered his nature as a vampire, so too Riley and his fellow commandos had their essential nature altered by the Initiative's interference, rendering questionable Riley's previous assertion, "I cannot be programmed! I'm a man!" (4.14, "Goodbye Iowa"). The Nazi-like science used by the Initiative makes it possible to program human beings, thus dehumanizing them. What Riley was trying to say is, "I am a man. I ought not to be programmed." Rob Breton and Lindsey McMaster, in their article in the first issue of *Slayage*, "Dissing the Age of Moo: Initiatives, Alternatives, and Rationality in *Buffy the Vampire Slayer*," argue, "To maximize its performance, the Initiative reconditions not only the monsters (to render them non-mystical and, more importantly, to harness their potential strength) but also their own soldiers through drugs and computer chip implants" (13). On the basis of this, they quite rightly conclude, "In an attempt to cleanse the divide between human and non-human, in order to eliminate the latter, the Initiative paradoxically compromises that divide in the physical manipulation of their own agents" (13).

We have been arguing, following our discussion of reason in Chapter One, that the applied science of the Initiative is not value neutral, that without proper constraints it can lead to the kind of horrors depicted by Whedon in Season Four of *Buffy the Vampire Slayer*, which we have been discussing. Madeline Muntersbjorn, in "Pluralism, Pragmatism, and Pals: The Slayer Subverts the Science Wars," argues with specific reference to Season Four, "*BtVS*'s characters rely more on magic than on mathematics, not because of some deep distrust of logical reasoning, but because they are so busy trying to save the world (while living lives worth saving) that they have little time to develop complete and consistent systems of axioms" (93). This, we suggest, fails to capture the very obvious fact that in the Whedonverse moral decisions rely more on existential choice than on systems of rules and axioms, either ethical or scientific. Riley does not decide to become an anarchist by consulting rules and axioms. How could he, given the meaning of anarchist? Though such decisions come close to improvisation, they still do not succumb to complete chaos. Riley's decision, for example, is based on accumulated personal knowledge both about how he has been treated and how he has treated others in the past. He is now in a position to react emotionally, but not unreasonably, to the situation. As Muntersbjorn admits, "the value of a rule or an exception depends on the context in which it occurs, and the context always changes" (96). Buffy and the Scooby Gang are not above choosing to use reason and science when they are useful. As we argued in Chapter One, Buffy actually uses reason in a mythical way. We argued that her wooden stake was a symbol of logic (the Tree of Knowledge), and this she wields with unerring skill and accuracy. Drawing on reason derived from the ancient Greek philosophers, the reason of Athens, Buffy is able to confront the logical absurdity of vampires, driving home the point that being undead is logically impossible. In Chapter One, we were making use of the distinction between Athens and Jerusalem. Buffy's wooden stake is, of course, totally bound up with the mythology stemming from Jerusalem, from the ancient Hebraic Torah, the basis of the Genesis story. The stake is thus paradoxically *both* Athens *and* Jerusalem. It is only by using both that the serpent's gift can be accepted without succumbing to the serpent's poison. The technology and applied science of the Initiative show where unbridled reason can lead us.

We have taken vampires in the Buffyverse as, at least in part, putting a face on the evil that Buffy must fight. James South, in "'All Torment, Trouble, Wonder, and Amazement Inhabits Here': The Vicissitudes of Technology in *Buffy the Vampire Slayer*," goes one step further, and regards vampires as symbols of the evils of technology and exploitation, citing Karl Marx's claim "capital is dead labor which vampire-like, lives the more, the more labor it sucks"(96). South describes Episode 3.9 ("The Wish"), which depicts an alternate reality where the vampires are victorious in Sunnydale and find technology most compatible, building an assembly line "blood extractor machine" (98) that mechanically drains blood from living human beings, turning them, in effect, into nothing but blood dispensers. South cites the Übervamp inventor, "humans with their plebian minds have brought us a truly demonic concept — mass production." South then goes on to argue, "there is present in *Buffy the Vampire Slayer* a real worry about the uses of technology and the ways in which it can dehumanize humans" (98). As South also argues, "It is significant that the show recognizes that technology cannot fight technology, since we would merely end up being subjugated by yet another technology. Hence, the significance of magic and witchcraft becomes apparent. There is something about magic that can in fact lead us to our liberation" (99). As Buffy has learned, "We can't beat evil by doing evil. I know that" (7.14, "First Date").

As South correctly points out, "magic is rooted in tradition" and the Scooby Gang gains access to this esoteric wisdom through the use of books, "tradition is signified by books" (99). For this reason, Muntersbjorn claims, "humanities scholars seeking to canonize a patron saint might consider *BtVS*'s creator Joss Whedon" (91). Muntersbjorn also recognizes that Buffy and the Scooby Gang use both reason and magic in their never ending fight against evil, and therefore argues that Whedon does not "champion the anti-science cause in the Science Wars," but rather "*BtVS* is a subversive challenge to arbitrary battle lines drawn in a needless debate" (91).

Not only is Buffy's stake a combination of reason and mythology, as we have argued above, but both magic and technology, the internet, are used by Willow to help the Scooby Gang battle the forces of darkness. In fact, her mentor is the "techno-pagan" Jenny Calendar who is not only her computer teacher, but also a Wiccan and part of the gypsy tribe that cursed Angelus with a soul. As Andrew Aberdein puts it in "Balderdash and Chicanery: Science and Beyond," "Jenny Calendar reminds Giles that 'bad old science' did not make the magic go away: 'the divine exists in cyberspace same as out here' ('I Robot ... You Jane'). Indeed, the show's most characteristic ambience is 'a creepy mix of magic and science' ('Beer Bad,' shooting script direction)" (85). As Aberdein quite rightly concludes, "Although the Scoobies can appropriate Initiative-style techniques when necessary ... the Initiative's ... perspective always prevents them from reciprocating" (86). The Initiative's exclusive reliance on reason and technology certainly precludes dabbling in the occult. In fact, as Breton and McMaster argue, "Buffy, Giles and the Scooby Gang ... are of the world that the Initiative, steeped in disjunctive reasoning, seeks to identify, compartmentalize, and destroy" (12). Just as the Initiative's exclusive use of reason and technology is the source of their difficulty and downfall, so Willow's story arc exposes the danger of becoming addicted to the magics. Still, Willow's magical abilities are required in order for Buffy and the Scooby Gang to defeat Adam.

It is only because of Willow's magic "enjoining spell" that Adam is ultimately defeated. Although Buffy (the anti–Eve) is strong enough to penetrate Adam and remove his nuclear power source, she cannot get close enough to him to do so because of his superior strength, agility, and built-in self-upgrading weaponry. Even the Initiative with all its military might is unable to defeat the "kinematically redundant, biomechanical demonoid" it created, because it is essentially a technologically enhanced *demon*. As Buffy tells them, "This is not your business. It's mine. You, the Initiative, the boys at the Pentagon — you're all in way over your heads. Messing with primeval forces you have absolutely no comprehension of.... I'm the Slayer. You're playing on my turf" (4.21, "Primeval").

However, just as the demon has been technologically enhanced, so the Slayer, in order to defeat it, becomes, through Willow's enjoining spell, magically enhanced. She is able to use a Sumerian paralyzing spell that Giles has unearthed through his research with ancient magical texts. The spell needs to be chanted in Sumerian by "an experienced witch." Giles can speak Sumerian, but is not an experienced witch. Willow has the Wicca experience, but is not fluent in Sumerian. Neither is powerful enough to fight Adam or even strong enough to rip out his power source once he is paralyzed. They therefore take seriously Xander's off the cuff suggestion: "So, no problem! All we need is combo Buffy. Her with Slayer strength, Giles's multi-lingual know-how, and Willow's witchy power" (4.21). This they accomplish through Willow's enjoining spell, "Make us mind and heart and spirit joined. Let the hand encompass us." The mind is Giles's contribution, the heart Xander's, the spirit Willow's and the encompassing hand Buffy's, which is able to reach in and remove Adam's uranium power source, as Buffy informs him, "You could never hope to grasp the source of our power" (4.21, "Primeval").

The use of this much magic constitutes an abuse of mystical power, which is almost as bad as the Initiative's exclusive reliance on science and technology. It upsets the balance and invokes the spirit of the First Slayer who, throughout the next episode, stalks each of the Scoobies in their dreams. As Giles explains, "Somehow our joining with Buffy and invoking the essence of the Slayer's power was an affront to the source of that power" (4.22, "Restless). The First Slayer reminds Buffy in her dream that Slayers work alone: "No friends! Just the kill.... We are alone!" (4.22). However, the moral of the story seems to be that Buffy has broken with the Slayer tradition and finds that Slayer power can be enhanced by befriending others. Certainly Buffy, by combining magic and technology with the help of the Scoobies, has lived more fully, fought longer, and, arguably, accomplished more than Slayers of the past.

Chapter Six

Darla, Spike, and Xander: Love and Self-Sacrifice

We have been discussing the existential love ethic implicit in the works of Joss Whedon, particularly in *Buffy the Vampire Slayer* and *Angel*, but also in his space westerns, *Firefly* and *Serenity*. While love is an emotion, it is also closely associated with a virtue, the virtue of care. Therefore any love ethics must necessarily be a virtue ethics, dealing primarily with moral character rather than with ethical judgments about specific actions. In such an ethics, we decide which actions are obligatory or permissible by referring to exemplary or ideal moral characters, asking what they would do in similar circumstances. Xander, for example, admits, "when it's dark and I'm all alone and I'm scared or freaked out or whatever, I always think, 'What would Buffy do?'" Of course, he also admits, "Ok, sometimes when it's dark and I'm all alone I think, 'What is Buffy wearing?'" (4.1, "The Freshman"). The point is that Xander regards Buffy as his hero and therefore tends to model his actions on hers. Xander, in treating Buffy as a moral exemplar, is, of course, attempting to imitate, or rather adopt, her virtues rather than her Slayer strength or her expertise in martial arts, which, of course, would not be possible, as Jason Kawal points out in his article, "Should We Do What Buffy Would Do?" (153ff). One of Buffy's essential virtues is her dedication to and care of others; that is, her willingness to sacrifice herself for the sake and safety of others. Jana Riess in her book, *What Would Buffy Do?: The Vampire Slayer as Spiritual Guide*, in her chapter amusingly titled "Be a Hero, Even When You'd Rather Go to the Mall: The Power of Self-Sacrifice," argues, "One theme of the Buffyverse is that for human beings to realize their full potential and make the world a better place, an element of sacrifice is essential" (12). Gregory J. Sakal, in his article in *'Buffy the Vampire Slayer' and Philosophy*, entitled "No Big Win: Themes of Sacrifice, Salvation, and Redemption," notes that etymologically, "to sacrifice" something is "to make it holy" or, more generally, "to

75

dedicate it to a higher purpose" (241). So, Buffy certainly is dedicating her life to such higher purposes as helping and protecting others, fighting evil, and making the world a better place.

In this chapter, rather than concentrating on Buffy, we discuss love and self-sacrifice by looking at three somewhat more minor characters in the Buffyverse: Xander, seemingly the least powerful and the least effective member of the Scooby Gang, and two vampires, one somewhat friendly (Spike), the other definitely not (Darla). Darla is, in fact, the first vampire we meet in the series. We actually meet her before we meet Buffy or any of the Scooby Gang. Even before the opening credits of the very first episode, though we don't yet know it's Darla, we are shown a night scene in which a boy and a girl are breaking into a science classroom through a window in Sunnydale High School. The classroom is obviously a biology lab, judging from the skeleton, vertebrae, specimens in formaldehyde, etc. over which the camera pans (1.1, "Welcome to the Hellmouth"). This also makes it a perfect setting for a horror movie. The young lad is obviously enticing the innocent schoolgirl into an isolated place where they can be alone, on the flimsy pretext that he wants to show her his old high school. Darla, in fact, is given the first line of the entire series *Buffy the Vampire Slayer*: "Are you sure this is a good idea?" (1.1). Of course, she actually thinks it is a really good idea. This is a work by Joss Whedon and nothing is as it seems. Though the boy may think that he is enticing an unsuspecting Darla to a place where he can have his way with her, she in fact is the one in complete control of the situation, with even more evil ideas of her own. As soon as she establishes that they are completely alone and unlikely to be disturbed, her vampire face emerges and she has her way with him, or, as the original shooting script puts it, "She bares HORRIBLE FANGS and BURIES them in his neck" (*Buffy the Vampire Slayer: The Script Book, Season One, Volume One*, 7). Later that day, his corpse is found in a gym locker in the girls' changing room. There are two bite marks on his neck and his blood has been drained, as Buffy reports to Giles once she has surreptitiously, if somewhat reluctantly, inspected the body (1.1).

We think it is important to note that the opening scene of the entire series takes place in a science lab which is also serving as a setting for a horror movie in which someone is killed (even if it's not the one the audience expects to be killed). The theme of science and mythology which recurs throughout the entire series is there from the very beginning, indeed from the opening teaser. We are thus set up from the very outset to see the high school, the knowledge-dispensing institution, as a locus for evil. The title of the first episode is not "Welcome to High School," or "Welcome to Sunnydale." It is, significantly, "Welcome to the Hellmouth." We learn that the high school is built on a hellmouth. Buffy is told that she is "standing at the mouth of Hell. And it's about to open" (1.1). The full implications of the close association between science and evil do not come out until Season Four in the episodes involving the Initiative, with its militarization of science and technology and unethical experimentation on both demons and humans. The fact that this is introduced so early in the series substantiates our claim that the evils of science, and indeed of reason itself (Athens), are principal themes in the Whedonverse, balancing the themes of love and self-sacrifice (Jerusalem).

It may well be asked what an evil vampire like Darla could possibly have to do with love and self-sacrifice. She is a very minor character in *Buffy the Vampire Slayer*. We learn in Episode 1.7 ("Angel") that she sired Angel and has had a long history of rampaging throughout Europe and Asia with him as companion and lover. She is killed in this episode by Angel who stakes her to prevent her from killing Buffy. We do not see Darla again (except in flashbacks which confirm her long history with Angel) until the evil law firm, Wolfram and Hart, in Season Two of the *Angel* series, magically brings her back to deal with Angel (*Angel* 1.22, "To Shanshu in L.A."). Until this point, love and self-sacrifice are the farthest things from Darla's mind and constitute no part of her character. The entire chronology of Darla's relationship with Angel from first bite to staking, and beyond, is outlined and cogently discussed in Joy Davidson's article "'There's My Boy...'" in the collection *Five Seasons of Angel: Science Fiction and Fantasy Writers Discuss Their Favorite Vampire*.

Stacey Abbott, in "From Madman in the Basement to Self-Sacrificing Champion: The Multiple Faces of Spike," claims that Wolfram and Hart bring Darla back as "a curious hybrid of her vampire and human selves" (331). We disagree. Though she is brought back in the form of a human being, soul and all, Darla nevertheless retains the memories of her lengthy and bloody career as a vampire. This is no different than Angel's status in *Angel* Episode 1.8 ("I Will Remember You"), when he is made human by the blood of a Mohra demon. Angel's heart then beats again, he loses all of his vampire strength, and is not in danger of losing his soul when achieving the climax of perfect happiness with Buffy. Nonetheless, he retains the memories of his double careers as Angelus, the most vicious of all vampires, and Angel, the champion dedicated to helping the helpless. Indeed, a return to the human state is, for much of the *Angel* series, the goal for which he strives, the prize at the end of his path of redemption. In Episode 1.8, however, he soon decides that in order to be an effective champion he must relinquish being human and asks to be restored to his vampire-with-a-soul condition, which, if anything, is the truly hybrid condition. This is an act of extreme self-sacrifice; he is giving up his long-sought goal. There is no suggestion that he is giving up a hybrid self of vampire and human. He is giving up his human self and the ability to consummate his love with Buffy for the sake of that very love (see our Chapter Two).

Athough she also remembers her vampire days, mostly nights, Darla is brought back as fully human, not as a curious hybrid of vampire and human. There is no suggestion that Darla is brought back as a hybrid in Davidson's article-length study of Darla. Presumably, Wolfram and Hart have brought Darla back in order to make Angel lose his soul and thus to restore the evil Angelus. They seem to assume that if Angel is sexually seduced by his former long-time lover, Darla, he will achieve a moment of perfect happiness, just as he did when he consummated his love for Buffy. Wolfram and Hart obviously know about the famous gypsy curse, which created Angel by giving Angelus a soul, with a rider that should Angel ever achieve a moment of perfect happiness, he would lose said soul and revert to his former evil self as the vampire Angelus. However, Darla does not seduce Angel at this point. It turns out that when Darla is brought back as a fully human being, her former human self as she was a prostitute in the early seventeenth century, this unfortunately includes her terminal case of syphilis, which she had evaded by being turned into a vampire. Her sire was the Übervamp known as the Master, the Big Bad of Season One of *Buffy*. Darla does try to talk Angel into turning her into a vampire once again, thus making Angel her second sire, in order to avoid both imminent death from the syphilis and the inconvenience of having a soul. Though Darla at this point is not a hybrid, she is, nevertheless, trying to be an evil human being, and her soul is functioning as a conscience, which is beginning to bother her. Abbott claims that when Angel refuses to sire Darla and thus remove her soul, "Wolfram & Hart bring in Drusilla to do the job" (331). But this is not quite accurate. Abbott ignores a crucial element in Darla's story arc. It is true that Darla begs Angel to turn her back, but this is in Episode 2.7 ("Darla"), two episodes before Wolfram and Hart bring Drusilla in to vamp her. In the meantime, Angel has convinced her that she has been given a second chance for a natural death, which can be seen as a form of redemption. Even in the earlier episode, Angel argues that humanity, mortal life, is a gift: "It's a gift. To feel that heart beat — to know, really and for once, that you're alive. You're human again, Darla. You know what that means?" (*Angel* 2.7, "Darla"). In the later episode, Darla finally comes to realize this and the second chance she has been given: "Maybe this is my second chance.... To die the way I was supposed to die in the first place" (*Angel* 2.9, "The Trial"). Angel accepts her choice and assures her that he will stay with her as she dies. It is important to emphasize that this is Darla's free choice. She is rejecting the evil life of the vampire.

At this point the goons from Wolfram and Hart burst in with Drusilla, subdue an obviously surprised Angel with a taser gun, and allow Drusilla to sire a struggling and resisting Darla. Angel can only look on helplessly, as he is repeatedly shocked by the taser and as he has had his hands bound behind his back. Again, the fact that Darla is struggling emphasizes the point that she had made the moral choice to reject being a vampire, that this is happening to her against her will. The scene is very different from the time that she was much more willingly sired by the Master, which we had seen in flashback just two episodes previously (2.7, "Darla"). To ignore, as Abbott does, the fact that Darla freely chose to reject life as a vampire, and in fact struggles against Drusilla's fangs, makes Darla's final act of self-sacrifice less intelligible, and actually misses its full significance. Even Joy Davidson, in her article dedicated to Darla, misses this crucial point.

Stacey Abbott is quite correct in the observation that it is most ironic, "Darla who was denied salvation and redemption as a human with a soul, finds it as a vampire when she becomes pregnant with Angel's human son" (331). Darla's redemption actually occurs when she stakes herself to save the life of her unborn child, whose soul within her has reminded her of the soul and life she had so recently re-experienced. Her experience of both of these souls has taught her to love and thus bond with her child. As she has told Angel, "I can't let it out. I-I can't. I love it completely. I-I-I don't think I've ever loved anything as much as this life that's inside of me.... I haven't given this baby a thing. I'm dead. It's been nourishing me. These feelings that I'm having, they're not mine. They're coming from it" (*Angel* 3.9, "Lullaby"). Shortly after this scene, she starts to refer to her unborn child as "he" rather than "it," but, as she tells Angel, "He's dying. Isn't he?... I can feel the life slipping away from me.... I told you I had nothing to offer this kid. Some mother ... can't even offer it life" (3.9). When she stakes herself, she is clearly sacrificing herself to save her child. This constitutes a tremendous change on Darla's part. When she first discovered she was pregnant, she went to every demon and shaman she could find to have it aborted, but found that they were all powerless to terminate this impossible pregnancy and relieve her of the soul within. The pregnancy is, of course, biologically impossible. Angel makes it clear that it is unheard of for vampires — the undead — to create life, to conceive children. There is something unnatural, even monstrous, about this pregnancy, even for vampires. Before returning to Angel to tell him about their impossible child, Darla has found herself not only craving the blood of children, but actually succumbing to this desire on many occasions: "Oh. I love children. I could just eat them up" (*Angel* 3.7, Offspring"). This means, incidentally, that their child, Connor, was in fact originally nourished, vampire-like, on the blood of innocent infants and children. Connor, of course, is not a vampire; in fact, he is more like a vampire-slayer, and one who at times hates his vampire father. Certainly, Angel finds him a troublesome teen. We think that Connor's story arc can be better understood when his dark origin is kept in mind.

Both Drusilla and Darla were conscripted by Wolfram and Hart to make Angel lose his soul and thus again to become the evil vampire Angelus. This is confirmed in the Fifth Season of *Buffy the Vampire Slayer*, which ran parallel to Season Two of *Angel*. As Spike puts it, in trying to clarify Drusilla's ramblings, "So, uh, let me get this straight. Darla got mojo'd back from the beyond ... you vamped her ... and now she and you are working on turning Angel into his own bad self again" (*Buffy* 5.14, "Crush"). This is a wonderfully concise summary of the storyline in Season Two of *Angel* appearing in Season Five of *Buffy the Vampire Slayer*, showing just how closely these two series work together as one complete narrative. The scene in which Darla actually has sex with Angel appears in one of the darkest episodes of the season. Angel has just been shown by Wolfram and Hart that the head office of the law firm, which everyone believed was located in Hell, is, in actual fact, the city of Los Angeles, here and now. Wolfram and Hart could not exist were it not for the perpetual existence of evil in everyone. Their job, it seems, is to bring this out, which we regard as a kind of opening of the Hellmouth. As the late Holland Manners, the lawyer explaining all this to Angel, says, "Welcome to the home office" (*Angel* 2.15, "Reprise"), as the doors of the elevator they had been descending in open onto the same street of Los Angeles they had apparently just left. The opening episode of *Buffy the Vampire Slayer* is, as we noted above, entitled "Welcome to the Hellmouth." The parallel here cannot be coincidental. The late Holland Manners also explains to an incredulous Angel, "I'm quite dead. Unfortunately my contract with Wolfram and Hart extends well beyond that." He goes on to explain, bleakly, "Our firm has always been here, in one form or another. The Inquisition. The Khmer Rouge. We were there when the very first caveman clubbed his neighbor. See, we're in the hearts and minds of every single living being.... See, the world doesn't work in spite of evil, Angel. It works with us. It works *because* of us" (*Angel* 2.15). This is why this episode of *Angel* is so dark. Angel becomes completely depressed. He has lost his reason to fight. Nothing matters.

When Angel returns to his apartment, he finds vampire Darla waiting for him there. He grabs her and kisses her violently. When she asks if this is what he really wants, he replies, "I just wanna feel something besides the cold.... It doesn't matter. None of it matters" (*Angel* 2.15). After he pushes her into the bedroom, shattering the French doors, and they have passionate sex, the episode ends, with the help of some discreet camera work, with Angel suddenly sitting up in bed with a gasp. There is a huge thunderstorm going on. This parallels closely Episode 2.13 ("Surprise") in *Buffy the Vampire Slayer*, in which Angel consummates his love with Buffy, loses his soul, and reverts to Angelus. In both episodes, he awakes, sitting up with a start. In both episodes, there is a fearsome thunderstorm. In both episodes, he goes out into the storm. Both episodes end leaving audiences hanging. The major difference, as we learn in the next episode of *Angel* ("Epiphany"), is that this time Angel has not lost his soul. This is a terrible affront to Darla's vanity. Having sex with her did not yield a moment of perfect happiness for Angel, the only thing that would make him lose his soul and become evil again. Darla says incredulously, "You're not evil. I-I don't understand. Was I ... Was it ... not good? Well, I don't accept that. You cannot tell me that wasn't perfect. Not only have I been around for four hundred years, but I used to do this professionally. And that was perfect" (*Angel* 2.16). This speech is a grim parody of Buffy's hurt and confusion when she finds Angel suddenly cold, uncaring, and coarse after they consummate their love. Buffy says, "I, I don't understand. Was it m-me? Was I not good?" Angel, now Angelus, responds cruelly, "You were great. Really. I thought you were a pro" (*Buffy* 2.14, "Innocence"). In this case, Angelus is using the word "pro" as a malicious put down. In the *Angel* episode, Darla was describing herself with a great deal of professional pride. But Darla's professional pride here has been hurt. Angel says, "It was perfect, Darla. It was perfect despair" (*Angel* 2.16).

Their child, conceived in despair, is the occasion of Darla's redemption, both sacrificing herself in absolute love for another, and escaping the hopelessness of vampire existence. The scene in which she stakes herself also takes place in the pouring rain. It is a most dramatic scene. Darla tells Angel, "Our baby is gonna die right here in this alley" and reminds him, "You died in an alley, remember?" This is significant, since she is referring to the time she sired him, killing him as a human being and creating him as an immortal undead creature. Before this moment, she had always thought that she had done him a favor by turning him into a vampire (see *Angel* 2.7, "Darla"). She now recognizes the horror of what she has done: "We did so many terrible things together. So much destruction, so much pain. We can't make up for any of it. You know that, don't you." As the rain beats down upon her, she is lying in the alley, and as she drives the stake into herself she disintegrates into dust, leaving her naked child crying on the bare pavement. She had come to the realization that their child is "the one good thing we ever did together" (*Angel* 3.9, "Lullaby"). What a nativity scene! Because of this child, she has learned to love, to care for someone more than for herself. This represents sacrifice in the etymological sense of dedication to a higher purpose.

Spike is another vampire who has learned the meaning of love and self-sacrifice. He, like Darla, sacrifices himself for a greater cause. At the end of Season Seven of *Buffy the Vampire Slayer*, in the concluding episode of the entire series, appropriately entitled "Chosen," Spike chooses to play a central role in once again sealing the Hellmouth, thus preventing evil from entering the world. Spike has finally achieved true existential freedom, which, as we have argued, "consists in the force and power not to admit evil into the world" (Shestov, *Athens and Jerusalem*, 256). The final battle scene takes place in the very mouth of Hell. It involves an army of Potentials, two Slayers (Faith and Buffy), and the Scooby Gang, now enlarged and enhanced from the original three supporters of Buffy. Buffy, with Willow's help, has magically shared her Slayer strength and abilities with each of the potential slayers gathered in Sunnydale from around the world. They have freely chosen to join the battle.

In the throes of battle, it becomes obvious that even this formidable army will go down to defeat without the essential help of Spike and his magic amulet, which was given to him by Buffy. When Buffy acquired this amulet it came with strict instructions that it must be given to a champion. There is, then, a very real sense in which Buffy has chosen Spike to be the champion. This means that when Spike chooses to sacrifice himself he is, in effect, like Buffy herself, choosing to be the chosen one. The title of the episode, "Chosen," draws attention to Spike's existential choice, as well as to that of the Potentials, all of whom are choosing to be the chosen ones. The amulet, it turns out, allows Spike to magically magnify and redirect sunlight, through his own body, into the Hellmouth. This destroys the seemingly invincible army of übervamps arrayed against them. When the Hellmouth was sealed at the end of Season Three, it involved only the destruction of the high school, the symbol of knowledge. Here, however, sealing the Hellmouth involves the destruction of the entire town of Sunnydale. The majority of the population has fled the rumblings of the Hell-mouth, leaving Sunnydale a ghost town, so to speak. Due to the amulet, the town collapses into the Hellmouth, thus sealing it completely. Spike is, of course, destroyed in the process, but not before Buffy has a chance to say, "I love you." Spike, in an uncharacteristic moment of insight, replies, "No, you don't. But thanks for saying it" (7.22, "Chosen"). Buffy, the surviving Potentials, and members of the Scooby Gang have managed to escape, driving to the edge of town in a schoolbus.

Jean Lorrah, in her *Seven Seasons of Buffy* article, "Love Saves the World," notes that it is ironic that Buffy and company "escape ... in a Sunnydale High schoolbus" (175). We agree, but we would argue that the reason for this irony is that this ending implies that the only thing surviving of the town is a bus belonging to the knowledge-dispensing institution, a vehicle of knowledge, which, we have argued, is inextricably linked to the Hellmouth and the admitting of evil into the world. Thus, a tiny bit of the evil of knowledge escapes the otherwise complete demolition of the Hellmouth, showing that evil, once admitted into the world, can never be completely destroyed.

Spike's self-sacrifice, like Darla's, is inextricably linked to love. Gregory Stevenson, in *Televised Morality: The Case of Buffy the Vampire Slayer*, puts it even more strongly. He argues, "Spike's story of redemption is a love story" (247). The fact that Spike is a vampire who has acquired a soul is also important. Though it is controversial, there is a suggestion that soulless vampires can learn to love. At least, Spike's long-time vampire paramour, Drusilla, replies to Buffy's claim, "You can't love without a soul," that vampires "can, you know. We can love quite well. If not wisely" (5.14, "Crush"). The truth of Drusilla's comment seems to be illustrated by Spike's entire amorous career. He has never, even as a human, loved very wisely. As a human, William, he was a foppish and sentimental poet who had a hopeless passion for one Cecily, who utterly despised both him and his verse. After Drusilla turns him into a vampire, he is equally infatuated with her, but also in the most sentimental of ways. Stevenson argues that possessiveness and selfishness are central features of Spike's love once he becomes a vampire (250), but in fairness we should point out that in Season Two, at least, he is very solicitous for Drusilla's well being. Gregory J. Sakal, in his article, "No Big Win: Themes of Sacrifice, Salvation, and Redemption," points out that Spike "demonstrates a kind of selfless love for his mate Drusilla, manifested in his steadfast willingness to put Drusilla's needs ahead of his own" (245). Indeed, we would have to conclude that Spike has a somewhat conflicted notion of love at this point.

Drusilla drops him, because Spike is simply not demon enough for her tastes: "Dru said I'd gone soft.... Wasn't demon enough for the likes of her.... I gave her everything: beautiful jewels, beautiful dresses with beautiful girls in them, but nothing made her happy.... I caught her on a park bench, making out with a chaos demon!... She only did it to hurt me ... and she said we could still be friends. God, I'm so unhappy!" (3.8, "Lover's Walk"). Spike considers forcing Willow to do a spell that will win back Drusilla, but in the end he decides instead to go back to what always works with her, "I want Dru back, I've just gotta be the man I was, the man she loved. I'm gonna do what I shoulda done in the first place: I'll find her, wherever she is, tie her up, torture her until she likes me again" (3.8).

When Spike initially falls in love with Buffy, he is once again conflicted. He expresses a genuine sympathy for her in Season Five when she is weeping over her mother's illness, a sign that Spike, the soulless vampire, can be concerned for others (5.7, "Fool for Love"). But at the same time, the root of his passion remains every bit as selfish and possessive as Stevenson argues, focused largely on Spike's desire for sensual gratification, the more instant the better. Hence, Spike's attempt to achieve satisfaction, first through a mere robot facsimile, called the Buffybot, and then later through his attempted rape of Buffy herself. Not surprisingly, both efforts fail. What is surprising is that by the time he attempts to rape Buffy, he is able to feel shock and revulsion for his own actions.

It seems that a combination of influences is at work here. In Season Four, a secret military research organization, called the Initiative, install a microchip in Spike's brain, which disables his ability to harm humans by causing him intense pain when he attempts to do so. The chip disables his ability to perform evil, but not his ability to enjoy evil or his desire to be evil; it also provides an opportunity to have other experiences and to develop new feelings of a more human nature. One of those other experiences is his love for Buffy, both in the sense of affection (his usual romantic sentimentality) and in the sense of physical gratification. His affection, however feckless, leads him to need to protect and help Buffy while she is doing good. Meanwhile he himself is refraining from evil hoping to impress Buffy by doing so. He is not at all aware that simply avoiding evil is not actually virtuous: "You want credit for not feeding on bleeding disaster victims?" (5.11, "Triangle"). Spike, like Faith when she takes over Buffy's body, gets to experience a reflection of the moral experience of being Buffy, in that he gets to develop some sense of how it can feel to be virtuous by helping others (even if it is at first just to impress Buffy). Whatever mixed motives drive him to acquire a soul at the end of Season Six, the immediate cause of the search is his self-loathing after the rape attempt, a loathing that recalls Faith's beating her own body (while in Buffy's) and labeling herself murderous and disgusting. This soul makes possible the completion of the process begun by acquisition of the chip and by his love for Buffy.

The possession of a soul endows Spike with the ability to make free, morally responsible, choices about his actions and thus about defining who he wishes to become. The soul does not make Spike good, any more than it makes anyone good (Xander has a soul when he leaves Anya at the altar), but it motivates him to choose to be good, rather than simply be programmed by debilitating impulses from a computer chip. And having a soul gives him the opportunity to understand what true love for Buffy really means: "only one thing I've ever been sure of. You.... I'm not asking you for anything. When I tell you that I love you, it's not because I want you, or 'cause I can't have you — it has nothing to do with me. I love what you are, what you do, how you try. I've seen your strength, and your kindness, I've seen the best and the worst of you and I understand with perfect clarity exactly what you are. You are a hell of a woman" (7.20, "Touched"). Spike's once demonic, that is to say, selfish and possessive love for Buffy has become something quite different: he now loves her as an ethical ideal, a moral exemplar.

Xander, too, as we have seen, comes to regard Buffy as a moral exemplar. Like Spike, Xander gets to save the world when it has become obvious that Buffy and the other Scoobies would fail without him. However, Xander's amulet is love itself. "Love will bring you to your gift," the First Slayer mysteriously tells Buffy (5.18, "Intervention"). Buffy finally understands the First Slayer's enigmatic explanation, "Death is your gift," when she realizes that she must sacrifice herself for her sister, Dawn. Xander, too, is motivated by love to offer his life to save the lives of others.

At the end of Season Six (6.22, "Grave"), Xander and Willow confront one another almost as a Christ and Antichrist. Willow has allowed the dark side of her Wiccan nature to get the better of her. She has become such a powerful witch that she can actually feel the pain of others. Unfortunately, it is the collective pain of everyone on earth that she is simultaneously tapping into: "It's incredible. I mean, I am so juiced ... it's like ... no ... mortal person has ... ever had ... this much power. Ever. It's like I, I'm connected to everything.... I can feel ... it feels like ... I ... I can feel ... everyone. Oh. Oh my God. All the emotion. All the pain. No, it, it's too much. It's just too much.... I have to stop this. I'll make it go away. Oh, you poor bastards! Your suffering has to end" (6.22, "Grave"). Like Christ, she has taken the pain of the world upon herself. Not only does she find this unbearable, but simply feeling the pain of others does nothing to take it away from others. She is sharing this pain, not removing it. Whether for the sake of others or for her own sake, she decides that life is not worth this much pain and so all must die.

Willow's Wiccan powers have grown to such an extent that she is fully capable of bringing about the end of the world. She is also strongly motivated to do so. This is why we argue she is functioning as an Antichrist. She is so powerful and enraged that neither Buffy nor Giles, who inadvertently provided her with this power, can stop her. Only Xander, her friend since childhood, is capable of doing so. Unlike Buffy, his only superpower is the power of love. He has known and loved Willow since they were in kindergarten together. Xander confronts her: "You're not the only one with powers, you know. You may be a hopped-up über-witch, but ... this carpenter can dry-wall you into the next century.... You've been my best friend my whole life. World gonna end ... where else would I want to be?... You're Willow.... First day of kindergarten, you cried because you broke the yellow crayon, and you were too afraid to tell anyone. You've come pretty far. Ending the world, not a terrific notion. But the thing is? Yeah. I love you. I loved crayon-breaky Willow and I love scary veiny Willow. So if I'm going out, it's here. If you wanna kill the world? Well, then start with me. I've earned that" (6.22, "Grave").

The more Xander tells Willow he loves her, the more she wounds him with magical lightning bolts from her veiny hands until love finally wins out, and black-haired, scary Willow once again becomes red-haired, gentle Willow, weeping quietly in Xander's arms. The Prayer of St. Francis is being sung in the background by Sarah McLachlan. It includes the words "Where there is hatred, let me sow love," and "for it is in giving that we receive."

Xander is certainly performing the Christ-like role. His reference to himself as a carpenter confirms this as does his name. The normal short form of "Alexander" is, of course, "Alex," not "Xander," just as the usual short form for Abraham is "Abe," not "Bram," as in Bram Stoker, the author of *Dracula*. The short form "Xander," we contend, conjures "Christ" in much the same way as "Xmas," the short form for "Christmas" does. "Xander" is then "Christ-ander," from "andros," the Greek for "man." Thus "Xander" is "Christ-man." However, many of us were erroneously taught in Sunday School that we should never write "Christmas" as "Xmas" because this is crossing the "Christ" *out of* "Christmas." We suggest that this also fits well with atheist Joss Whedon's attempt to use a Christian love ethics without its metaphysical and theological foundations. He wishes both to invoke the Christian tradition and yet to maintain his atheism, so Christianity is invoked under a kind of Derridaean ~~erasure~~, as if the term were written and then crossed out, thus appearing in the text with a line through it. With the name "Xander" then, Christianity is both invoked and not invoked at the same time. This apparently logically impossible proposition, as we have argued in Chapter One, is in fact possible under the mythos of Jerusalem but not under Athens, the logic of the Greek philosophers. Rhonda Wilcox, in her 2005 book *Why Buffy Matters: The Art of "Buffy the Vampire Slayer,"* notes, quite correctly, that Xander's name is "a curtailed form" of the name of one of the most famous Greek generals, Alexander the Great (47). We argue further that Xander has the heroism of Alexander the Great, but instead of relying on the power of Athens (reason), he uses the much gentler power of love derived from Jerusalem. Xander is able to reach Willow only through love. As Giles says of Willow, "the magic she took from me tapped into the spark of humanity she had left. Helped her to feel again. Gave Xander the opportunity to reach her" (6.22). Xander, the Christ-man, thus uses love to save the world.

However, this is not the first time that the humble Xander has saved the world. In Episode 3.13 ("The Zeppo"), Xander's apparent marginality as the least effective and least powerful member of the Scooby Gang does not prevent him from single-handedly saving the world (sort of). The whole "Zeppo" episode centers on Xander, with the rest of the Scooby Gang in the background dealing with yet another impending apocalypse. Both Buffy and the others keep telling Xander to stay out of danger's way. After a battle in which Xander is almost killed, Buffy and Faith express concern, saying, "Xander, one of these days, you're gonna get yourself hurt.... Or killed.... Or both. And, you know, with the pain and the death, maybe you shouldn't be leaping into the fray like that. Maybe you should be fray-adjacent" (3.13). The episide contains several pointed reminders of Xander's alleged inadequacy, culminating in Cordelia's cruel summary: "It must be really hard when all your friends have, like, superpowers — Slayer, werewolf, witches, vampires — and you're, like, this little nothing.... Xander, you're the, the useless part of the group. You're the Zeppo" (3.13).

Xander is certainly ordinary and represents those of us without superpowers. Xander is bullied by Jack O'Toole and his high school friends. Most of us have experienced being bullied by high school zombies. In Sunnydale, of course, these bullies really are zombies, though, as Rhonda Wilcox points out in *Why Buffy Matters*, they move and act more like regular high school kids (138). They force Xander at knife-point to take them cruising at night in the convertible he has rented from his uncle in order to appear cool. Xander has to wait outside a hardware store while the bullies break in and steal the makings of a powerful bomb (though it is some time before Xander finds out what they stole). As he sits behind the wheel, he says to himself nervously, "Okay. Now I'm involved in crime. I'm the criminal element. Having a car sure is cool!" When the members of his his new-found gang return from the hardware store and dump what they call the "cake mix" into the back seat of the car, Xander is able to get away by literally running from their death threats and circling back to leap into the car and take off. He later discovers the ingredients for a bomb sitting on the back seat of his car. He bravely returns to the hardware store, but the bullies are long gone. He assumes that they have acquired more ingredients for a bomb, and wonders where they will set it off. He seeks out Buffy (and eventually Giles), since, after all, "Buffy'll know what to do" (3.13). But he finds that they are preoccupied with the coming apocalypse, so he must decide for himself what Buffy would do.

He has already rescued Faith from a demon of the Sisterhood of Jhe, the perpetrators of tonight's apocalypse. As Giles has discovered, "The Sisterhood of Jhe is an Apocalypse cult. They exist solely to bring about the world's destruction" (3.13). Xander encounters Faith in a losing battle with one of these demons, and runs it over, immobilizing it long enough for Faith to leap into his car so they can both flee the danger. He takes her back to her motel where he helps set her dislocated shoulder. She then tells him, "A fight like that and ... no kill.... I'm about ready to pop" (3.13). Faith always finds that fighting makes her "hungry and horny" (3.3, "Faith, Hope, and Trick"). Good taste prevents us from discussing the ensuing scene in much detail, but it's Xander's first time, or, as Xander puts it, "I've never been up with people before" (3.13). He also asks Faith, "Did I mention that I'm having a very strange night?"

The night gets stranger still. Xander feels duty-bound to seek out the zombie bullies and attempt to find out where they have placed the bomb. Again, his car comes in handy. He bravely drives up to them and then speeds away, hesitating just long enough for one of them to grab on to the driver's door and be swept along with him, holding on for dear life (or whatever zombies have). Xander, driving with one hand, and holding the zombie with the other, discovers that the bomb is in the boiler room of the high school, but drives too close to a mailbox and accidentally decapitates the zombie before finding out how to defuse the bomb. Two of the zombies follow Xander to the school, where he has a difficult time avoiding them. Buffy, Giles, and the other members of the Scooby Gang are in the school library fighting the Sisterhood of Jhe and a three-headed snake, which have emerged from the Hellmouth directly below the library floor. Xander is so busy he doesn't even notice his friends in the library, though one of the zombies does. We see him looking wide-eyed through a window in the library door, as he exclaims, "Wow!" (3.13). While the apocalyptic battle rages upstairs, Xander confronts the zombies and their bomb downstairs in the boiler room. He has managed to kill one of them, and finds himself face-to-face with their leader, Jack O'Toole, over the ticking bomb. There are only minutes left on the timer, and Xander has been unable to force Jack to tell him how to disable the bomb. They are no longer fighting, but both are watching the timer while Xander blocks the door. They both realize that neither of them can get out of the school before the bomb explodes. To Jack's bluster that he is not afraid to die because he is already dead, Xander responds, "Yeah, but this is different. Being blowed up isn't walking around and drinking with your buddies dead. It's little bits being swept up by a janitor dead, and I don't think you're ready for that" (3.13). When Jack asks Xander if he is ready for such a death, Xander replies, quite in character, "I like the quiet." Xander has always been the quiet hero. With only two seconds left on the timer, Jack caves in and disconnects it.

It is important to recognize that it is not just the high school that Xander is saving here. If the Scooby Gang upstairs cannot defeat the Sisterhood of Jhe, with help of a binding spell by Willow, the entire world will come to an end. The Sisterhood, but not the Scooby Gang, seem powerful enough to survive the destruction of the high school. We can conclude, then, that without Xander we would have the final apocalypse. He has not merely helped the Scooby Gang prevent this apocalypse, but he has enabled them to do so. He never tells them of his role in the night's proceedings and they continue to try to protect him from danger, keeping him "fray-adjacent." Xander alone has learned what he is capable of and is quite satisfied. We now know, as does Xander, that he is an integral part of the Scooby Gang.

Rhonda Wilcox, in *Why Buffy Matters*, gives a Freudian/Jungian reading of the "Zeppo" episode. She sees the basement of the high school as the individual's subconscious id lying at the base of "the highly intellectual Giles and Willow in the library" above, and argues, "Buffy and company cannot save the world unless Xander saves the school they are in: the battle with self must be won first" (144). She also notes that Joss Whedon has admitted that Xander is the character who most closely represents him as well as the rest of us (144). If Xander is Everyman, then we are all quite capable of saving the world as well as ourselves, and are responsible for doing so, whatever the sacrifice required.

Chapter Seven

Willow and Tara: Love, Witchcraft, and Vengeance

How can Buffy's best friend, Willow Rosenberg, develop from a shy, studious high school girl who has seen the "softer side of Sears" (1.1, "Welcome to the Hellmouth") into the world's wickedest Wiccan, hell-bent on apocalyptic destruction with the power and will to incinerate all life on earth? James B. South, in *Buffy the Vampire Slayer and Philosophy: Fear and Trembling in Sunnydale*, argues that Willow's decision to destroy the world is totally irrational and thus, at least to him, quite unintelligible. South, as a professional philosopher trained in the Anglo-American analytic tradition, seems totally unable to cope with the upsurge of the irrational, and he proposes instead "to sketch a philosophical framework that recognizes the truly unintelligible side of irrationality" (133). We must admit that we find South's argument itself quite unintelligible. We have no difficulty in understanding and explaining both Willow's transition to the dark side and her redemption. Nor are we alone in this. Gregory Stevenson, in *Televised Morality: The Case of Buffy the Vampire Slayer*, does admit, "it is like the experience of having ... a close friend suddenly and inexplicably descend into darkness." However, even Stevenson goes on to argue, "the truth is that such self-destructive turns are rarely sudden or inexplicable. The seeds are always sown earlier, growing slowly beneath the surface until sprouting forth." He concludes, "With Willow, the signs were there all along" (236). Similarly, Jana Riess, in *What Would Buffy Do? The Vampire Slayer as Spiritual Guide*, argues, "the series' most interesting downfall by far is that of Willow.... Even toward the beginning of the series, there are hints that she's sometimes more interested in acquiring knowledge and power, and avoiding emotional pain, than she is in doing the right thing" (103). Both Stevenson and Riess are approaching Willow's unreason from the theological perspective, Christian and Buddhist, respectively, rather than from the philosophical (the Anglo-American analytical) angle. In Chapter One, we drew upon the distinction between Athens and Jerusalem as a key to understanding the underlying meaning of the entire show *Buffy the Vampire Slayer*. We suspect that South is blinkered by his training in the philosophical traditions stemming from ancient Greece (he even begins his article with a reference to "Raphael's famous painting, *The School of Athens*," 131). Stevenson and Riess are following more in the line stemming from Jerusalem, using the magical-mythical tradition of the ancient Hebrew mystics, or in Riess' case, the Eastern traditions as well. Given their approach, both Stevenson and Riess seem better able than South to understand Willow Rosenberg, who is, incidentally, the only explicitly Jewish major character in the series.

Stevenson notes that in the Buffyverse "magic is treated to the same principle of moral evaluation as technology" (128). Given our distinction between Athens and Jerusalem, we have argued that the technology stemming from the exclusive acceptance of reason is not in fact morally neutral, but rather is responsible for the opening of the Hellmouth and thus allowing evil to enter the world. Nonetheless, as we have shown, both reason and technology are used, on more than one occasion, to help humanity, to save the world, and even, periodically, to close the Hellmouth and thus prevent evil from entering the world. For example, there is, in 1.4 "Teacher's Pet," Buffy's use of Giles' recording of bat sonar to disorient a teacher who is in actuality a giant praying mantis (Buffy having remembered from science class that bat sonar has this effect on smaller versions of the bug). There is also the use of a rocket launcher in 2.14 "Innocence" to kill an enemy who could not be killed by "any weapon forged." There is the use of the internet on numerous occasions to find information needed to save the day. And, most dramatically, at the end of Season Three, there is the blowing up of the high school (the knowledge-dispensing institution), filling the Hellmouth with its rubble. This can even be seen as stuffing the rational back from whence it came. In a typically Joss Whedon reversal, he has demonized the rational rather than the magical. As Stevenson argues, "Identifying the very depiction of magic and witchcraft as a glorification of the occult misses the point" (174–175). For Stevenson, the metaphorical function of magic on *Buffy the Vampire Slayer* is to represent power, its use and abuse. "Because magic is a source of power, its use becomes a moral issue ... misuse of that power is immoral on *Buffy*, represented by the consequences that follow" (175).

The source of power is not as important as the consequences resulting from its use. Even the power of the Slayer to fight evil has been shown to originate in the demonic (7.15, "Get it Done"). As Buffy acknowledges,

"It's about power. Who's got it ... who knows how to use it" (7.1, "Lessons"). Whedon refuses to demonize the demonic. The magical-mythical rather than the strictly rational is seen to be morally neutral. The ethical issue is about its use or abuse. This is the clue to understanding both Willow's descent toward world-destroying evil, and her subsequent redemption and central role in permanently changing the world for the better. We see Willow's relationship with Oz as providing her with an example to follow in controlling her own inner demons. As we argued in Chapter Two, Willow's werewolf boyfriend, Oz, recognizing that he must learn to control the wolf within him, learns and practices the appropriate spiritual exercises, meditation techniques, and so forth. But the self-discipline he acquires is not quite powerful enough to deal with the emotional turmoil which overcomes him when he learns of Willow's love for Tara, and he then makes the most difficult sacrifice of all: he relinquishes his relationship with Willow, while continuing to love her intensely, and leaves Sunnydale permanently in order to ensure that he will not pose a threat to either Willow or Tara (4.19, "New Moon Rising"). Oz's story arc here reflects and reinforces the major plot line in which Angel also chooses to leave Sunnydale and the one great love of his life. It will be remembered that because of a gypsy curse Angel cannot risk having even one moment of true happiness with Buffy for fear of losing his soul and reverting to the evil vampire, Angelus. Both Oz and Angel, then, show that tremendous self-sacrifice is sometimes required in order to prevent evil from entering the world.

Willow, too, as we shall see, must learn this difficult lesson, but she cannot do it without the help of others. Her relationship with Tara is one of the most important. As Gregory Stevenson notes, the Willow-Tara relationship "lasted longer and was treated more positively than almost any other relationship on *Buffy*" (13). Stevenson remarks that this may be the reason "why many evangelical Christians reject, ignore, or attack *Buffy*" since the loving friendship between Willow and Tara was depicted as an obvious "lesbian relationship between two witches" (13). Since, as we have noted, Whedon does not demonize witchcraft, his linking of lesbianism and witchcraft cannot really be read as a negative portrayal of lesbianism per se, as some critics have suggested (cf. the varied studies of this issue by Kryzywinska, 2002; Bartlem, 2003; Beirne, 2004; Wilts, 2004; Battis, 2005; and Jowett, 2005). Buffy herself, though denying being "freaked out" by Willow's coming out, when first told does respond with surprise and confusion: "Oh! Oh. Um ... well ... that's great. You know, I mean, I think Tara's a, a really great girl, Will.... Well, there you go, I mean, you know, you have to, you have to follow your heart, Will. And that's what's important, Will.... I'm glad you told me" (4.19, "New Moon Rising"). Again, we do not see this as in any way a negative portrayal of lesbianism. In the same episode, Buffy has already accused her boyfriend, Riley, of bigotry, when he comments on Willow's dating a werewolf (Oz). When he defends himself, saying, "Whoa, hey, how did we get to bigot? I'm just saying it's a little weird to date someone who tries to eat you once a month," Buffy responds, "Yeah, well, love isn't logical, Riley" (4.19).

It is important to note and keep in mind the explicit reference to love as non-rational in a program which, we contend, is developing a love ethic rather than a moral philosophy based on reason.

In the previous season, when Willow is still going out with Oz, she discovers she has an irresistible attraction to her longest-standing friend, Xander. The negative consequences of giving in to this mutual attraction are dramatically illustrated when Xander's girlfriend, Cordelia, and Willow's boyfriend, Oz, find them kissing in an abandoned factory when they arrive to rescue them from Spike. While tearfully running away from the scene, Cordelia trips and falls, impaling herself on a piece of rebar (3.8, "Lovers Walk"). What a wonderful portrayal of the pain of betrayal! Willow, too, finds it impossible to deal with the pain of losing a lover, when Tara is accidentally shot (6.19, "Seeing Red"). As a number of commentators have noted, there are hints of Willow's inability to deal with strong emotions right from the outset of the series. As Stevenson puts it, "Willow's later troubles all grow out of her deep-seated insecurity and lack of emotional control" (237).

One of our earliest encounters with Willow is highly instructive in a number of ways. The first piece of information we receive about her is that she is a brainy high school student, one Xander turns to for help with his math. This presentation of Willow could indicate that she may be either a person of confidence and ability, or that she is the stereotypical nerd (or a combination of the two). Shortly after that brief scene, we see Willow having a drink from the water fountain, and addressed by Cordelia: "Willow! Nice dress! Good to know you've seen the softer side of Sears." After Willow nervously indicates that her mother selected the outfit, Cordelia mockingly says, "No wonder you're such a guy magnet." Jes Battis, in his book *Blood Relations: Chosen Families In Buffy The Vampire Slayer And Angel*, draws our attention to this scene as his means of explaining Cordelia and her sense of entitlement, as popular, attractive rich girl, to bluntly speak whatever she sees as the truth. He explains that the "softer side of Sears" was in fact part of a 1997 Sears advertising campaign to stress that the store sold clothing and bedding as well as major appliances and electronics. Cordelia is thus putting Willow down by saying, in effect, that her clothing style comes from an appliance store rather than from Bloomingdale's (Battis 116, 174 n.4). Later, when Cordelia finds Buffy and Willow in conversation, she intrudes, "I don't mean to interrupt your downward mobility...." She has already welcomed Buffy to Sunnydale High School by noting that she will "be OK" in her new school if she hangs with Cordelia and her cool crowd, then, with pointed reference to Willow, advises, "Once you can identify [the losers] all by sight they're a lot easier to avoid" (1.1, "Welcome to the Hellmouth").

Although Battis uses these Cordelia-Willow encounters to characterize Cordelia's rich girl, fashion-conscious status, we would argue that they also show how Willow's negative self-image is determined from the outside. Buffy ultimately decides to hang with Willow, rather than with Cordelia. Willow, as we know, becomes part of the Scooby Gang, helping to fight evil and the forces of darkness. Battis, in fact, goes so far as to argue that Willow is "given form ... purely by the perceptions of others." His point is that Buffy and Xander "have constructed a Willow who is always available, always ready with an innovative solution ... Xander's best friend, and Buffy's best friend, and 'she of the level head'" (6.22, "Grave")" (32–33). Willow is, then, being constructed by two conflicting sets of what we have called outside view predicates, those imposed on her by Cordelia and the Cordettes on the one hand, and those associated with the more positive acceptance by the Scooby Gang on the other. But, as we explained in Chapter Three, to allow yourself to be determined by the Look of the Other, by outside view predicates, is to live in Bad Faith. We would argue that Willow does not approach anything resembling an authentic existence until she achieves redemption through existential choice in Season Seven. This would explain her insecurity and lack of emotional control in the earlier seasons. She is so insecure that she confesses to Buffy her inability to engage in meaningful conversation with the opposite sex, the site of crucial emotional tensions for teenagers: "Well, when I'm with a boy I like, it's hard for me to say anything cool, or, or witty, or at all. I-I can usually make a few vowel sounds, and then I have to go away" (1.1, "Welcome to the Hellmouth"). Willow certainly gets over her stage fright with boys by the time she has her relationship with Oz.

It is, however, Willow's relationship with Tara that is the most telling, and quite different from that with Oz. In her relationship with Oz, Willow derived her sense of identity and validation from Oz's standing in the social hierarchy of high school: "my boyfriend's in the band!" (2.16,

"Bewitched, Bothered and Bewildered"). In other words, he is both male and occupies a prestigious position as a guitarist in a locally popular band. With Tara, for the first time, Willow attempts to exert control over the relationship, to be the one who defines its essential characteristics, so much so, in fact, that Tara complains, "But you don't get to decide what is better for us, Will. We're in a relationship, we are supposed to decide together" (6.8, "Tabula Rasa"). Tara is here objecting to Willow's attempt to control her mind by means of a magic spell to make Tara forget that she and Willow had been quarreling. This sort of intrusion into Tara's mind is a very dramatic illustration of the attempt to possess the freedom of the Other, which Jean-Paul Sartre characterizes as the essence of sexual relationships. It is, of course, impossible to possess another's freedom because, as soon as you possess it, it is no longer freedom. You have, in effect, made a slave out of your lover.

The paradox is that the relationship cannot be satisfying unless the Other freely gives herself/himself to you. This Sartrean point is portrayed literally in the Buffyverse in episode 5. 15, "I Was Made to Love You," in which techno-nerd Warren Mears builds himself a robot girlfriend, whom he calls April. Warren, at least at first, is quite insistent that this object is not a sex toy, but an actual girlfriend. Much to his surprise, Warren does not find a relationship with a lovebot satisfying: "I didn't make a toy. I made a girlfriend.... I really thought I would be [in love] ... I mean, she's perfect. I don't know, I ... I guess it was too easy. And predictable.... You know, she got boring. She was exactly what I wanted, and I didn't want her" (5.15, "I Was Made to Love You"). Warren's difficulty is, of course, that the robot, being a mere thing, is not capable of freely giving itself to him, it does not possess freedom. As Sartre argues in *Being and Nothingness*, "The man who wants to be loved does not desire the enslavement of the beloved.... The total enslavement of the beloved kills the love of the lover ... if the beloved is transformed into an automaton, the lover finds himself alone." Sartre's point is "the lover does not desire to possess the beloved as one possesses a thing; he demands a special type of appropriation. He wants to possess a freedom as freedom" (478).

Warren's frustration and the Sartrean explanation of it are echoed in Spike's disappointing relationship with the Buffybot (also built by Warren, but to Spike's specifications). After a particularly energetic (and to the viewer, quite comic) session of lovemaking, the Buffybot says, "Spike, I can't help myself. I love you." The besotted Spike replies, "You're mine, Buffy," only to be completely deflated by the Buffybot's impeccably timed, "Should I start this program over?" The now irritated Spike responds, "No programs. Don't use that word. Just be Buffy" (5.18, "Intervention"). This, of course, is the very thing that the robot cannot be, since the real Buffy possesses freedom, and is more than a mere thing. What's missing in both Spike's and Warren's relationships with their lovebots is the notion of the lover freely giving herself to the beloved.

This form of possession is sensitively illustrated in a conversation between Willow and Tara, in which Willow tells Tara that she likes being a member of the Scooby Gang, but that what she really wants is to have someone who is just hers, and Tara replies freely and fondly, "I am, you know.... Yours" (4.16, "Who Are You?"). From a Sartrean perspective Tara's freely choosing to be possessed by Willow is deeply significant. Sartre, in *Being and Nothingness*, within two pages of introducing his automaton to explain the freedom required in a loving relationship, actually uses the phrase "*the chosen one*" to characterize the paradox that although we require free choice from our lover we also believe our lover to be our one and only, chosen specifically for us by fate as it were. "[I]f I am to be loved by the Other, this means that I am to be freely chosen as beloved. As we know, in the current terminology of love, the beloved is often called *the chosen one*" (482, italics in original; in the French it is "*élu*," *L'Être et le Néant*, 438). Sartre goes on to make it quite clear that this means not simply chosen randomly from among many, but rather chosen by the universe or God or fate to be the only choice possible. The lovers were somehow meant to be together, made for each other. Love, it seems, wants the logically impossible. It requires free choice, as the experience with the lovebots makes perfectly clear, but it also needs each of the lovers to have found *the chosen one*, the one person in all the world meant just for them. It may not be rational to want *the chosen one* to freely choose, but then love is not rational, not logical, as Buffy keeps reminding Riley, her hyper-rational boyfriend. Love is an emotion, and therefore more akin to the magical.

We would argue that one of the implicit goals of the entire series, *Buffy the Vampire Slayer*, is to illustrate just how someone designated as *the chosen one* can have the kind of free choice necessary for an authentic existence. Giles keeps reminding Buffy that it is no coincidence that both Watcher and Slayer have arrived in Sunnydale at the same time: "You really have no idea what's going on, do you? You think it's coincidence, your being here?" (1.1, "Welcome to the Hellmouth"). As Giles tries to explain, "You are the Slayer. Into each generation a Slayer is born, one girl in all the world, a Chosen One, one born with the strength and skill to hunt the vampires...." It is here that Buffy interrupts by joining in "...with the strength and skill to hunt the vampires, to stop the spread of their evil blah, blah,

blah.... I've heard it, okay?... I've both been there and done that, and I'm moving on "(1.1, "Welcome to the Hellmouth"). It really doesn't matter if *the chosen one* is Slayer or lover, the "problem of freedom" is the same. We are not suggesting that Whedon is consciously and deliberately attempting to solve a problem raised by Sartre. When we discussed Sartre's *Being and Nothingness* in Chapter Three, we stopped short of claiming any kind of direct Sartrean influence on Whedon, in spite of Whedon's admission that Sartre is the author of the most important book he has ever read. Nor are we going to try to substantiate any such claim of direct Sartrean influence here. We do, however, suspect that some sections of *Being and Nothingness* could be read as kind of convoluted storyboards for at least a few of the episodes in *Buffy the Vampire Slayer*. Certainly Sartre's description of the automaton and his discussion of the freedom necessary for both a lover and a beloved has clear echoes in Warren's dissatisfaction with the robot girlfriend he constructed, and also in Spike's frustration with his Buffybot. By the time we are introduced to the lovebot in Whedon's futuristic movie *Serenity*, we are ready to see that the complete acceptance of the lovebot as wife and lover by the character called Mr. Universe serves only to underline the loss of freedom under the totalitarian regime of the Alliance.

If the beloved can choose to be possessed by the lover, then the beloved can also choose to leave the relationship, not because the love affair is over but, more importantly, for the sake of that very love. We have in fact seen both Oz and Angel do just that. Tara too actually leaves Willow at one point, because Willow abuses Tara's freedom through manipulation. Tara sees Willow's increasing use of magic for selfish purposes, and her dependence on it for all sorts of things that can be dealt with by normal means, as Willow's growing loss of freedom and morality as well as a form of addiction to magic. When Willow insists on performing a spell to raise Buffy from the dead, Tara warns her, "It is wrong. It's against all the laws of nature" (6.1, "Bargaining, Part One"). Willow, nevertheless, goes ahead and successfully performs the spell, though, of course, there are consequences. There are always consequences.

Tara, unlike Willow, is keenly aware that there are ethical constraints to using the power of magic. This is, in part, what makes Tara a better, if less powerful, witch than Willow. It also makes her a better person. Tara's death is all the more tragic because of the person she is and is seen to be. She may be the most empathetic person on the show. She helps Buffy deal with the death of her mother because she has lost her own and knows what Buffy is suffering. She is like a surrogate parent to Buffy's little sister, Dawn, because she knows what it feels like to be on the outside, not quite a full member of the Scooby Gang. It is also Tara to whom Buffy turns and confesses when she is having a self-destructive affair with the vampire, Spike, complete with gratuitous sex and violence. While living with Willow, Tara begins to see herself as a codependent, the enabler of Willow's addiction to magic, and tries to help her gain self control. Willow, unfortunately, fails to respond, dismissing Tara's helpful interventions as attempts to control and limit her own freedom. Willow's addiction is itself a growing loss of freedom.

In some significant ways, Willow's loss of freedom through addiction to magic is reminiscent of Christopher Marlowe's *Doctor Faustus*. We have already noted that Willow is consistently presented as the brainy one of the Scoobies, quick to learn everything that Sunnydale High has to offer, quick to master the computer and the internet, intrigued by the chance to learn magic, and eager for what she sees as the opportunity for a massive increase in knowledge when she gets to college: "It's just in high school, knowledge was pretty much frowned upon. You really had to work to learn anything. But here, the energy, the collective intelligence, it's like this force, this penetrating force, and I can just feel my mind opening up — you know? — and letting this place thrust into and spurt knowledge into.... That sentence ended up in a different place than it started out in" (4.1, "The Freshman"). In Christopher Marlowe's play *Doctor Faustus*, we find some interesting parallels to Willow's unnatural addiction to magic. In the very first scene of the play, Faustus delivers a soliloquy in which he appraises himself and his knowledge, declaring that he has fully mastered philosophy, medicine, law, and theology and found them all wanting. Despite his learning, he is still "but Faustus and a man" (1.1.21). Faustus knows that knowledge is power, and concludes that a full knowledge of magic is what he needs:

> But his dominion that exceeds in this [magic]
> Stretcheth as far as doth the mind of man:
> A sound magician is a demi-god! [1.1. 57–59].

The crux of the matter for Faustus' career is in that term "sound," when he calls himself a "sound magician." Faustus has already revealed throughout his survey of his learning that he has in fact not mastered or even understood the basics of the disciplines he claims are beneath his talents. Not surprisingly, his knowledge of magic is no more sound than his knowledge of anything else; he fails to distinguish among the types of magic available to him, and foolishly opts for the variety that requires selling one's soul to the devil; his incantation to summon Mephistopheles is a garbled mess of languages that both invokes and abjures the Trinity; and, finally, when Mephistopheles arrives, he tells Faustus that the details of the conjuration were irrelevant in any case, and did not in any way force the demon's arrival, since all that is required to summon a devil is to deny God:

> For when we hear one rack the name of God,
> Abjure the Scriptures and his savior Christ,
> We fly in hope to get his glorious soul.
> Nor will we come unless he use such means
> Whereby he is in danger to be damned.
> Therefore the shortest cut for conjuring
> Is stoutly to abjure the Trinity
> And pray devoutly to the prince of hell [1.3.46–53].

In short, Faustus is what Giles would call a "rank, arrogant amateur." This is his condemnation of Willow upon hearing that, in order to bring Buffy back from the dead, she has used a magic whose "ferocious and primal" power is beyond her understanding (6.4, "Flooded"). Faustus ignores the advice of the good angel, makes the worst possible choice, and signs, in blood, a pact with the devil, even despite the urgings of his own body that makes thick his blood to impede his signing of the contract. This contract requires that Faustus relinquish his soul for all eternity, but gives him only 24 years of doing, with demonic help, whatever he wishes. So, what does Faustus wish for? Right away, he declares he is "wanton and lascivious," and asks for a wife, but is presented with a female demon instead (2.1). Mephistopheles tells him that marriage is a "ceremonial toy" (2.1. 153) and promises him the fairest courtesans of Europe instead.

What Mephistopheles calls a "ceremonial toy" Marlowe's audience would have understood as a sacrament, so naturally the devil will have no truck with that. In his first request, Faustus shows that he neither understands the nature and limitations of devils, nor the nature of marriage in a Christian context. Faustus next tries to expand his knowledge, and after receiving some astronomy lessons that simply repeat what every educated person of the time would know, asks who made the world. Mephistopheles refuses to even answer on the grounds that he is bound to tell Faustus only what is "not against our kingdom" (2.2. 77).

Frustrated in his desires to get authentic knowledge, frustrated because authentic knowledge was thought to lead ultimately to the love of God and is hence not the devil's arena, Faustus instead spends his 24 years not using his alleged power to benefit humankind, or even himself: he plays practical jokes on the Pope, torments a horse dealer, fetches out-of-season apricots for a pregnant duchess, etc. In short, his performance does not live up to his hype in any sense, and he completely wastes both his 24 years and his soul. At one point (5.1), he even takes as his paramour a demon made up to look like Helen of Troy. (If Whedon had written the play, it might have been a Helenbot! The point is similar.)

The similarity of Willow's path to that of Faustus is unmistakable, as are some crucial differences. Unlike Faustus, Willow is authentically brainy, but like Faustus, she is more than willing to reach way beyond her grasp to try complicated spells before she is ready. Willow may not sell her soul to Mephistopheles, but she does the next worst thing: she goes to a magic "pusher" by the name of Rack to get power that overwhelms her, but for which she has no useful application (6.10, "Wrecked"). Hence she uses her power, both before and after having it augmented by Rack, to do silly, trivial things, or things that can be done just as well without magic. For instance, in Episode 6.9 ("Smashed"), Willow and her witch friend, Amy, go to the Bronze and play pool telekinetically rather than with a cue stick; humiliate a couple of annoying guys by making them, against their will, dance in cages while wearing skimpy loincloths; change the sex of the singers in the band (significantly, the male singers, just prior to being changed into female, are singing the refrain "What is wrong here?"); change some of the customers in the Bronze into sheep; change the sizes of others; and so on. Finally Willow and Amy get bored and return everything to normal (as the singers become male again, the male lead singer's line is "What is wrong with you?"). And, just as Faustus gets his demon Helen, so Willow inflates and animates Tara's clothing, to make a shell of a Tara for herself that she then hugs pathetically, since Tara herself has already left her because she had been abusing magic in just this way (6.10 "Wrecked"). Willow, like Faustus, is addicted to magic because she is addicted to herself; she has been the überstudent, the computer hacker extraordinaire, and finds that magic is all that is left to possibly satisfy her desire for power, dominance, control, recognition, self-image, etc., a desire that really can never be satisfied.

Tara is also a powerful witch, but she does not become addicted to magic, nor do the members of the powerful English coven who are instrumental in Willow's later recovery. The problem, therefore, must lie in Willow as an individual, rather than in the nature of magic itself. So, what is it in Willow? Why does she become Faustus-like in these ways? She moves from seeking dominance and power in academia and computers to seeking it in magic and witchcraft, so we need to be alert to early hints of a tendency to go overboard in the pursuit of knowledge and its attendant power.

We see, for example, that Willow quite probably keeps bits of the evil robot Ted ("Not any big ones," she says, 2.11); keeps the Buffybot after Buffy takes it away from Spike; and fixes it so that it can be used in the fight against Glory, the big bad of Season Five. Willow seems to have been doing illicit hacking even before Giles asks her to "wrest some information from that dread machine" (1.2, "The Harvest"). She experiments in magic quite early on even when counseled to be wary because it is too dangerous. She does a good job of replacing Jenny Calendar as both teacher and techno-pagan. We see Willow using her specialized expertise to get revenge when she tells Cordelia and Harmony to press the "deliver" button ("del"), when Cordelia asks how to save their computer homework (1.2, "The Harvest"). It vanishes like magic of course. Willow's later addiction and serious drive for revenge are signs of her lack of emotional control. We are given hints of this early on as well. Stevenson, in *Televised Morality: The Case of Buffy the Vampire Slayer*, notes two principal instances. The first is from 3.16, "Dopplegängland," "when Willow floats a pencil while lecturing Buffy on how magic requires emotional control.... Willow becomes upset during the conversation, [and] the pencil suddenly spins out of control and buries itself in a tree" (238). As Stevenson notes, this is our first inkling "that Willow's combination of magic and passion may prove lethal" (238). The second instance is in Episode 4.9, "Something Blue," when her emotions lead to a more or less unconscious casting of spells that harm her friends, prompting the überdemon D'Hoffryn to offer Willow a position as a vengeance demon.

Willow reacts in shock and horror at the suggestion she could be anything like a vengeance demon, because that does not fit her image of herself. However, after Tara's death, Willow becomes something even more frightening than a vengeance demon. She seeks out Tara's killer, Warren Mears of lovebot fame, and actually tortures and murders him. Using dark magic, she takes the bullet that wounded Buffy, not the stray one that killed Tara, and drives it slowly and painfully into Warren's body, saying, "One tiny piece of metal ... ripped her insides out ... took her light away. From me. From the world." Willow then flays him alive, magically tearing his skin off in one piece, and leaves his body suspended between the two vines with which she had magically entangled him. She then incinerates the body, again using magic (6.20, "Villains"). From this point, she seeks out even greater magical powers, which continue to grow until she begins to feel not only her own pain and grief, but also the pain of everyone in the entire world, "It's incredible. I mean, I am so juiced ... it's like ... no ... mortal person has ... ever had ... this much power. Ever. It's like I, I'm connected to everything.... I can feel ... it feels like ... I ... I can feel ... everyone. Oh. Oh my God. All the emotion. All the pain. No, it, it's too much. It's just too much.... I have to stop this. I'll make it go away. Oh, you poor bastards! Your suffering has to end" (6.22, "Grave"). Willow has now acquired both the desire and the power to end the suffering of the world.

Unfortunately, she decides to accomplish this by destroying herself and the entire world. Jana Riess, in *What Would Buffy Do?: The Vampire Slayer as Spiritual Guide,* like most commentators, states that Willow's desire to destroy the world results from her anger and grief at Tara's death. However, Riess does admit, "It can be argued that this is a morally ambiguous act. Not purely evil, it may come out of a sense of misguided altruism: she seeks to end the terrible misery and suffering of others" (10). We argue for this alternative interpretation. Willow has the power to end the suffering of others, but chooses to do so as an Antichrist, destroying the good as well as the pain, by an act of self-sacrifice that allows the ultimate evil to enter the world.

It is her life-long friend, Xander, who plays the role of Christ in this crisis. Xander confronts her, saying, "You may be a hopped-up über-witch, but ... this carpenter can drywall you into the next century.... You've come pretty far. Ending the world, not a terrific notion. But the thing is, yeah. I love you.... If you wanna kill the world, well, then start with me. I've earned that" (6.22, "Grave"). Willow continually knocks him to the ground with her magic, inflicting great pain, but he repeatedly offers her his unconditional love, and Willow's dark magic weakens with each successive offer until he finally gets through to her humanity. Willow then abandons her ill-conceived plan and collapses in Xander's arms. As Jana Riess observes dramatically, almost melodramatically, "Xander, the show's gentle carpenter, has saved the world with his demonstration of unconditional love, echoing the sacrifice of another gentle carpenter of another time.... In one of the show's most explicitly Christian references, the Prayer of Saint Francis of Assisi is sung [by Sarah McLachlan] after Xander's moving display of heroism." As Riess concludes, Xander offers hope and forgiveness in return for repeated injury, and such love and compassion constitute "the strongest remedy of all for fighting evil" (11). This, we contend, is one of the foundations of Whedon's existential love ethics.

Willow does find redemption. Giles takes her to England for rehabilitation under his guidance and that of the very powerful coven of English witches, from whom Willow had indirectly gained some of her magical power. Willow, at first, does not really understand why she has been taken to England. She tells Giles that she thought it might be for punishment, even execution: "I thought it was to kill me. Or lock me in some mystical dungeon for all eternity" (7.1, "Lessons"). When Giles then asks, "Do you want to be punished?," Willow replies, "I wanna be Willow" (7.1). This is the first sign of her redemption. When she was at the height of her evil power and about to destroy the world, she proclaimed, "Willow doesn't live here anymore" (6.22, "Grave"). The black magic had possessed her completely. It seems that she has been brought to England in order to learn how to live with the magic she has actually become. Giles tells her, "everything's connected. You're connected to great power, whether you feel it or not.... This isn't a hobby, or an addiction. It's inside you now, this magic. You're responsible for it" (7.1). It thus turns out that the magic for Willow is, in a way, what Angelus is for Angel and what the wolf is for Oz. Magic, however, unlike Angelus and the wolf, is not unambiguously evil, and Willow must learn to use this power for the benefit of others.

Interestingly enough, when Willow realizes that Giles is there as her teacher, not her judge and jailer, she tells him, "Instead, you go all Dumbledore on me" (7.1). Dumbledore is, of course, the kindly headmaster of Hogwarts School of Witchcraft and Wizardry in the popular *Harry Potter* series. There are a number of references to Hogwarts in *Buffy the Vampire Slayer* (5.2, "Real Me"; 7.1, "Lessons"; and 7.19, "Empty Places"). It is significant that Dumbledore is seen as a kindly headmaster and teacher only by Harry Potter and many of the staff and students at Hogwarts (the good guys). From the perspective of Voldemort (the "big bad") and his followers, Dumbledore is seen as a vicious opponent, the only wizard powerful enough to be any kind of threat to Voldemort. The fact that Willow sees her guide and teacher, Giles, as her Dumbledore shows that she is no longer dominated by evil, that Willow finally lives here again. Still, this is only a first step in her path toward redemption. She must still learn to let go of her late lover, Tara. She is still haunted by the magical murder of Warren, Tara's killer, not to mention her attempt to destroy the world. She must overcome the fear that doing magic will result in possession by the black arts once again.

When Willow returns to Sunnydale, she learns that she is still not in complete control of her magic. She is not sure of her acceptance by the Scooby Gang after all that has happened, and unconsciously casts a spell which both prevents them from seeing her and prevents her from seeing them (7.3, "Same Time, Same Place"). As we noted above, she had previously done something similar which resulted in harm to her closest friends (4.9, "Something Blue"). This time her unintentional spell, besides creating confusion at the Sunnydale airport, results in Willow's capture by a demon, Gnarl, who looks and speaks suspiciously like Gollum from the film *Lord of the Rings*. Ironically, Gnarl feeds by slowly skinning his victims alive, devouring each morsel with much too loquacious pleasure. This torment puts her in the same position as Warren when she skinned him alive during her grief-fueled rampage. We cannot stop ourselves from observing that she now knows what it is like to be in Warren's skin, as it were. This constitutes a further step towards her redemption and ability to deal with her conscience and her grief. Her invisibility does rather impede her friends' efforts to rescue her, though they do eventually succeed before too much of Willow's skin is consumed. By the end of the episode, Willow is welcomed back into the Scooby Gang: "It's nice to be forgiven. Too bad I need so much of it" (7.3).

During Season Seven, the final season of *Buffy the Vampire Slayer*, the Scooby Gang and Sunnydale become Slayer central for the "Potentials," girls who might become the Chosen Ones to succeed Buffy, and other Slayers, upon their death. Potentials from all over the world are gathering for protection in Sunnydale because someone or something has been trying to eliminate potential Slayers in order to terminate the Slayer line. One of these Potentials, by the name of Kennedy, falls in love with Willow, and plays a crucial role in her redemption. When they first kiss, Willow is magically transformed into Warren, Tara's killer (7.13, "The Killer in Me"). The transformation does not take place all at once, though she does immediately look and sound like him, much to the surprise and consternation of both herself and Kennedy.

They soon learn that the transformation has been caused by Willow's former friend and fellow witch, Amy, who has cast a "Standard Penance Malediction" on her. The special feature of this hex is that it allows its victim to unconsciously choose the precise form that the penance will assume. The victim will always create something more imaginative and exquisitely painful than the spellcaster herself could possibly conceive of. Willow, of course, is punishing herself for the murder of Warren. We naturally think back to the battle between Buffy and Faith, when Faith taunts Buffy by saying that if Buffy kills her, she becomes her (3.17, "Enemies").

Sartre would say that killing someone is the ultimate form of possession. Willow is certainly finding out what it is like to be inside Warren's skin. Fortunately, the spell is reversed before Willow is completely transformed into Warren. With a most fairytale-like kiss, Kennedy is able to bring back the true Willow. Willow returns changed for the better. She had half believed that she was also being punished for betraying Tara by being attracted to Kennedy. Now, she is finally able to let go of Tara and get on with her life.

Kennedy, though not a witch herself, also plays a crucial role in anchoring Willow, who is still afraid that performing magic may transform her back into the evil Willow who tried to destroy the world. In the series' final episode, Willow is called upon to perform magic more powerful than any she has yet attempted, a spell that will turn all Potentials world-wide into Slayers. Buffy has come to realize that her power, or for that matter the power of any single Slayer, is not enough to confront the "First Evil" which is now threatening to erupt into the world: "In every generation one Slayer is born because a bunch of men who died thousands of years ago made up that rule. They were powerful men.... [Willow] is more powerful than all of them combined. So I say we change the rule" (7.22, "Chosen").

Willow, who is central in actually bringing about this change of rules to empower all the Potentials, is extremely anxious about the task, uncertain that she has yet mastered the magic fully enough to accomplish it and still remain Willow, since it involves magic that will take her to "what lies beyond" the "darkest place" she has ever been (7.22, "Chosen"). Kennedy says she will be there to keep Willow grounded, and even to kill her if necessary (that is, if something goes horribly wrong and the dark Willow emerges). As Willow performs the spell, an aura of white light surrounds her. Her hair turns completely white and an ecstatic expression appears on her face. This is in stark contrast to the black-haired, black-eyed, scary, veiny Willow who nearly destroyed the world. Indeed, Kennedy declares that Willow has become a goddess, and we almost believe it. When the spell ends, Willow regains her normal red-haired appearance, but it is clear that both she, and, more importantly, the entire world, have been changed forever. This concluding episode of *Buffy the Vampire Slayer* emphasizes in a most dramatic way another important aspect of Joss Whedon's existentialist love ethics. It is a communitarian ethics, not an ethics of radical individualism.

Chapter Eight

Angel and Spike: Soul Mates and Moral Responsibility

By following the development of a soulless undead evil creature as he seeks to have his soul restored or of the creature who has his soul forced upon him, the shows *Buffy the Vampire Slayer* and *Angel* are both able to explore in some detail the concepts of freedom and power of the will as well as the related notion of moral responsibility. Angel and Spike are both vampires with souls. At least, that's how they end up. This is the main, but we argue not the only, reason that they are soul mates. They both come to love the same woman, Buffy. Further, both vampires were called "William," or variants thereof, before being sired — William, the bloody awful poet (Spike), and Liam, the bloody awful son (Angel/Angelus), at least in his father's eyes. Rhonda Wilcox, in *Why Buffy Matters: The Art of 'Buffy the Vampire Slayer,'* makes much of the fact that both were named "William," or (Wil)Liam, noting that "William" can mean "a willing protector" (51–52). We would add that "Will" is also related to free-will and to the act of will, as in will power, and that these significations are just as relevant to Angel and Spike as is the one that indicates their status as willing protectors of Buffy and the world.

When the good demon, Whistler, takes Angel to secretly watch Buffy, then an incompetent, novice slayer who actually misses the heart on her first try at staking, Angel is moved to say, "I wanna help her. I want ... I wanna become someone" (2.21, "Becoming, Part One"). Whistler has already offered Angel a choice: "I wanna know who you are.... I'm looking to find out. 'Cause you could go either way here.... I mean that you can become an even more useless rodent than you already are, or you can become someone. A person. Someone to be counted" (2.21). The implication here is clearly that Angel, through his own act of will, can choose to make himself someone other than, better than, he is. He has wasted the last ninety years, during which he has been ensouled, living on the streets, eating rats (rodents) because he can no longer bring himself to kill humans, and feeling tremendous guilt about his prior life as Angelus, the evil soul-less vampire who murdered his own family and left a trail of misery and corpses across Europe and Asia. Angel cannot change on his own, even though he has a soul. He needs the motivation provided by Whistler in order to make the choice. As Whistler puts it to Angel, "You see, and then you tell me what you wanna do" (2.21). Introducing Buffy to Angel amounts to providing a potential moral exemplar for Angel to emulate. Whistler himself seems to be working for the Powers-That-Be. As we have argued throughout this study, Joss Whedon does not demonize demons. Whistler tells Angel, "I'm not a bad guy. Not all demons are dedicated to the destruc-tion of all life" (2.21). When Buffy asks Whistler, "What are you, just some immortal demon sent down to even the score between good and evil?" he responds, somewhat whimsically, "Wow. Good guess" (2.22, "Becoming, Part Two). Whistler's role, insofar as Angel is concerned, is to help Angel see that his goal or purpose is to fight evil, if he so chooses. He and Buffy can work together to seal the Hellmouth, thus preventing evil from enter-ing the world and achieving for themselves the kind of freedom which goes beyond merely choosing between good and evil.

Just as Angel feels motivated to protect and care for the novice Slayer, Buffy, so Spike, even before he acquires a soul, finds himself loving and caring for the insane vampire Drusilla (2.3, "School Hard"). Drusilla was driven insane by the evil vampire Angelus's forcing her to watch as he mur-dered her entire family before turning her into a vampire on the day she was to take holy orders and become a novitiate in the Church (2.7, "Lie to Me"). (Angel/Angelus seems to have a thing for novices.) Spike's love for Drusilla is not normal for vampires. A truly evil creature says of this odd couple, "You two stink of humanity. You share affection and jealousy" (2.13, "Surprise").

It is significant that the emotion of love can make even vampires seem more human. The first time that Spike fights on the side of good by help-ing Buffy fight Angelus, it is for the sake of love. Interestingly enough, it is still for the love for Drusilla, not Buffy. He makes a deal with Buffy to help her with the Angelus problem if she will allow Spike to take Drusilla safely away. The Angelus problem for Spike has little to do with the end of the world, though he says it does. Instead, Angelus has been horning in on his girlfriend, Drusilla, and Spike is jealous: "I want to stop Angel. I want to save the world.... I want Dru back. I want it like it was before *he* came back" (2.22, "Becoming, Part Two"). This is, significantly, the first time, though it won't be the last, that Buffy makes any kind of deal with the dark side.

We have argued that vampires in general represent the dark side. They are, in the Buffyverse, simply the personification of evil. The fact that at least two of them acquire souls and are thus better able to make moral choices suggests that the distinction between good and evil in the Buffyverse is no more straightforward than it is in real life. This is of the utmost importance, since much of the Buffyverse is about fighting evil. We ourselves have no moral qualms about the killing of vampires on the show, because we see vampires as symbols of evil, and *Buffy the Vampire Slayer* is, after all, about fighting evil.

Other critics of *Buffy*, Kent A. Ono, for example, argue that vampires in the Buffyverse symbolize the oppressed Other, particularly Blacks, in American society. Ono criticizes the show for thoroughly marginalizing Blacks by making them "'killable' characters" (170). Rhonda Wilcox in *Why Buffy Matters* suggests that such "racial/ethnic implications are debatable" (73). We agree. Mary Alice Money, in her article "The Undemonization of Supporting Characters in *Buffy*," argues that the undemonization of vampires like Angel and Spike also demarginalizes them (102).

We see vampires as simply symbolizing evil. We don't see vampires as symbolizing Blacks, and we certainly don't see Blacks as symbolizing evil, in the way that Ono's interpretation of the Buffyverse would imply. Ono himself has difficulty with the fact that most of the actors portraying vampires are Caucasian. The majority of the ones who are individualized to any extent, in fact, seem to be Irish or English. Ono attempts to get around this by adding a footnote suggesting that when they show their vampire face, they are truly evil and showing their real colors. He sees the actors in what he calls "vampireface," and argues, "I am, of course, implicitly referring to the racist practices of Blackface and Yellowface, for instance — media strategies primarily used to allow white actors to play roles of Blacks and Asian Americans in derogating ways" (184). Ono's article was published in the year 2000, well before Season Five of *Angel* where we see, in a flashback to the Second World War, Spike in a Nazi officer's uniform (*Angel* 5.13, "Why We Fight"). The sight of a blonde vampire in a Nazi uniform suggests the evils of the white supremacist, an image of the ultimate oppressor, rather than of the oppressed Other. This, we suggest, confirms our reading of vampires as symbolic of evil in general.

Milly Williamson, in "Spike, Sex and Subtext," in fact sees Spike as symbolizing the experience of "marginality and disappointment that is the majority experience" (295). She argues that individual fulfilment and stardom are valorized in an American society that maintains "the conditions that ensure that its achievement is unattainable" (294). Vampires thus represent not the oppressed minority, but rather the majority of us in a capitalist society, an oppressed majority, in Marxist terms the proletariat.

Interestingly enough, James South in "'All Torment, Trouble, Wonder, and Amazement Inhabits Here': The Vicissitudes of Technology in *Buffy the Vampire Slayer*," uses vampires to symbolize the capitalist oppressor, sucking the blood from the unwary proletariat (98). Brian Wall and Michael Zryd, in "Vampire Dialectics: Knowledge, Institutions and Labour," also argue that vampires, indeed the supernatural more broadly in the Buffyverse, symbolize the evils of capitalism in general, "the hidden forces and systems of economy and ideology" (69). We think, therefore, that it is more plausible to say that the soulless vampire "represents everything that is evil and disgusting," as Dee Amy-Chinn argues in "Queering the Bitch: Spike, Transgression and Erotic Empowerment" (325). In sum, as Wilcox argues in *Why Buffy Matters*, the "vampires in the *single* text of *Buffy* carry as many meanings as they do in a *variety* of texts worldwide" (92, emphasis added).

When we first meet Spike, he is a soulless vampire. In our first glimpse of him, "we see only his vampire visage, an unattractive prosthetic face which deflects the erotic presentation of his body" (Amy-Chinn, 317). We do not see his handsome human face until he is with his beloved Drusilla (2.3, "School Hard"). The fact that he loves Drusilla makes him more human. When his fellow demons react to their love by saying that Spike and Drusilla "stink of humanity," it turns out to be a rather backhanded compliment, at least from the human point of view. It certainly suggests that Spike is a vampire capable of radical transformation, that he is, in some important way, fundamentally different from all the other vampires in the series. Spike is certainly given the opportunity to have experiences which could lead to moral development. A covert government institution, the Initiative, had captured him, labeled him "Hostile 17," and experimented on him, installing a computer chip in his brain which has prevented him from harming humans by causing him to experience intense headaches whenever he attempts even to strike a person. Once he discovers that he can, instead, fight demons and vampires with impunity (even with gusto), he finds himself fighting alongside the Slayer and her team of Scoobies, doing battle against his own kind.

This working in close conjunction with human beings (both those with and those without superpowers) gives Spike the opportunity for various experiences that would be otherwise totally inaccessible to him (as they are to all other soulless vampires). Spike, being by nature a somewhat sensitive and observant sort (even if his poetry stinks, but not of humanity, just of incompetence), is almost inevitably going to learn something, even if merely by osmosis. He could not work closely with the Slayer without coming to admire her fidelity, dedication, courage, caring, etc.; in effect, she is virtually bound to become a moral exemplar for him, quite apart from the frustrating and destructive sexual passions he also develops for her.

Actually, Wall and Zryd argue, "Spike, motivated by his erotic love for Buffy, has cultivated a soul ... his goodness is built, not given" (62–3). Spike does eventually tell Buffy, "I'm not asking you for anything. When I tell you that I love you, it's not because I want you, or 'cause I can't have you — it has nothing to do with me. I love what you are, what you do, how you try.... I've seen your strength, and your kindness, I've seen the best and the worst of you and I understand with perfect clarity exactly what you are. You are a hell of a woman" (7.20, "Touched"). He imitates her only to impress her at first, but ultimately starts to really become what he is initially just play-acting at. If you act like a champion often enough, you eventually become a champion. This is how virtues are acquired. The close association with, and imitation of, humans gives Spike the same kind of ultimate goal in life that Angel develops when guided by Whistler towards Buffy. Spike even admits at one point that although he is still a monster, Buffy treats him like a man, and implies that he is grateful for that experience (5.22, "The Gift").

This indicates a transformation in his character, because when he is first turned into a vampire, and turns his mother into one too, he wonders if the newfound monster in him will triumph over the failed poet he once was. He is not encouraged when his vamped mother tells him, "Darling, it's who you'll always be. A limp, sentimental fool" (7.17, "Lies My Parents Told Me"). As Gregory Stevenson argues in *Televised Morality: The Case of Buffy the Vampire Slayer*, "All of Spike's swaggering menace and violent bravado is an attempt to hide the fact that underneath he is still the same sentimental fool" (249). Stevenson discusses this in some detail. A principal difference between Spike and Angel is due to the kind of people they were before they were vamped. Liam, the boozing, wenching layabout, becomes Angelus, one of the wickedest vampires in history, whereas William, the bloody awful poet, though known to the Watchers' Council as William the Bloody, actually becomes the very conflicted vampire who stinks of humanity and takes the name Spike. It would seem that the person that one was has an influence on the kind of vampire one turns into once bitten. As Darla tells Angelus, "What we once were informs all that we have become" (*Angel* 1.15, "The Prodigal"). Scott McLaren notes in his *Slayage* article, "The Evolution of Joss Whedon's Vampire Mythology and the Ontology of the Soul," "Darla consistently appeals to the existential view that there is a close connection between the host human and the vampire across the whole of both series from her earliest attempts to convince Angel to reassume his killing ways in *BtVS*'s first season to her insistence, after Wolfram and Hart resurrected her as a human, 'It's still me'"(note 9).

Another difference between Spike and Angel that is mentioned by some commentators is that Spike chooses to go on a quest to regain his soul, whereas Angel has had his soul thrust upon him through a gypsy curse as punishment for killing one of their tribe. At least Rhonda Wilcox argues in *Why Buffy Matters*, "Whether the reader believes Spike chose to undergo horrendous trials from a conscious or subconscious desire for a soul, certainly it is significant that he is given the soul as a result of his own agency (as opposed to Angelus, who had his soul forced upon him)" (37). Peter S. Beagle, in "The Good Vampire: Angel and Spike," speaks of Spike setting out "in search of a soul" (117). Similarly, Nancy Holder, in "Death Becomes Him: Blondie Bear 5.0," says of Spike, he "left Sunnydale to win himself a conscience — a soul" (156). Stevenson, in *Televised Morality: The Case of Buffy the Vampire Slayer*, speaks of Spike's "retrieval of his soul" (88). This certainly makes it sound like a conscious choice, and there is no indication in Stevenson, Holder, or Beagle of any ambiguity concerning this choice. However, Stacey Abbott, in "From Madman in the Basement to Self-Sacrificing Champion: The Multiple Faces of Spike," argues in some detail, "the dialogue in the scene when Spike requests the restoration of his true self is deliberately written so that it can be interpreted either as the removal of the chip or the return of his soul" (333). She also insists that James Marsters, the actor playing Spike, "delivers his lines with clear intent ... as a monster, not a hero" (333). She notes that Spike never once mentions a soul, but repeatedly refers to the chip the Initiative had placed in his head to render him harmless to humans.

It should be noted that the chip does not work to curtail Spike's violence when it comes to Buffy. He has discovered, with some surprise, that he can strike Buffy and suffer no ill effects as a result. Naturally enough, he concludes, "Nothing wrong with me. Something wrong with her" (6.9, "Smashed"). This eventually leads to violent sex with Buffy, with Buffy as the aggressor (6.9). This, indeed all of Season Six, represents a very low

ebb in Buffy's life, because she has been the victim of Willow's resurrection spell, bringing her back from what she believes was Heaven and
depositing her in what she feels is a living Hell. Her affair with Spike is
undertaken just so she can escape the numbness of life and feel something,
anything. She ultimately breaks it off, recognizing, and telling Spike in no
uncertain terms, that she is just treating him as a means: "I'm using you.
I can't love you. I'm just being weak, and selfish ... and it's killing me. I
have to be strong about this. I'm sorry William" (6.15, "As You Were").

Buffy's calling him "William" here, although she is trying to be sensitive, brings to mind Cecily's constant rejection of the bloody awful poet,
William (5.7, "Fool for Love"). Both Slayer and Cecily use exactly the same
words in their rejection of his first advances: "You're beneath me" (5.7).
The fact that Buffy goes on to have her affair with Spike indicates just how
low she has sunk, and the depth of her despair. As Rhonda Wilcox, following Delores Nurss, points out, Spike often functions as Buffy's darker
or shadow self, in a kind of Jungian sense (82). This means that much of
Spike's story arc is there really to tell us something about Buffy, and ultimately, we contend, about ourselves.

Buffy's termination of the affair hurts and angers Spike deeply, resulting in his failed attempt to rape her (6.19, "Seeing Red"). This is a crisis
for Spike. He has allowed the monster within him to emerge, attacking
the woman he loves. Yet he is conflicted. He seems both sorry to have
attempted such an evil act and at the same time puzzled, if not completely
sorry, that he was unable to carry it out: "What have I done? Why didn't
I do it? What has she done to me?" (6.19). He does not really know who
is the victim and who is the victimizer. He is a monster after all. Ultimately,
he blames the chip: "It isn't supposed to be this way! It's the chip! Steel
and wires and silicon. It won't let me be a monster. And I can't be a man.
I'm nothing" (6.19). We contend that it is this crisis of identity which
drives Spike to seek his soul. We agree that the quest scenes were written
with deliberate ambiguity. This is confirmed by Rhonda Wilcox, who cites
Joss Whedon's answer to the question of whether Spike was really just trying to get his chip removed: "Noo — but you were meant to believe that
he was. This is just a thing that I personally have devised called a 'plot
twist.' I think it's going to catch on with the young people" (213, n. 9).
We suggest that the real question is *why* the deliberate ambiguity in Season Six?

When the newly ensouled Spike returns in Season Seven, he certainly
speaks as if he believes that he went in deliberate search for a soul to make
him worthy of Buffy. He tells Buffy most explicitly, "I got my soul back

so I could be the kind of person you could care for, the man you would come to, the man you could love" (7.2, "Beneath You"). Stacey Abbott confirms that Spike does indeed talk this way, not only in the final season of *Buffy* but also after his miraculous reappearance at the beginning of Season Five of the *Angel* series: "Throughout Season 7 of *BtVS*, as well as the final series of *Angel*, Spike claims that he *chose* to regain his soul, which separates him from the other 'ensouled' vampires of the series and makes him a truer champion than Angel, who had his soul thrust upon him" (333). Abbott, however, does not entirely believe Spike: "This argument assumes that we believe him when he says that he went in search of his soul" (333). Abbott argues that the final episodes of Season Six are not all that ambiguous as "they clearly suggest that Spike went to hell and back again to have the chip removed and be once again what he was: a vampire" (333). Her final argument in support of this interpretation is that in the DVD commentary on the episode where Spike earns his soul, the writer and producer, David Fury, claims that the line "We will return your soul," which Abbott says is "a line clearly designed to shock audiences," was deliberately omitted from the shooting script "so that all involved (and we assume that this means James Marsters himself) believed that Spike's intention was to become a monster again" (334). In other words, Abbott would have us believe that Spike, at the end of all the excruciating trials of his quest, was expecting nothing more serious than a chipectomy.

Yet, the chip is finally removed by the medical team from the Initiative, using what seems to be a fairly minor bit of surgery. The Initiative's former operative, Riley Finn, left orders that all "decisions regarding Hostile 17 are to be left in [Buffy's] hands" (7.13, "The Killer in Me"). Buffy justifies her decision to have Spike's chip removed, telling a skeptical Giles, "He has a soul now, Giles. That's what's going to keep him from hurting anyone. I'm going to trust that before I trust some chip we already know can go bad on him.... He can be a good man, Giles. I feel it. But he's never going to get there if we never give him a chance.... Just look in his eyes and you'll see he's changed. There's ... there's a person in there now" (7.14, "First Date"). That there is indeed a person inside Spike now is confirmed by Anya before Spike has admitted that he has had his soul restored. Looking deep into Spike's eyes, Anya exclaims in shock, "Oh my God.... How did you do it?... I can see you" (7.2, "Beneath You"). Anya's question, "How did you do it?" certainly assumes that this is something Spike chose deliberately.

Even before Anya's discovery, the First Evil, in the guises of the late Mayor Richard Wilkins III and Drusilla, taunts Spike, who is hiding in the basement of the rebuilt Sunnydale High School, trying to escape the overwhelming feelings of guilt descending on him because of his soul: "So what'd you think, you'd get your soul back and everything would be jim-dandy? Soul's slipperier than a greased weasel. Why do you think I sold mine? Well, you probably thought that you'd be your own man. And I respect that. But you never will" (7.1, "Lessons"). The reference to expecting to be "your own man" certainly suggests that this is something Spike chose of his own free will.

The fact that Anya, a reformed vengeance demon with human experience, and the Big Bad of Season Seven, an incorporeal hell god with exceptional power and knowledge, both assume that Spike chose to seek the return of his soul seems to resolve the ambiguity of Spike's quest on the side of soul restoration as opposed to chip removal. We reject therefore Abbott's claim that the ambiguity is resolved in favor of the chipectomy. We think it makes more sense to accept that the intended ambiguity remains unresolved in Season Six, and we return therefore to the important question raised before: "*Why* the deliberate ambiguity in Season Six?"

What is gained by portraying Spike's quest as ambiguous? We argue that it draws attention to the radical transformation Spike undergoes while working with Buffy and the Scooby Gang. By Season Seven, and probably not before, Spike has adopted completely new goals in life (OK unlife, he's still a vampire after all). Like Angel, he is faced with an existential choice which could well lead to the radical transformation of his very being. As Whistler put it to Angel, "you could go either way here.... I mean that you can become an even more useless rodent than you already are, or you can become someone. A person. Someone to be counted" (2.21). When Spike told Buffy that he set out deliberately to regain his soul, he might have been lying just to impress her, as Abbott's interpretation of events implies. And who could blame either Buffy or Abbott for not believing him? After all, Spike has lied to Buffy before just to seduce her. He might well be doing so again. On the other hand, he might have changed. When be behaved badly before, he did not have a soul. Now he does. Of course this is no guarantee that he is now more trustworthy, as Giles is at pains to point out, sometimes, in desperation, reduced to pure sarcasm: "Well, of course you trust Spike. He has slaughtered thousands, and therefore probably knows all about how not to do it" (7.14, "First Date). Still, as we have seen, Buffy learns to trust Spike enough to allow his chip to be removed so that he is free to choose of his own free will to become a champion and fight evil by Buffy's side. We know that this is the choice he makes.

It is here that an existential analysis of the situation is most relevant and most revealing. Throughout this study, we have been analyzing Whedon's work from an existential perspective. The existential analysis here allows us to answer the question about the ambiguity of Spike's quest for his soul in a way that tells us something important about the human condition. We are all capable of radical transformation, of making moral choices that, given our past character and behavior, no one would have expected, and certainly no one could have predicted. This is what existential freedom is all about, the freedom to become better than we were, to transform ourselves completely by adopting new life-defining goals, as both Spike and Angel ultimately do. As the existential philosopher Jean-Paul Sartre points out, one important implication of such radical transformation of the self is that it draws attention to the often overlooked fact that our memories themselves are actually interpretations of what we have experienced. Changing ourselves by changing our goals in life can also change these interpretations, change the way we remember the past, and thus change the way the past influences us, our feelings, our emotions, our behavior. As Phyllis Sutton Morris explains in *Sartre's Concept of a Person: An Analytic Approach*, "Sartre is not saying that we are able to change the brute facts of the remembered past; his point, rather, is that there is an element of choice in our remembering.... We decide what our past means by acting in the present to achieve one kind of goal as opposed to some other kind of goal" (73). This is in part how existential freedom subverts any kind of causal determinism which wrongly insists that freedom is an illusion because all our actions are caused, and thus explained, by past events. However, we do have freedom; even though in a narrow sense the past may determine the present, it is also the case that the future (in terms of our sometimes newly chosen goals) reaches into that past to produce the present. In other words it is our choice of goals that really determines who we are. As Morris puts it, "What links present action to memories of past events is, at least in part, an interpretive connection which can only be understood in terms of the individual's chosen future end" (73). Given this existentialist understanding of memory as interpretive, we contend that the reason for the deliberate ambiguity of Spike's quest for a soul (or chipectomy) is not simply as Whedon says, "just a thing that I personally have devised called a 'plot twist.'" Rather, the so-called plot twist allows Spike's interpretive memory of his quest to confirm that he has undergone a radical transformation of self by choosing to become a champion, and, as we have seen, ultimately to sacrifice himself in the sealing of the Hellmouth.

Scott McLaren, in "The Evolution of Joss Whedon's Vampire Mythology and the Ontology of the Soul," also gives a Sartrean analysis of Whedon's treatment of soul-acquisition, "Whedon, a self-described existentialist with Sartrean leanings (Whedon, "Commentary for 'Objects in Space'"), advances an understanding of the soul as a metaphor for individual moral agency" (para 1). Actually, in the DVD commentary cited by McLaren, Whedon denies being an intellectual of any sort and admits to having read only two existentialists, Albert Camus and Jean-Paul Sartre. As we noted in our chapter on Faith and Bad Faith, Whedon does tell us that Sartre's *Nausea* is the most important book he has ever read. In our chapter on Faith and Bad Faith, we presented internal evidence which suggests that Whedon might also have read Sartre's major existentialist study, *Being and Nothingness.* We would agree with McLaren, therefore, that Whedon could be described as an "existentialist with Sartrean leanings." Unfortunately, McLaren, in his otherwise cogent study, fails to notice Sartre's analysis of memory as interpretive. This is an important oversight, because Sartre's notion of interpretive memory is not just an implication of his position; it is, rather, an integral part of his existentialist philosophy, without which the notion of existential freedom would be impossible. Further, Sartre's notion of interpretive memory would have helped McLaren solve the problem of moral responsibility that he quite rightly raises in his paper.

McLaren actually notes that there are at least two concepts of the soul at work in Whedon's mythology. The first is the existentialist understanding mentioned above in which, McLaren says, the soul serves primarily "as a metaphor for individual moral agency" (para 1). The second is "a more traditional concept of the soul as the reified and ontological seat of individual identity and conscience" (para 1). This Neoplatonic Christian concept of the soul, as McLaren rightly notes, seems to be the official account adopted by the Watchers' Council. Giles explains it to the Scooby Gang, stressing the fact that vampires are demons: "The books tell that the last demon to leave this reality fed off a human, mixed their blood. He was a human form possessed, infected, by the demon's soul. He bit another, and another and so they walk the earth, feeding. Killing some, mixing their blood with others to make more of their kind" (1.2, "The Harvest"). Buffy herself seems to accept the account given by the Watchers' Council. In explaining why being vamped would be a poor way to achieve personal immortality, she argues, "That's not how it works. You die. And a demon sets up shop in your old house. It walks and talks and remembers your life, but it's not you" (2.7, "Lie to Me"). Wesley Wyndham-Pryce, a former watcher, confirms that we are "more than just memories" (*Angel* 5.18, "Origin").

As McLaren quite rightly points out, if Spike and Angel have acquired the kind of thing that the Watchers' Council describes as a soul, why should they then feel guilty about their previous lives as soulless vampires? As we have seen, Angel spends at least ninety years agonizing about the harm Angelus had done before acquiring a soul. Once Spike regains his soul, we see him hiding in the basement of Sunnydale High School being driven mad with guilt, though he seems to become reconciled to his monstrous past more quickly than Angel does to his. But the point is that both do feel guilty. McLaren's question is why: "Here then is the crux of the dilemma: if Angel was stripped of his soul, his personhood, and therefore his human identity, when he was turned into a vampire by Darla, then how can he be held accountable for the actions of the demon who 'took over' or assumed command of his body during the soulless hiatus between his human life and his ensouled vampire life?" (para 10). McLaren's concern here has probably been noticed by every careful viewer of *Buffy* and *Angel*. If, once you are vamped, your soul which has something to do with your personal identity, leaves, and a demon "sets up shop" in your body, why should you feel guilty about, or take responsibility for, anything the demon does in your absence? As Angel explains at one point, "When you become a vampire, the demon takes your body. But it doesn't get the soul. That's gone. No conscience, no remorse ... it's an easy way to live" (1.7, "Angel"). It would seem to follow that ensouled vampires like Spike and Angel contain two warring souls, a human one and a demon one, while regular vampires are possessed by only one, the demon soul. McLaren's solution to this problem of moral responsibility is to emphasize the two different conceptions of soul used in the Buffyverse, the existentialist and what he calls the ontological. He claims that Whedon plays on the ambiguity of the term "soul," using whichever best fits the context at the time. Given this, McLaren argues that the ensouled vampire "[t]hough ontologically innocent, ... remains somehow existentially culpable because he chooses to be so" (para 14). Given that the existential interpretation of the soul is simply a metaphor for moral choice, McLaren argues that this minimizes the inconsistency between the two concepts of soul at play: "the ongoing tension between the ontological and the existential — the soul reified and the soul as metaphor for moral choice — that Whedon consistently maintains throughout the whole of *BtVS* and its spin-off *Angel*, far from detracting from the verisimilitude of the series, contributes to the much vaunted and provocative ambiguity that has been one of the Whedonverse's most commented upon and defining features" (para 2). McLaren, in other words, never successfully reconciles these two inconsistent conceptions of the soul.

We contend that McLaren does not sufficiently explore the full implications of the existential conception of the soul. An existentialist approach is by its very nature phenomenological. That is, it relies upon our subjective experience as individual agents. Just as the demon soul inherits and exploits the memories of the human it possesses, so the returning human soul must, with some minor exceptions (cf. *Angel* 4.9, "Long Day's Journey"), also endure and learn to live with the memories of the demon possessor. As we argued before, memories are always interpretive, depending upon the goals of the individual remembering; change the goals, change the way things are remembered. Both Angel and the ensouled Spike now want to do what is right and good; both want to become champions, helping the helpless.

Given such goals, it is not difficult to imagine how horrified and guilty they must feel remembering what they had done. It is important to note that Angel, for example, remembers doing the monstrous things Angelus did. It is not the case that Angel merely remembers Angelus doing such awful things; rather, from a phenomenological or experiential perspective, he actually remembers doing them, and so must own them himself, making such amends as he can. This is why Angel seeks redemption. The goal of redemption, in turn, would result in an even more negative interpretation of his memories, resulting in more intense feelings of guilt and remorse. Peter S. Beagle describes the guilt of having done "what Angel remembers doing every moment of his life-in-death" and its consequences: "Wiping out families, ravaging entire towns and villages, sadistically seducing the innocent and turning them into gleefully undead horrors like himself ... immortal as he is, Angel understands that there is no way for him ever to atone for his crimes. All he can do is devote his eternity to trying" (117).

Note that Beagle too refers to all these crimes as Angel's crimes, not those of Angelus. Angel not only accepts the sins of Angelus as his own; at one point he actually admits with considerable shame and embarrassment that this monster within him is in some sense what he really is. When Angel journeys with friends to an alternate reality called Pylea, he discovers that not only can he go out into the daylight (of its two suns) without bursting into flames as he would back in Los Angeles, but he can also see his reflection. Vampires, of course, are not supposed to be able to cast a reflection (forcing Whedon's cameramen to be extremely careful with camera angles on the normal set). In Pylea, Angel does not show his vampire nature by the simple emergence of vampface. Rather, much to his surprise and dismay, an entire demon bursts forth, much like a werewolf transformation, but with less fur and much scalier. This monster is a good deal more hideous than the mere vampire face viewers have grown accustomed to over the many seasons of both *Buffy* and *Angel*. As Angel's friends remark, "So that's what the thing inside of him really looks like.... In its purest form.... That's nasty" (*Angel* 2.21, "Through The Looking Glass"). When Angel sees his monstrous self reflected in a pool of water, he is shocked and embarrassed that his friends have seen him like this: "They, they saw it. They, they looked right at it. They saw it.... The monster. They, they saw what I really am" (*Angel* 2.21). We take this as evidence that Angel fully accepts and reluctantly identifies with Angelus, the monster within him. This is not unlike Prospero in Shakespeare's *The Tempest*: "This thing of darkness I acknowledge mine"(5.1. 275–276).

In the Pylea reality, Angel finds it difficult to control his inner demon, yet it is only when this demon is manifested that Angel has the strength to win the battle he knows he must face. The problem, from Angel's perspective, is the fear that the demon, once manifested, will remain so, permanently suppressing Angel's good side. His friends encourage him, telling him they have faith in the Angel they know (rather than the demon they don't): "We know you. We know you're a man with a demon inside — not the other way around. We know you have the strength to do what needs to be done, and you will come back to us" (2.22, "There's No Place Like Plrtz Glrb"). This certainly confirms the account of ensouled vampires as beings with two warring souls. Further confirmation of this is found in Season Four of *Angel*, when Angel's friends use a shaman to remove Angel's human soul to a magical vessel for safe-keeping so that they can access Angelus, the demon soul. They believe Angelus has crucial information they need and which Angel seems unable to access. Angelus, of course, gets free and we find the Big Bad of the season threatening to return his human soul if he does not cooperate. The Big Bad taunts Angelus, reminding him what it is like to be imprisoned in a body with a human soul, "you're the voice in there, aren't you? Just beneath the surface, buried under all that goodness, fully conscious, fully aware, but trapped. Unable to move or speak, powerless to act on your desires. So thirsty, so helpless. It must be agony" (*Angel* 4.14, "Release"). This a wonderful description of how our inner demons must feel once we have gained control of them. The point is that in order to control them, we must first acknowledge them as ours, as part of what we really are.

We are morally responsible for our actions, whether or not we attribute them to our inner demons. Being drunk or being under the influence of recreational drugs, for example, is not considered an extenuating circumstance in the ascription of moral responsibility for actions done under such influence. When Willow, for example, while addicted to magic, injures Dawn in a car accident, she assumes responsibility and does not plead extenuating circumstances, but rather, admits that she needs help (6.10, "Wrecked"). Vampires with souls are simply Whedon's way of dramatizing such questions of moral responsibility.

The reified soul, the ontological question, as McLaren puts it, is really just a metaphorical way of dealing with the ethical issue. These are metaphors made literal, as so much of the Buffyverse is. As is often noted, everyone believes that high school is Hell, but Whedon makes this literal by placing Sunnydale High School on a Hellmouth. Buffy and the Scooby Gang spend much of their time attempting to seal the Hellmouth. We all have inner demons and keeping them under control is each individual's way of sealing the Hellmouth, and thus taking responsibility for ourselves. Though McLaren is right to say that the existentialist account of the soul is a metaphor for moral choice, there is much more to the existentialist analysis than this.

In our chapter on Faith and Bad Faith, we examined Sartre's account of the illusion of a soul separate from the body. For Sartre, if we are to speak of soul at all, we must speak of an embodied soul. From a phenomenological perspective, Sartre would prefer to talk about the body as subject as opposed to the body as object. There is not literally a soul within the body. Sartre would call this the "illusion of immanence," i.e., erroneously thinking of a non-corporeal soul's being literally within the body. (Sartre 1961, 5). The only sense in which it is meaningful to say that the soul is "in" the body is in the same sense that we can say, for example, that a knot is "in" a piece of rope. We cannot take the knot out of the rope and put it elsewhere as we can, for example, take a pen out of our pocket and put it on the table. The rope is, as it were, a knotted rope. There is no knot apart from the rope. In a similar way, a living human body can be said to be an ensouled body, but there is no soul apart from the body.

In the Fourth Season of *Angel* when the shaman places Angel's human soul in a magical vessel for safe-keeping, this is, of course, a metaphorical way of accessing Angel's inner demon. The important point is that it is *Angel's* inner demon. Whatever it does, Angel remembers doing and is morally responsible for. How often have we said "I'm not myself today" when having a bad day? Yet we are still morally responsible for whatever this self did. We don't take such expressions literally, nor should we take soul-talk in the Buffyverse literally. For example, though we refer to Angelus and Angel as if they are two persons, they are in fact only one insofar as moral responsibility is concerned. In a similar way, though everyone refers to an ensouled Spike and to a Spike prior to earning his soul, it is still the one and only Spike they have in mind. This point is driven home by the fact that he is called "Spike" in both states. Common English usage recognizes, and ordinary language analysis confirms, that there is a continuity of identity here, whereas the Angel/Angelus terminology actually confuses the matter.

McLaren's discussion of soul in *Angel* and *Buffy* relies heavily on discussions of ancient Greek philosophers and the subsequent interpretations of their theories in the early Christian tradition (Plato, Aristotle, and the Neoplatonists). We have traced the existentialist tradition back to Dostoevsky and the distinction between Athens (the ancient Greeks) and Jerusalem (the pre–Hellenic Hebraic tradition). Certainly Sartre's account of the soul is closer to that found in the Old Testament, in spite of his atheistic leanings. As Hastings' *Dictionary of the Bible* clarifies, the "Biblical concept of soul appears in the Hebrew *nephesh*.... The soul is not an entity with a separate nature from the flesh and possessing or capable of a life of its own. Rather it is the life animating the flesh.... Adam was made of the dust, but when God gave him breath he *became* (not obtained) a living *nephesh*. Man does not 'have' a soul, he is a soul" (932).

This is much closer to Sartre's embodied soul of existential phenomenology than to the Neoplatonic Christian concept of the soul. It may also explain why, in the Buffyverse, a vampire immediately turns to dust as soon as the demon animating its soulless body is destroyed. Though McLaren, in his article on ensouled vampires, has difficulty reconciling the existential phenomenological and the reified ontological accounts of the soul, he might take solace in the fact that the subtitle of Sartre's major existentialist study, *Being and Nothingness*, is *A Phenomenological Essay on Ontology*.

Chapter Nine

Angel in Hell:
Love and Moral Choice

"What is Hell?" According to Dostoevsky, who raises the question in *The Brothers Karamazov*, "It is the suffering of being unable to love" (169). This particular definition of Hell has particular relevance to Buffy's major love interest, the 250-year-old vampire with a soul, Angel. Angel does not *dare* to love once he realizes the full implications of the gypsy curse that restored his soul. Prior to having his soul thrust upon him, Angel was known as Angelus, one of the wickedest vampires on record with the Watchers' Council. The Big Bad of Season One, the übervamp known as the Master, fondly remembers Angelus: "He was the most vicious creature I ever met. I miss him" (1.7, "Angel"). When he realizes that Angelus is lost forever, the Master says with regret, "He was to have sat at my right hand, come the day. And now..." (1.7). In the same episode, Giles tells us what the Watchers' Council knows about this notorious vampire: "There's mention some two hundred years ago in Ireland of ... Angelus, the one with the angelic face.... Angelus leaves Ireland ... wreaks havoc in ... Europe for ... several decades, and then ... about eighty years ago, the most curious thing happens. He ... comes to ... America ... shuns other vampires, and ... lives alone. There's, there's no ... record of him hunting here" (1.7).

It is obvious that Angelus, like Liam, the human he once was, has never loved, and indeed has scorned love. Angelus's relationship with Darla, his sire, mentor, and companion in carnage, is very different from that of Spike and Drusilla, which, as we noted in the previous chapter, was observed to "stink of humanity." In *Angel* 2.9, "The Trial," Angel admits that he was Darla's "lover" for 150 years, but that he never actually loved her. He states explicitly that as Angelus, "I wasn't capable of it" (2.9). Darla herself admits that for 400 years she too was incapable of love (*Angel* 3.9, "Lullaby"). As we also noted in the previous chapter, the kind of vampire you become is determined by the kind of person you were before being vamped. The emotionally crippled drunkard, Liam, had not been capable of love and, accordingly, neither was the vampire he became, and Darla had been an unfeeling syphilitic prostitute before she became a vampire. Dostoevsky implies that we are given earthly existence in order to experience at least "a moment of *living* love" (169). For Dostoevsky, in his ambiguously Christian interpretation, if love is scorned on earth and we remain callous, we risk spending eternity thirsting for love, wanting to sacrifice the life we no longer have for the love of another, "Even though I would gladly give my life for others, it can never be, for that life is past which can be sacrificed for love" (169). Liam, it seems, was given a second chance, not, of course, through Angelus, but rather through Angel.

Angelus regains his human soul through a gypsy curse. In 1898, he kills a daughter of the gypsy tribe, and in anger and vengeance, the Elders retaliate with the curse: "Neither dead, nor of the living, I invoke you, spirit of the passing. Return to the body what distinguishes Man from the beast!" (2.21, "Becoming, Part One"). As another gypsy Elder later explains to Jenny Calendar, "Angel is meant to suffer, not to live as human. One moment of true happiness, of contentment, one moment where the soul that we restored no longer plagues his thoughts, and that soul is taken from him" (2.14, "Innocence"). Angel's soul does indeed plague his thoughts. The gypsy Elders warn him the moment he gets his soul: "It hurts, yes? Good. It will hurt more.... You don't remember everything you've done for a hundred years? In a moment, you will. The face of everyone you killed ... our daughter's face ... they will haunt you, and you will know what true suffering is" (2.21, "Becoming, Part One"). As Angel confesses to Buffy in telling her about the gypsy curse, "You have no idea what it's like to have done the things I've done ... and to care" (1.7, "Angel").

No one suspects, least of all Buffy and Angel, that the moment of true happiness could be the consummation of the love these two have developed for each other. In fact, the episode in which this occurs is appropriately entitled "Surprise" (2.13). As we explained in the previous chapter, Angel is given the opportunity to begin to work towards redemption by choosing to help and protect the novice Slayer, Buffy. He seizes this opportunity. In working with Buffy to fight evil and close the Hellmouth, Angel finds himself falling in love with her. Their first kiss is a premonition of things to come. Rhonda Wilcox, in *Why Buffy Matters*, calls it a "precap" or precapitulation (115). The first kiss occurs in Buffy's bedroom. They have been chased by "The Three," a trio of warrior vampires, and take refuge in Buffy's house. Angel explains, as Buffy slams and locks the door against The Three, that vampires cannot enter your home unless you invite them in. Buffy has just shouted to Angel to "Get in! Come on!" not know-ing that he too is a vampire. He certainly seems to have a first-hand knowl-edge about vampires. Buffy tells him that she had heard that vampires cannot enter uninvited but that she had never "put it to the test before" (1.7). As The Three seem to be lurking outside the house, and Angel is wounded, they decide that he should remain overnight. Buffy introduces him to her mother, Joyce, as a study partner, or rather tutor from the col-lege, pretends that he has left, and hides him in her bedroom so that her mother will not discover that her study partner is spending the night, inno-cent as it is. When they kiss, Angel erupts into vampire face, and as a hor-rified Buffy screams, he jumps out the bedroom window, does a safety roll down the porch roof, lands on the ground, and runs away.

The eruption of Angel's vampire face here can be read on many lev-els. He has certainly lost, at least momentarily, control of the monster within. Teenage boys watching the show can relate to a somewhat lower eruption in similar circumstances and understand and sympathize with the need to leap out the window in a dramatic effort of self-restraint. As Xander observes concerning a not unrelated problem, "I'm seventeen. Looking at linoleum makes me wanna have sex" (2.14, "Innocence"). The inconvenient emergence of Angel's vampire face here certainly invokes the show's central theme about controlling our inner demons and how difficult this sometimes is.

Buffy and Angel are star-crossed lovers. Angel had already told her that he was too old for her. Buffy, at this time, does not realize how much too old he is for her (it is something like 224 years, as Buffy finally real-izes near the end of 1.7, "Angel"). But this is not simply the problem of a seventeen-year-old girl in love with an older man. This is the Slayer, who had begun to care for someone she has now discovered to be a vampire, the very thing that it is her duty to hunt down and destroy. Even Darla, his sire, chides Angel, "You love someone who hates us" (1.7). Thus, it would seem, they could not be more unsuited for one another.

Buffy's scream as the vampire-faced Angel leaps out the window brings her mother into her room to see what is wrong. As they both look out the window, Buffy tells her mother that nothing is wrong, "I saw a shadow" (1.7). Rhonda Wilcox and a number of other commentators draw atten-tion to the fact that Angel, and indeed vampires generally, can be read as Buffy's shadow in a quasi–Jungian sense, or as Donald Keller puts it in "Spirit Guides and Shadow Selves" as "Buffy's counterpart ... or Jungian shadow" (116). Wilcox and Lavery begin their book, *Fighting the Forces: What's at Stake in "Buffy the Vampire Slayer,"* with the premise that the

Slayer's "strength incorporates the Shadow" (xvii). Wilcox, in her own study, *Why Buffy Matters*, is not sure whether the Jungian concept should be Shadow, Animus, or Anima, but she is certain that vampires, particularly those with souls, constitute the dark counterpart of the Slayer herself (82). We are not arguing that all this follows from Buffy's dismissive remark that "I saw a shadow" (1.7), but this statement does, ironically, refer to Angel at the very point that Buffy is shown his dark side. If Angel is indeed Buffy's dark counterpart or shadow self, this raises questions about just how star-crossed, how impossible, this love really is.

Elizabeth Krimmer and Shilpa Raval, in "'Digging the Undead': Death and Desire in *Buffy*," compare the story of Angel and Buffy with "works of art ranging from *Romeo and Juliet* to *Tristan and Isolde*," and argue that while they "seem on the surface to celebrate the power of love, they are in fact driven by a desperate conviction of its impossibility" (153). Upon discovering that Angel is a vampire, and particularly after finding Angelus in full vampire face holding her mother's limp body, Buffy's intense love turns into an equally intense hatred. As Buffy herself puts it, "I've killed a lot of vampires. I've never hated one before" (1.7). Unbeknownst to Buffy, it is Darla who has attacked Joyce and set Angel up (don't worry, Joyce is OK; her doctor thinks she fell on a barbecue fork). Ultimately, Angel stakes Darla to prevent her from shooting Buffy. Buffy finally learns that Darla set him up and, more importantly, that Angel has been cursed with a soul, a conscience, by the gypsies: "Fed on a girl about your age ... a favorite among her clan.... Romany. Gypsies. The Elders conjured the perfect punishment for me. They restored my soul.... I haven't fed on a living human being since that day" (1.7). After their victorious battle with Darla, Buffy and Angel make up. Their words to one another suggest that they know that their love is doomed, that a Slayer and a vampire cannot be lovers, but their actions tell another story. Angel tries to tell Buffy, "Look ... this can't..." and Buffy completes his sentence, saying, "I know, ever be anything. For one thing, you're, like, two hundred and twenty-four years older than I am" (1.7, *Scriptbook, Vol. Two*, 64). They both agree that they must "walk away from" this relationship, but each stays rooted to the floor even though Buffy says, "One of us has to go here" and Angel agrees. What follows is the second kiss between these star-crossed lovers. This time, it is more passionate, longer, and Angel is able to control the demon within. As the shooting script says, "finally they break. She looks up at him, the cross he gave her glinting at her throat" (65). They both agree that this is "painful." As she turns and leaves, "he watches her go, pain playing on his features" (65). The camera pans slowly from his face to his chest "where we now see the smoking IMPRINT OF THE CROSS she was wearing — *burned into his chest*" (65). These are star-crossed lovers indeed.

Angel and Buffy attempt to stay away from one another, though Angel continues to help Giles, for example, finding the important ancient document, the Pergamum Codex, for him and rescuing the Scoobies from a gas-filled room (1.11, "Out of Mind, Out of Sight"). At the end of Season One, in Episode 1.12, "Prophecy Girl," it is revealed that the Master is about to complete his project of opening the Hellmouth, and it is prophesied in the Pergamum Codex that as part of this process, the Master will also kill the Slayer. Oddly enough, it is Xander, who has just been rejected as a romantic partner by Buffy and remains jealous and mistrustful of Angel, who pleads with Angel to help Buffy and himself combat the Master: "I don't like you. At the end of the day, I pretty much think you're a vampire. But Buffy's got this big old yen for you. She thinks you're a real person. And right now I need you to prove her right" (1.12). When they discover Buffy drowned by the Master in a pool of water, it is Angel who must now ask Xander for help, when Xander suggests using CPR: "You have to do it. I have no breath" (1.12). The fact that vampires do not breathe made it possible for Angel to rescue people from the gas-filled room, but here this seeming advantage left Angel in need of help, unable to save the woman he loves. He loves her enough to ask for help and, as we know, she does fully recover. Buffy and Angel do eventually, one might say inevitably, consummate their love, get "groiny" as Cordelia would later put it (*Angel* 1.8, "I Will Remember You"). Of course, the full consequences of the gypsy curse ensue. These too can be read, indeed have been interpreted, in many ways. Certainly Buffy awakens the next morning to find that her lover no longer respects her, has turned into a monster, and that, yes, this is the end of the world. These greatest of teenage fears are of course made quite literal in the Buffy-verse. Still, we would argue that this is not really meant as a parable moralizing about the dire consequences of teenage sexual activity. Throughout our study we have maintained that a consequentialist ethics is not at work in either *Buffy the Vampire Slayer* or *Angel*. In fact, we have argued that both programs constitute, or at least can be read as, moral arguments against consequentialist ethical theories such as, for example, utilitarianism.

When Buffy confesses *all* to Giles, her Watcher and father figure, and whimpers that it is all her fault, he replies, "No. I don't believe it is." Although he agrees that she acted rashly, he lets her know that he believes that she and Angel truly loved each other, and goes on to tell her, "if it's guilt you're looking for, Buffy, I'm not your man. All you will get from me is, is my support. And my respect" (2.14, "Innocence"). These words do prove somewhat ironic as Angelus, now out of control, attacks and kills Giles's own love interest, Jenny Calendar, and kidnaps and tortures Giles himself in an attempt to get information from him about how to awaken the demon Acathla who, we learn, if and when awakened, will suck the world into Hell, will literally end the world. None of this may be Buffy's fault, but it is still up to her to rescue Giles and to save the world (again).

Teenage angst, especially concerning disasters associated with the crossing of sexual thresholds, can certainly seem like the end of the world. However, the love story of Buffy and Angel is much more profound than this. Rhonda Wilcox, in *Why Buffy Matters*, argues that in the two episodes in which Buffy loses her innocence and Angel simultaneously loses his soul, "Surprise" (2.13) and "Innocence" (2.14), "Whedon, Noxon, and Co. take on the myth of Original Sin, the conflation of sex, knowledge, and the stain of evil" (126). We partially agree, but also suggest that Wilcox is somewhat misleading, since it is not just these two episodes, but rather the entire Whedonverse that presupposes the myth of Original Sin, partaking of the fruits of the Tree of Knowledge. Moreover, Wilcox does not utilize the Russian existentialist interpretation of the Tree of Knowledge as Reason itself (the logos), which, as we argue in Chapter One, is foundational to our reading of the Buffyverse.

At one point Wilcox does come close, when explaining how Buffy must learn to cope with the repercussions of her night with Angel/Angelus: "To pretend that sorting out the feelings should be a clear-cut, rational process would be mere propaganda for a certain social view" (126). Buffy had already begun to sort out her feelings about Angel as early as when deciding whether or not to sleep with him, though we would not characterize it as an especially "clear-cut, rational process." Buffy seeks Willow's advice concerning further developing her relationship with Angel. When Willow asks her what she really wants to do, Buffy replies, "I don't know. I... I mean, 'want' isn't always the right thing to do. To act on want can be wrong." Buffy then goes on to consider the question, "But ... to not act on want ... What if I never feel this way again?" (2.13, "Surprise"). Wilcox, in discussing this scene, notes that Willow's advice is to give back to Buffy the *carpe diem* philosophy that Buffy herself espoused during their first meeting in the Bronze (1.1). Wilcox draws attention to the fact that when Willow then followed that advice, she left the Bronze in the company of an apparently nice boy she had just met who, unfortunately, turned out to be a vampire. Wilcox wants us to see the parallel between this event and Buffy's seizing the day with Angel. In both cases, the girls end up being confronted by monstrous vampires (117).

Buffy does not let her experience with the monster sour her attitude towards love, as her subsequent advice to Willow illustrates. In episode 4.19, "New Moon Rising," Willow is herself crossing a sexual threshold, in discovering that she really loves her new girlfriend, Tara, rather than her old boyfriend, Oz, who, having been away learning to master his lycanthropy, obviously wants to get back with her. (In the Buffyverse, many boyfriends seem to have a monster within that needs controlling.) Buffy tells Willow that no matter what she does, someone is going to get hurt, but that the important thing is "you have to follow your heart." It is revealing that Buffy can offer this advice even after the pain she has experienced following her own heart with Angel. As she has told her new boyfriend, Riley Finn, earlier in this same episode, "love isn't logical, Riley. It's not like you can be Mister Joe Sensible about it all the time" (4.19). The love ethics implicit in the Buffyverse is most certainly not a moral theory based on reason.

Whistler, the emissary from the Powers-That-Be, tells Buffy that even he thought that Angel had come Sunnydale to stop the demon Acathla from destroying the world. No one could have predicted that meeting and helping Buffy would result in Angel's losing his soul, becoming Angelus and actually awakening Acathla. Given these circumstances, Whistler asks Buffy, "Now, what are you gonna do? What are you prepared to do?" He has no doubt that Buffy and he are both partially responsible for the mess they are in. He brought them together after all. Speaking of Angel's duty to stop Acathla, he tells Buffy, "I figured this for Angel's big day. But I thought he was here to stop Acathla, not to bring him forth. Then you two made with the smooches ... now he's a creep again." When Buffy replies that she is prepared to do anything to stop Angelus, Whistler responds prophetically, "Maybe I should ask, what are you prepared to give up?" (2.22, "Becoming, Part Two"). Buffy must give up a great deal indeed.

Buffy's wiccan friend, Willow, tries to help by using her developing powers as a witch to restore Angel's soul. She has found the words to the needed gypsy spell on a computer disk left by Jenny Calendar, the late (thanks to Angelus) high school computer teacher. Willow is so advanced in her knowledge of computers that she has been asked to take over the computer class in the absence of Miss Calendar. It turns out that Miss Calendar was a member of the gypsy tribe that had cursed Angelus in the first place. It is no coincidence that she was teaching in Sunnydale at the same time Angel arrived up there, since the gypsies were keeping an eye on him. Besides being a computer teacher, Jenny was also a powerful witch in her own right, a technopagan as she called herself. As she told the stuffy and bookish librarian Giles, "You think the realm of the mystical is limited to ancient texts and relics? That bad old science made the magic go away?... The divine exists in cyberspace same as out here (1.8, "I Robot ... You Jane").

Willow hopes to be able to restore Angel's soul before Angelus awakens Acathla, and she almost succeeds. Almost but not quite. It is Buffy the Vampire Slayer who must save the day (and the world). Angelus has discovered that his blood will awaken Acathla and open the mouth of Hell. Buffy attempts to stop him, and almost succeeds. Angelus successfully removes the sword embedded in the chest of the magical stone statue of Acathla, which immediately begins to come alive, slowly opening a portal to Hell. Buffy and Angelus are fighting with swords. She has learned from Whistler, "Angel's the key. His blood will open the door to Hell. Acathla opens his big mouth, creates a vortex. Then only Angel's blood will close it. One blow will send 'em both back to Hell (2.22, "Becoming, Part Two"). It is of course Angelus, not Angel, who awakened Acathla. As Buffy fights Angelus, Willow's magic succeeds in restoring the vampire's soul. Buffy is now confronted by Angel, not Angelus. As with the first time his soul is restored, Angel does not immediately remember his life as Angelus: "Buffy? What's going on? Where are we? I-I don't remember" (2.22). She recognizes that her true love, Angel, is standing before her. They embrace and kiss. The vortex in Acathla's mouth of Hell begins to rumble and grow larger. Buffy knows what she has to do, she knows where her duty lies, and she knows what she must choose to give up. Before plunging her sword into Angel, she says, "I love you.... Close your eyes" (2.22). Angel is immediately sucked into the vortex, the Mouth of Hell closes, and Acathla turns back to stone.

Audible in the background is the song "Full of Grace" by Sarah McLachlan, which captures perfectly Buffy's desolate mood (2.22). There is a sense in which both Buffy and her lover have been sucked into Hell. Buffy has never felt so low. This she confirms in confessing to Giles and the Scoobies how she felt at the moment she realized in the midst of battle that it was Angel before her, "When I killed him, Angel was cured. Your spell worked at the last minute, Will. I was about to take him out, and, um ... something went through him, and he was Angel again. He-he didn't remember anything that he'd done. He just held me. Um, but i-it was, it was too late, and I, I had to. So I, I told him that I loved him, and I kissed him, and I killed him" (3.3, "Faith, Hope, and Trick"). Having sent her first love to Hell, it is little wonder Buffy feels like she herself has gone to Hell by the end of Season Two.

In the first episode of Season Three, "Anne," Buffy has run away to Los Angeles where she quite literally enters a Hell dimension, which jolts her into resuming her Slayer duties and saving the homeless people of Los Angeles held captive and rendered nameless in this dimension. It is this experience which gives her the courage to return to Sunnydale and to continue being the Slayer, as we explain in some detail in Chapter Four, "Slayer Authenticity: Constructing Reality Through Existential Choice."

Though Angel haunts Buffy's dreams (3.1, "Anne"; 3.2, "Dead Man's Party"; and "3.3, "Faith, Hope, and Trick"), he does not actually return from his Hell dimension until the end of 3.3, though Buffy does not learn of this until the next episode (3.4, "Beauty and the Beasts"). Angel is not quite himself upon his return, and Buffy nurses him back to both physical and mental health, without telling Giles and the Scooby Gang of his arrival. She does ask Giles, purely hypothetically, what he might be like if he were to return, and learns, "From what is known about that dimension, i-it would suggest a world of ... brutal torment. And time moves quite differently there, so ... he would've been down there for hundreds of years ... of torture." Giles tells her that only someone of "extraordinary will and character" could survive such an ordeal, and would likely be a monster. There would, however, be some hope, he tells her, because "there are two types of monster. The first ... can be redeemed, or more importantly, wants to be redeemed," while the second "is void of humanity, cannot respond to reason, or love" (3.4, "Beauty and the Beasts").

From the standpoint of the existential love ethics implicit in the Buffy-verse, if Angel is to recover from Hell, he must want to be redeemed, that is, he must exercise existential choice and he must be able to respond to both reason and love. Angel does respond to Buffy's love; however, we contend that in one sense he never really escapes from Hell at all. He dares not consummate his love with her again now that he knows the consequences of the gypsy curse. According to Dostoevsky's definition of Hell, it is "being unable to love" (169). We contend that Buffy's sending Angel to Hell through the portal opened by Acathla can be read as a metaphor for the impossible love that Angel develops for her. On another level, Angel is still able to follow his love for Buffy by leaving her, an act that is paradoxically motivated by both passion and reason.

Angel thinks with both his head and his heart. In conversation with Buffy's mother, Joyce, Angel is told, "when it comes to you, Angel, [Buffy is] just like any other young woman in love. You're all she can see of tomorrow. But I think we both know that there are some hard choices ahead. If she can't make them, you're gonna have to. I know you care about her. I just hope you care enough" (3.20, "The Prom"). In breaking up with her, Angel tells Buffy that he is just trying to be rational: "I've been thinking about our future. And the more I do, the more I feel like us, you and me being together, is unfair to you.... I'm trying to do what's right here, okay? I'm trying to think with my head instead of my heart" (3.20). We should point out that this is a choice which Buffy has already reluctantly made herself by stabbing Angel and sending him to the Hell dimension in the first place, though she may not have been completely conscious of the full implications at the time. So in one sense, these star-crossed lovers do have an impossible love, but in another, more profound, sense they are making the most difficult sacrifice of all, for the sake of that very love. Their love is, then, both impossible and possible, indeed necessary, at one and the same time, in that they can and must sacrifice themselves for love. Dostoevsky, as we have seen, characterizes this as the "*living* love," the highest love of all. It is, we contend, is an important part of the overall theme of the entire series.

Reflecting this theme, Buffy is constantly sacrificing herself to save the world. For example, at the end of Season Five, as we have seen, Buffy quite literally sacrifices her life to save her sister, Dawn, and close an opening Hellmouth (5.22, "The Gift"). Either Dawn's death or her own would have saved the day, but Buffy chose to sacrifice herself rather than the sister she loves, finally understanding the First Slayer's prophesy "Death is your gift" and "love will bring you to your gift" (5.18, "Intervention"). At this point, the First Slayer, aka Buffy's Spirit Guide, reassures Buffy that she is not losing her ability to love: "You are full of love. You love with all of your soul. It's brighter than the fire, blinding.... Love is pain, and the Slayer forges strength from pain. Love, give, forgive. Risk the pain. It is your nature" (5.18).

Though Buffy can never be with Angel, it does not follow that they have ceased to love one another or that this kind of living love is impossible. Buffy's chosen death to save Dawn out of love is just the most extreme example of Buffy's life of self-sacrifice. In fact, everything she does by choosing to be the Slayer involves at least the sacrifice of a normal life. For instance, in the episode in which Angel announces his plan to leave (3.20), she in fact sacrifices her very normal and important teenage desire to have a memorable and wonderful prom in order to protect the school from an impending threat: "You guys are going to have a prom. The kind of prom that everyone should have. I'm going to give you all a nice, fun, normal evening if I have to kill every single person on the face of the earth to do it" (3.20).

Stacey Abbott, both in the introduction to her book *Reading Angel: The TV Spin-off with a Soul* and in more detail in the article "Walking the Fine Line between Angel and Angelus," argues, "the series *Angel* undermines the distinction between Angel and Angelus and presents the hybrid Angel/Angelus as a self-defining existentialist protagonist" (para 4). Drawing on Robert Porfirio's study, "No Way Out: Existential Motifs in the *Film Noir*," Abbott argues that although there is no direct existentialist influence, the *film noir* genre on which *Angel* is partially based "was influenced by the American hard-boiled school of fiction and the 'symbiotic relationship they had with the French existentialist writers'" (para 7).

Though we agree with Abbott that an existentialist reading of the *Angel* series is appropriate, we cannot accept her further claim that this distinguishes the character of Angel as he appears in his own series from the Angel in *Buffy the Vampire Slayer*. As noted above, we give an existentialist interpretation of *Buffy the Vampire Slayer* as well as of *Angel*. Abbott, on the other hand, argues that, on *Buffy*, Angel "represents an essentialist definition of good" (para 2). The concept of essentialist definition here is derived from Rhonda Wilcox's "Every Night I Save You: Buffy, Spike, Sex and Redemption." The essentialist, as opposed to the existentialist, definition of good suggests that because Angel "has a 'good' soul, he has no desire to harm people" (para 2), as Richard Greene and Wayne Yuen put it in "Why Can't We Spike Spike?: Moral Themes in *Buffy the Vampire Slayer*" (para 2). In other words, in *Buffy the Vampire Slayer* we are faced with "polar oppositions: the good Angel versus the evil Angelus" (Abbott, para 1), or "tortured soul" as opposed to "soulless demon," as Beth Braun expresses it in "*The X-Files* and *Buffy the Vampire Slayer*: The Ambiguity of Evil in Supernatural Representation" (90). Abbott clearly supports the essentialist interpretation of *Buffy the Vampire Slayer*. She states explicitly of Wilcox, Braun, Greene and Yuen, "these readings of Angel's character on *BtVS* are sound" (para 3).

Yet Abbott goes on to contradict herself by supporting a much more existentialist reading of *Buffy the Vampire Slayer*: "it was not the curse and the return of his soul that set Angel onto the path of goodness, but rather it was Buffy. Through her, his mission was clear. Without her, he is alone on a path struggling to walk a fine line between Angel and Angelus and to make the right *choices*" (para 17). We think this is a much more cogent interpretation of the Buffyverse than the essentialist one. As noted in our previous chapter, Whistler offered Angel a fundamental existential choice when he first presented him with the possibility of helping Buffy: "I wanna know who you are.... I'm looking to find out. 'Cause you could go either way here.... I mean that you can become an even more useless rodent than you already are, or you can become someone. A person. Someone to be counted" (2.21, "Becoming, Part One"). Angel, as we know, makes the choice to help Buffy.

His soul does not force him to make this choice; rather, it allows him the possibility of making such a choice. As with all existentialist choice, it is one which must be made continuously, as it is that which makes us who we are, and we are always "in progress." We can see that Angel is constantly tempted by human blood, and must continuously resist such temptations. For example, when Darla sucks blood from Buffy's mother, Joyce, and dumps her unconscious body into Angel's arms, we can see that he has to fight not to give in to Darla's suggestion that he really wants feed on warm human blood: "I just had a little. There's plenty more. Aren't you hungry for something warm after all this time? Come on, Angel. Just say 'Yes!'" (1.7, "Angel"). According to the shooting script, "Angel MORPHS into a vampire ... he is staring at the pinpricks of blood on Joyce's neck.... Angel shuts his eyes, trying to control himself. Opens them. Moves his head down towards Joyce's neck —" (41). Fortunately, as we noted above, Buffy comes home just at this moment.

The point is that Angel is both tempted and struggling with his inner demon. We will actually never know what would have happened if Buffy hadn't arrived just at that moment, though most of us believe that Angel would have done the right thing, not because he has a "good" soul, but because he had chosen as his project to help the Slayer fight evil. This choice is part of that larger choice which is forming Angel's character. Angel Investigations, in Los Angeles, is in fact a continuation of this character-determining existential choice. We see it as Angel's way of carrying on his love for Buffy by carrying on her good works, "helping the helpless," as the motto of Angel Investigations proclaims.

That the existential choice that Angel makes in the *Buffy the Vampire Slayer* series must be a continuous one is confirmed in the first season of the *Angel* series. In *Angel* 1.8, "I Will Remember You," Buffy, in one of her rare visits to Los Angeles, helps Angel fight an evil Mohra demon. It is extremely powerful, and Buffy and Angel together succeed only in wounding it. During the battle, some of the Mohra demon's blood is spattered on Angel. Blood, of course, is the life-giving substance, but Mohra blood has the magical quality of giving life to anyone it touches. The effect on Angel is dramatic. His heart starts beating, he is breathing normally — he becomes an ordinary mortal, as opposed to a vampire.

The effect on his relationship with Buffy is also dramatic. The gypsy curse no longer applies. Their love is no longer impossible, and they are able to be together as a normal couple. Unfortunately, Angel also discovers that he no longer has vampire strength, and this leaves Buffy to deal with the Mohra demon alone. If they could not defeat it together, Buffy stands less of a chance of defeating it alone, and if it is not defeated more of its kind will come and take over the world. Angel, therefore, petitions the Powers-That-Be to restore him to his former state, a vampire with a soul.

After much debate, the Oracles, agents of the Powers-That-Be, reluctantly grant his wish in spite of the fact that they do not, as a rule, do such things for what they consider "lower beings." They justify making such an extraordinary exception by pointing out that Angel "is willing to sacrifice every drop of human happiness and love he has ever known for another. He is not a lower being" (*Angel* 1.8). Their solution is to "swallow this day, as though it had never happened. Twenty-four hours from the moment the demon first attacked you, we take it back." Only Angel is allowed to remember these events; during them he also learns the Mohra demon's one weak point and, as the day begins again and as events start repeating themselves, he is able to slay it. It is, of course, only Angel who knows that events are starting to repeat themselves and who is thus able to stop them from doing so. Only Angel will remember the normal life he could have had with Buffy. Once again, he has sacrificed his love, and, furthermore, now he has sacrificed his human life as well for the sake of love in the same way that Buffy is constantly choosing to sacrifice her normal life to fulfill her duties as the Slayer.

We think it is also important to note that Angel's sacrifice is judged by the Oracles to be based on love, and this makes him a superior being. The fact that it is love, not reason, that sets Angel apart and makes him a champion corroborates our contention that a love ethics is implicit in the Buffyverse. Angel's choice is also a tremendous sacrifice, the pain of which comes from the fact that only he will remember the happiness he is giving up. As the Oracles warn, "You. You alone will carry the memory of this day. Can you carry that burden?"

In our previous chapter, "Angel and Spike: Soul Mates and Moral Responsibility," we raised the question of whether Spike was a more worthy champion than Angel because Spike chose to have his soul restored whereas Angel had his soul thrust upon him by a gypsy curse. Given, as we have seen, that Angel too *chooses* to be an ensouled vampire, we would have to conclude that Spike does not have the advantage in this argument. From a human perspective, at least, it would seem that Angel is making the greater sacrifice. However, it is clear that both these existential choices were motivated by love. These important choices also contribute to the continuous moral growth of both Spike and Angel.

Stacey Abbott, in her existentialist analysis of the *Angel* series, quite rightly emphasizes the fact that in an existentialist concept of person, who we are is determined largely by the goals which we choose to pursue. We define ourselves by the choices we make. Drawing on Jean-Paul Sartre's "Existentialism and Humanism," Abbott claims that for the existentialist "man's existence pre-dates his essence" ("Walking the Fine Line..." para 5). Though Sartre does say that we are given our existence and then must decide who or what we are to become, he does not actually mean this in a temporal sense. Rather, our existence precedes our essence in a logical, or rather ontological, sense. In other words, Sartre uses "precedes" in a logical or ontological sense, as opposed to a temporal one. Abbott's use of the word "pre-dates" is somewhat misleading, since it implies that we make our choice and thus acquire an essence. But, as Buffy would say, "it doesn't work that way." An authentic life is one of continuous and difficult choices, often involving intolerable sacrifices, as the characters of Buffy, Angel, and others dramatically illustrate, contrary to Abbott, throughout both *Buffy the Vampire Slayer* and *Angel*.

Some commentators, notably Scott McLaren in "The Evolution of Joss Whedon's Vampire Mythology and the Ontology of the Soul," have suggested separating the existential from the ontological concept of soul in discussing the ensouled vampires Spike and Angel. We discuss this issue in more detail in the previous chapter. Though McLaren argues that Angel is morally responsible for the crimes of Angelus, he never successfully establishes the ontological connection between the two. Rather, he argues that the ensouled vampire "[t]hough ontologically innocent, ... remains somehow existentially culpable because he chooses to be so" (para 14). Here we would point out that the Buffy episode 2.22, "Becoming, Part Two," discussed above, establishes the ontological connection missing in McLaren. Angel, having lost his soul and reverting to Angelus, has used his blood and a magic spell to awaken Acathla. Only the sacrifice of the person who awakens Acathla can stop him and close the Hellmouth. Hence, it is doubly significant that Willow's soul restoration spell works at the instant it does; it both magnifies the pain of the sacrifice Buffy must make, and clarifies the identity underlying both Angel and Angelus. It is the sacrifice of Angel that seals the Hellmouth opened by Angelus. This certainly suggests that they are, indeed must be, an ontological unity.

After Angel moves from Sunnydale to Los Angeles, Buffy's main love interests — Riley Finn and Spike (of all things) — can be seen as Buffy's unconscious and futile attempt to regain Angel. The rational Riley, a good boy from Iowa who attends church regularly, could represent to Buffy Angel's restored soul. The passionate vampire Spike could be Buffy's representation of Angelus. Spike certainly tells Riley, "You're not the long haul guy and you know it.... The girl needs some monster in her man, and that's not in your nature ... no matter how low you try to go" (5.10, "Into the Woods"). When Spike reveals that Buffy needs some monster in her man, he is sharing a bottle of booze with Riley and the two are commiserating with each other about how Buffy does not love either of them. Spike tells Riley, "Sometimes I envy you so much it chokes me. And sometimes I think I got the better deal. To be that close to her and not have her. To be all alone even when you're holding her. Feeling her, feeling her beneath you. Surrounding you. The scent. No, you got the better deal" (5.10).

Buffy does not love either Riley or Spike because neither of them is the complete Angel, the only man she truly loves. The fact that as early as Season Two of *Buffy the Vampire Slayer* Angel/Angelus, Buffy's first and only true love, is seen as ontologically and existentially one and the same man, also illustrates the problem with Stacey Abbott's claim that an essentialist concept of a good Angel and a bad Angelus is at work in *Buffy the Vampire Slayer*. We have shown that an existentialist interpretation of both *Buffy the Vampire Slayer* and *Angel* shows how love and the continuous necessity for moral choice help us determine our moral character and thus our selves as authentic persons.

Chapter Ten

Firefly and *Serenity*: Two Forms of Freedom

In this chapter we argue that the concept of freedom found in *Firefly* and much of the spinoff movie, *Serenity*, is a very limited concept of freedom, appropriate only for the tragic hero. It is very different from the ideal of freedom found in *Buffy the Vampire Slayer*, which we have described in Chapter One, with the help of Dostoevsky and the Russian existentialist, Lev Shestov, who argue, "freedom consists in the force and power to prevent evil from entering the world" (*Athens and Jerusalem*, 256). As we have seen, this ideal of freedom is portrayed most dramatically in *Buffy* through various attempts to prevent the Hellmouth from opening, or to seal it if and when it has been opened. This is very different from merely choosing between good and evil, or choosing the lesser of two evils. Of course, the notion of the tragic hero appears in *Buffy* as well as in *Firefly* and *Serenity*, though it is important to note that it is usually introduced in *Buffy* in order to contrast the freedom of the tragic hero with the ideal of freedom we have just described. For example, at the end of Season Five, Giles finds it necessary to kill the character Ben, who, through no fault of his own, is the vessel which the Hellgod Glory must use in order to manifest herself and destroy the world by means of a ritual that will melt all dimensions into one. Giles is a tragic hero because he is faced with a choice between two evils, killing an innocent person or allowing the destruction of the entire world. The sacrifice of the individual in this case would certainly seem to be the lesser of the two evils. It is important to remember, however, that Giles is not happy about being forced into the position of choosing between evils: "I've sworn to protect this sorry world and sometimes that means saying and doing what other people can't. What they shouldn't have to" (5.22, "The Gift"). People should not have to be forced to choose between evils, lesser or otherwise. It constitutes a lack of freedom as the ethical ideal in *Buffy* makes perfectly clear, since freedom involves preventing evil from entering the world. Being forced to choose between evils is what makes the existentialist tragic hero tragic, because it is still choosing evil, allowing evil to enter the world. Our true hero, Buffy, it will be remembered, refused to kill Ben, which is why Giles felt it was left up to him.

Giles quite rightly asserts that the world ought not to be such that we are forced to choose between evils. This is, nevertheless, the way the worlds are portrayed in both *Firefly* and *Serenity*. They are governed by a totalitarian regime calling itself the Alliance. This Alliance seems to be a confederation between China and the United States of America, which were presumably the two dominant powers on "earth that was." The flag of the Alliance is a combination of the stripes of the U.S. Stars and Stripes and the gold stars on red background from the flag of Communist China (the flag is seen in passing in the episode "The Train Job"). The setting of the Alliance worlds is some five hundred years in the future in a new solar system consisting of planets and moons that have been "terraformed" in order to replicate terrestrial conditions and environments. The Alliance has firm control over the central planets, which are regarded as "civilized," but its hold over settlements on the outer planets and moons is somewhat tenuous. As a result of the weak hold the Alliance has on these territories and of its inability and/or unwillingness to provide them with the same levels of supplies and services that the inner planets have, these remote regions have developed at different rates socially, economically, and polit- ically. Many of these far-flung regions (like the frontier towns of the "Old West" or rural Afghanistan today) seem to be governed by local warlords and mercenaries. As Mercedes Lackey argues in "*Serenity* and Bobby McGee: Freedom and the Illusion of Freedom in Joss Whedon's *Firefly*," "The dystopian society in which the crew of *Serenity* operates feels *real....* It resonates because the rules by which this dystopia operates are famil- iar.... The Alliance uses a lot of the same psychological weapons on its own people that all the major governments of the world ... are ... using today" (63–64). Lackey sees *Firefly* as a criticism of modern industrial society. We agree. Although the setting is five hundred years into the future, human nature and human relations (personal and political) seem not to have changed and certainly have not evolved for the better.

Though people under the Alliance have the illusion of freedom, they are very careful not to upset the status quo for fear of losing that very free- dom (though they are, of course, clinging to an illusion). For example, in the episode "Safe," we learn in various flashbacks that Simon and River Tam come from a respected family living under Alliance rule. Both brother and sister were stellar students. Simon is on his way to a brilliant medical career. His sister, River, at this point has been sent to a government-sponsored school for gifted children. Simon learns that this so-called school is in fact a covert government experimental institution which is dedicated, among other things, to turning child prodigies into government agents, through psychological, as well as biomedical, interference. Simon cannot convince his parents that River is a victim of this kind of government exploitation. Simon and River's parents appear to have just too much to lose (their status in this society) to question what the government is doing with their daughter. Simon is thus left on his own to attempt to rescue his sister. And he is willing to risk his entire medical career to do so. At one point, he is arrested in what is called a "blackout zone" and his father is forced to bail him out. The father is most concerned that this will go on the family's permanent record. The fact that this "civilized" society both has blackout zones and keeps permanent records on its citizens suggests that the kind of freedom available to its citizens is, if not completely illusory, at best severely curtailed. Simon's father certainly feels threatened when his son steps out of line in this way. We can only wonder what happens to the family after Simon, with his contacts from the blackout zone, rescues River from the government's experimental facility. Simon and River, in fact, end up fleeing the Alliance by booking passage with Captain Malcolm Reynolds and his crew of malcontents aboard Serenity.

Serenity is a firefly-class spaceship, which Captain Malcolm Reynolds is using as an independent transporter, finding odd jobs supplying goods to the outer planets, sometimes legally, sometimes not. He can certainly be regarded as a smuggler, though he would be the first to insist that many of the jobs he undertakes are perfectly legal and in fact sanctioned by the Alliance. As Lackey points out in her essay "*Serenity* and Bobby McGee," it is likely that far more of these activities than Mal realizes are sanctioned, or at least tolerated, by the Alliance. The Alliance's resources are stretched far too thinly to provide adequate services to the outer planets, so the Alliance is quite happy to allow smugglers like Reynolds to keep the populations somewhat contented by moving required goods such as food and medical supplies illegally. Malcolm Reynolds is unwittingly helping the Alliance govern the outer planets, or at least preventing their populations from rebelling. Mal thinks he is free, and the Alliance is more than willing to let him persist in this delusion, since he and those like him are performing a useful service for their imperial administration (66–67). So, Mal thinks he is flying under the radar of the Alliance, but they are in fact letting him do so, at least until he welcomes the fugitives, Simon and River

Tam, on board. In doing this, Mal "crosses that invisible boundary — the point past which the Alliance has to notice him and do something about him" (Lackey 68). He must now avoid inspection by Alliance ships and watch out for both covert government operatives and bounty hunters, a necessity that begins to reveal to him the tenuousness, and indeed the illusory nature, of his freedom.

All of Mal's major decisions are in fact the decisions of a tragic hero in that he is constantly forced to choose the lesser of two evils. Both *Firefly* and *Serenity* are space westerns. Folks on the frontier, the outer planets, tend to shoot each other on occasion, and it seems to be permissible to shoot bad guys, if you need to. There is certainly not the respect for human life we find in the *Buffy* and *Angel* series (most vampires and demons excepted, of course). For example, in the two-hour pilot, "Serenity Parts One and Two," Mal is selling stolen Alliance foodstuffs to Patience, a female outlaw leader in a remote outpost. Mal expects her to try to bushwhack him with snipers rather than make an honest deal, and so sends the toughest member of his crew, Jayne, to quietly take out the sniper and take over the sniper's position. This, Mal hopes, will give him the advantage. It is an amusing scene, with Mal and his second-in-command, Zoe, standing on the ground facing Patience and several members of her gang, all on horseback. After money has exchanged hands, Patience informs Mal that there are complications: she doesn't like to part with money she doesn't have to. Of course, she thinks she has the advantage with her sniper hiding up in the hills. When the shooting begins, she realizes the sniper is targeting her own men, and Mal and Zoe have drawn their pistols. Mal and Zoe kill most of Patience's men, though both he and Zoe are slightly wounded. Mal shoots Patience's horse, which she was using for cover, and as she is trapped beneath the horse, he takes back the sack of money which he had returned, ostensibly to avoid trouble: "I did a job. I got nothing but trouble since I did it, not to mention more than a few unkind words as regards to my character. So let me make this abundantly clear. I do the job. I get paid. And that's all" ("Serenity, Part 1 & 2").

This tells us something about Mal's moral character. Although he has shot a number of her henchmen, he refrains from killing Patience. Unlike Patience, he is willing to live up to the terms of the contract even though in these remote regions such contracts are legally unenforceable. Patience also knows that she was purchasing illegally salvaged Alliance goods, so she knew that she could get away with swindling Mal. There was no way he would report her to the authorities even if the authorities had an effective presence in this region. Mal is not governed by external moral rules, but has rather an internal moral discipline, such as it is. Comparing Mal and Patience, Mal is obviously the one with the better moral character, though this may not be saying much. Mal, after all, is willing to undertake illegal jobs, such as train and bank robbery. These illegal acts are usually against the Alliance, which Mal once regarded as the enemy since he was a volunteer soldier with the Independents, who in fact lost the war with the Alliance at the battle of Serenity Valley. The fact that he has named his ship "Serenity" suggests that he has not entirely forgotten the conflict against the Alliance. Alliance targets seem to be fair game. Mal seems to be content just surviving without the Alliance telling him what to do. At the end of the "Serenity" episode, he tells Simon that — in spite of being pursued by the law, criminals, and savages (reavers); having half the people on the ship, including himself, "shot or wounded"; and deciding to harbor "known fugitives" (Simon and River) — he has had "a good day" because he is still flying. Simon responds, "That's not much." Significantly, Mal replies, "It's enough." But by the end of the movie *Serenity*, Mal finds that it is not enough. His concept of freedom has expanded. We contend that it becomes in actual fact much closer to the ideal of freedom we have detected in *Buffy the Vampire Slayer* and *Angel*.

In order to see how freedom develops in *Serenity*, it is important to examine more closely the concept of freedom in *Firefly* and how it relates to Mal's moral integrity. We have seen that although Mal is in a sense free (and somewhat motivated) to kill Patience, he spares her life. Why does he do so? Mal, after all, seems more than willing to kill anyone whom he considers evil and who gets in his way. In the "Serenity" episode, upon returning to the ship (immediately after having spared Patience's life), Mal finds that a government lawman is holding River with a gun to her head, keeping Simon, Kaylee and the rest of the crew at bay. Without breaking his stride, Mal draws his gun and unhesitatingly shoots the lawman dead. It appears that he has re-holstered his gun by the time the lawman hits the floor. Mal and Jayne then unceremoniously dump the body out the hatch as it's closing and the ship is taking off. Jayne remarks, "Buzzards're the only ones gonna find him..."

So what are the crucial differences between these two cases, Patience and the lawman? Interestingly enough, on the DVD commentary on this episode, by Joss Whedon and Nathan Fillion (who plays Mal), we are told that when the lawman breaks out of the brig where the crew had him confined and knocks Shepherd Book out, they have him hit the good Book two more times when he is down just to establish that the lawman is bad, because Mal's going to shoot him at the end of the episode. So both Patience and the lawman may be considered evil. The crucial difference seems to be that the lawman, at the time, constituted a clear and present danger, while Patience was no longer a threat.

Once things settle down, Mal asks Jayne if the lawman had tried to make a deal with him. The lawman had been a passenger on Serenity for some time though, at first, no one knew he was after River. When Jayne doesn't reply, Mal asks, "How come you didn't turn on me, Jayne?" Jayne's response is certainly meant to tell us a great deal about his moral character, "Money wasn't good enough." Jayne is obviously both evil and dangerous, not to mention unreliable. Mal, however, does not shoot him, unhesitatingly or otherwise, but simply asks "What happens when it is?" They both agree that that will be an "interesting" day.

Though Jayne is dangerous, he is obviously of some use to Mal and probably worth the risk. Mal is constantly living on the edge like this. For example, just before facing Patience and her henchmen, Zoe comments to Mal on the location of the meeting place, "I don't think it's a good spot, sir. She still has the advantage over us." Mal quips in reply, "Everyone always does. That's what makes us special"("Serenity, Parts One and Two").

Mal is even willing to accept jobs from vengeful lunatics, of which this 'verse has its fair share. For example, in the episode, "The Train Job," Mal is hired by a character called Niska who shows him a tortured corpse he has hanging in an adjoining room, and explains, "Now, for you, my reputation is not from gossip. You see this man, he does not do the job. I show you what I do with him and now, my reputation for you is fact, is ... solid. You do the train job for me, then you are solid. No more gossip. That is strong relationship." In response to Niska's further question about whether or not Mal approves of Niska's killing this man, Mal says, "Well, I'm sure he was a ... very bad person" ("The Train Job").

Though this may have been meant ironically, there can be no doubt that Mal considers it permissible to kill very bad persons. In fact at the end of the episode, Mal kills Niska's man, Crow (the one responsible for torturing the victim seen in Niska's office). After carrying out the train job, and subsequently discovering that the "loot" was much needed medical supplies for a remote settlement, Mal returns the cargo to its rightful owners. He then unsuccessfully tries to persuade Crow to take the advance payment and return it to Niska. Mal also promises to stay out of Niska's way in the future, arguing that that solution would be "best for everyone." Crow refuses and threatens Mal, telling him to use the money for his own funeral since no matter where Mal goes, no matter how far he flies, Crow will hunt him down and "the last thing you see will be my blade." With a resigned "darn," Mal pushes Crow into the intake of the ship's fast idling engine, which results in an instant and gruesome death. Mal turns to another of Niska's henchmen and begins his speech again, but this hench-man has learned the lesson quickly: "Oh I get it. I'm good. Best for every-one. I'm right there with you."

The death of Crow, then, has some value for Mal in that it softens up Crow's colleague in crime, who, as we have seen, is much more coop-erative. Mal is also taking Crow's threat seriously and dealing with it expe-ditiously, ridding the world of a murderous torturer in the process. John Wright, in his paper on this episode, "Just Shove Him in the Engine, or The Role of Chivalry in *Firefly*," argues that Crow's death is unrealistic. Aside from a captain's jeopardizing the engine of his ship with the harder body parts, Wright suggests that Mal, himself a petty criminal, should, and indeed would, know that a crime boss could not let the murder of one of his men go unpunished (165–166). We would argue, on the contrary, that Mal knows full well that Niska will be out to get him, just because Mal has not completed the train job as instructed. The tortured corpse in Niska's office made that perfectly clear.

This is just another example of Mal's living on the edge. We disagree with Wright's criticism that this is unrealistic (though we are curious about the use of what look to be jet turbine engines on a craft designed for the vacuum of space). Regardless, Mal has acted exactly as we would have expected him to, given his character. We have already seen this facet of his character when Mal chooses to invite Simon Tam to become a member of his crew as the ship's doctor. Mal welcomes Simon and River in spite of being explicitly warned by the late lawman they had held captive that such an action will make Serenity a constant target of the Alliance, since River Tam is one of the Alliance's prize experimental projects: "That girl is a pre-cious commodity. They'll come after her. Long after you bury me they'll be coming" ("Serenity, Parts One and Two"). Mal is quite well aware that both Niska and the Alliance will be out to get him and the crew of Seren-ity. He knows the risks and is willing to live with them.

Mal is actually willing to spare the life of a combatant even when the rules of engagement require the death of the opponent as a matter of pro-tocol. As Inara complains, "Mal, you always break the rules. It doesn't mat-ter which 'society' you're in! You don't get along with ordinary criminals either! That's why you're constantly in trouble!" ("Shindig"). Inara is a Companion, licensed by the Alliance to serve as a high-class geisha, who has rented a shuttle aboard Serenity in order to serve clients on the vari-ous worlds to which Mal and his crew fly. In the episode, "Shindig," which takes place on a planet which seems to support what looks like a mid–18th century genteel society complete with fancy-dress balls, Mal feels it necessary to defend Inara's honor and finds himself challenged to a duel with swords. Significantly, it is Inara who shows Mal the basics of fencing during a quick lesson the night before the duel. The training of the Companion seems to be very comprehensive.

Though Mal disapproves of her profession, often calling Inara a "whore" to her face, he tells her he is defending her honor because he respects her as a person, explaining why he challenged her insensitive client: "I might not show respect to your job, but he didn't respect you. That's the difference, Inara. He doesn't even see you." Unfortunately, this particular client is well known as an experienced and expert swordsman. Mal is only able to win the duel by grabbing his opponent's sword by the blade and turning the duel into a fist fight. This is enough to leave his opponent on the ground with Mal's sword at his throat. Mal is told by the local official who volunteered to be his second, "You have to finish it, lad. For a man to lie beaten and yet breathing, it makes him a coward." Mal responds, "It would be humiliating, having to lie there while the better man refuses to spill your blood. Mercy is the mark of a great man." Mal then stabs his opponent, wounding him slightly, and says that he guesses he is just a good man, as opposed to a great one. He then gives his victim another painful stab, saying, "Well, I'm all right," as opposed to either good or great.

We would argue that Mal is here, as usual, the tragic hero, having to choose among evils. His own internal discipline and moral sense prevent him from killing an opponent who is no longer a threat, yet the rules of the society he happens to be in require that he do so, because not killing this person shows lack of respect for both the individual and the society.

In this episode, we also learn something about the nature of Inara's freedom and power. The victim, her former client, calls her a whore and spitefully tells her that he will see to it that she will never work again. She replies, "Actually, that's not how it works. You see, you've earned yourself a black mark in the client registry. No Companion is going to contract with you ever again."

Mercedes Lackey argues in "*Serenity* and Bobby McGee," that, in fact, Inara's "freedom is as thin as the piece of paper her license is printed on. Without it, she's no longer respected or respectable; she goes from being a sought-after professional to nothing but a lovely and exquisitely trained whore" (69). Mal has, in actual fact, already cautioned Inara that following Alliance rules may buy her a nice life, but these same rules simultaneously make her a slave ("Shindig"). We would add that Inara has no more freedom than Simon and River Tam's parents, who also regard themselves as respectable members of society. It is interesting that Mal is able to see the illusory nature of Inara's freedom much more quickly than he discovers that he himself is subject to similar self-deception.

It is not until Mal finds himself and his crew pursued by the relentless and extraordinarily committed Operative, an agent of the Alliance sent to capture River, that Mal begins to learn the true nature of the Alliance and how it maintains and perpetuates its control. This occurs in the movie *Serenity*, where Mal finds his eyes becoming opened to depths of Alliance evil that even he had not previously suspected. River has learned the secret failure the Alliance has been attempting to hide. In the terraforming of the extremely remote planet, Miranda, the Alliance scientists had added G-32 Paxilon hydrochlorate to the artificial atmosphere in order to pacify the population and thus make it malleable to Alliance control, easier to govern. Paxil is in fact a widely used anti-depressant today, though we are sure that the resemblance of names is purely coincidental, well purely amusing at least. The Alliance's experiment with "Pax" as they call it ("peace" in Latin) was in some ways too successful. Mal and his crew, partly to escape the pursuit of the Operative, travel to Miranda with some considerable danger to themselves since it lies on the other side of Reaver territory. Miranda turns out to be a ghost planet, not for the reasons given officially by the Alliance (terraforming failure), but rather because the entire transplanted population of several million had simply died, having become so passive under the influence of the Pax that they were unable and uninterested in doing anything required for survival (such as working, or even eating and drinking). The Alliance has, in fact, removed Miranda from official charts and histories, effectively removing it from existence in an Orwellian manner.

The Alliance also denies the existence of the Reavers, constantly broadcasting that no evidence of Reaver existence has ever been found, and teaching in the schools of the central planets that Reavers only appear in stories or myths, like the Bogeyman. On Miranda, Mal and his crew find a holographic recording in a crashed Alliance research ship. This recording contains not only the truth about how the G-32 Paxilon hydrochlorate catastrophe led to the deaths of the planet's colonists, but also how the Pax had the opposite effect on 0.1% of the population, making them aggressive beyond madness, with insatiable desires to rape, murder, and cannibalize their victims (sometimes eating them alive). These are the Reavers whose existence the Alliance is understandably so eager to deny. They have created them through their unethical experimentation and manipulation of unsuspecting populations.

What does Mal decide to do with this new knowledge? In the strictest sense, it is irrelevant to his means of making a living, so he could just simply ignore it and continue with business as usual, with its unspoken and only half-understood principle of not bothering the Alliance too much. However, for a personality like Mal's, with his degree of moral integrity, "business as usual" is not now an option any more than keeping the stolen medicines in "The Train Job" would have been. Knowing how deeply people have been meddled with by the Alliance, how the Alliance has, in fact, attempted to make people "better" through their Pax modification, and knowing that the Alliance is more than likely to try it, or something similar, again, Mal realizes that he and his crew cannot be the only ones to be exposed to the information on the holographic recording. He resolves to broadcast this recording as widely as possible throughout the 'verse: "So, no more running. I aim to misbehave" (*Serenity*).

He decides to use the resources of an old friend, calling himself Mr. Universe, who has both listening and broadcasting equipment capable of "broadwaving" the hologram, putting it "on every screen for thirty worlds." The only difficulties are that Mal suspects the Operative pursuing River will be waiting for them, with an Alliance fleet, at Mr. Universe's moon and that to get to that moon they must again pass through Reaver territory. To deal with the Alliance fleet, Mal decides to irritate the Reavers on his way by, an easy thing to do. As he expected, he is pursued by many Reaver ships, and when he emerges at Mr. Universe's moon, the Reavers and Alliance ships attack one another, keeping each other busy while Serenity slips through.

Mr. Universe has already been killed by the Alliance Operative, who will stop at nothing to capture River in order to keep the Alliance's secrets safe. The Operative at this point has no idea what secrets River is carrying; he is simply operating on faith. He is helping to build a better world and believes the Alliance is the key to that utopia. Indeed, as Shepherd Book had pointed out to Mal, it is the strength of that belief that makes the Operative especially dangerous as an enemy: "Sorta man they're like to send believes *hard*. Kills and never asks why" (*Serenity*).

Mal, too, now has something to believe in, something for which he is even willing to sacrifice his life. He must get the message out. As Mr. Universe had been fond of saying, "You can't stop the signal" (*Serenity*). The Alliance had attempted to destroy his broadcasting equipment, but fortunately, they had missed his backup unit hidden above the power generator deep within the moon. Before he died, Mr. Universe was able to program his robot wife, the lovebot Lenore, to tell Mal its location. While

Mal's crew attempts to hold off the invading Reavers who are now trying to break into the broadcasting complex, Mal attempts to get the message out. He is forced to fight the Alliance Operative, who has also been told the location of the hidden broadband equipment (lovebots are not really programmed to know to whom they are talking). After some difficulty, Mal gets the upper hand, and actually spares the Operative's life, leaving him to watch the Miranda holograph message now being broadwaved "on every screen for thirty worlds."

This shatters the Operative's illusions imposed on him by the Alliance, and more than challenges his belief in the better world that he thought he was sacrificing himself to help bring into being. Just as well, because once the Reavers are defeated, the Alliance troops capture Mal and his crew. The troop commander radios the Operative, "Targets are acquired! Do we have a kill order? Do we have a kill order?" (*Serenity*). They are told in response to stand down. The Operative has completely lost faith in the Alliance. River is no longer a threat to them, as the secrets she might have been carrying are now widely known.

The utopian world the Alliance had attempted to develop with the help of G-32 Paxilon hydrochlorate (Pax) is strikingly similar to that offered by the goddess Jasmine in Season Four of *Angel*. She promises, "the best of all possible worlds, without borders, without hunger, war, or misery. A world built on love, respect, understanding, and, well, just enjoying one another" (*Angel* 4.21, "Peace Out"). She actually brings this about, at least within the city of Los Angeles. She certainly has Angel and his crew completely enthralled. Just gazing upon her beauty seems to produce instant love and adoration, together with a feeling of euphoria.

Jasmine, certainly a beautiful goddess, is portrayed by Gina Torres, the actor who plays Zoe in *Firefly* and *Serenity*. Everyone who meets Jasmine seems to believe that she will make their world and their lives as beautiful as she is. However, as Steven Harper argues in his article, "Jasmine: Scariest Villain Ever," all this "bliss doesn't come without a price. Once you see Jasmine, you lose all will to do anything but serve her" (51). Harper is, quite rightly, genuinely troubled by the kind of world Jasmine presents us with. We achieve world peace and so forth, but, like the Alliance, she has deprived her followers of freedom in the process. As Angel puts it, "The price was too high, Jasmine. Our fate has to be our own, or we're nothing" (4.21).

However, the loss of freedom is only part of the price for the utopia Jasmine offers. This is a Whedon horror-comedy after all. It turns out that Jasmine eats people, but not that many (between eight and twelve people a day). What Harper finds truly frightening is that he feels almost willing to pay this price for what she offers, "and seems able to deliver — an end to death by violence ... no wars, no genocides, no holocausts, no murders, no spouse abuse, no child abuse, no drive-by shootings, and no suicides" (51). As Jasmine herself says, "I murdered thousands to save billions" (4.21).

This does constitute a genuine moral dilemma. As Harper perceptively puts it, "She offers a better world at an affordable price. Scary to the marrow" (51). We have already seen Faith using this kind of cost-benefit analysis to exonerate herself when she inadvertently kills a human bystander: "In the balance, nobody's gonna cry over some random bystander who got caught in the crossfire" (*Buffy* 3.15, "Consequences"). But, as we saw, this was Faith's first step toward the dark side. Choosing the lesser of two evils is still choosing evil. The dilemma presented by Jasmine constitutes Whedon's acute and devastating exposure of the problems presented by a utilitarian ethics with its cost-benefit approach to moral issues.

Interestingly enough, Jasmine also raises difficulties for the kind of love ethics Whedon seems to favor. She inspires love in her followers, preaches that they should love one another, and seems herself to love people (in more than the culinary sense). However, her followers are so besotted that they become fanatical and are willing to hunt down and kill those who do not accept Jasmine and her message of love. As Harper points out, "Jasmine's followers take on a wild-eyed fanaticism similar to the kind that powered the Inquisition ... they see unbelievers as dangerous" (54). Though Jasmine does not encourage such violence, she knows it exists and does nothing to stop it, if it means the elimination of those who have begun to see her as the demon she truly is. The individual under Jasmine's spell has no way of seeing her for what she is, and because everyone is under the same spell, skepticism cannot arise.

It is only by sheer chance that Fred discovers the ugly reality beneath Jasmine's façade of beauty. Fred is subsequently, with some difficulty, able to pass this knowledge on to Angel, who discovers the magical means to make this revelation universal with the more mundane help of radio and television broadcasting. The point is that Fred had to work extraordinarily hard, risking her very life, to dispel Angel's illusions. He could not have done this by himself. He needed to have his beliefs challenged, and was most reluctant to give them up. The Jasmine story suggests that a love ethic without a diverse communitarian base, one that allows skepticism and encourages the exchange of ideas and perspectives, can be easily perverted, or even turned into its opposite. A free and open press is also required to maintain such a diverse society. Angel is able to expose Jasmine for the demon she really is as she is about to broadcast her offer of a false paradise over radio and television to the entire world. Instead, the media expose her at the last moment. Still, she almost got away with it.

We are horrified by Jasmine, but can console ourselves by saying that that story is merely a myth, and that such events could never happen here. What Jasmine represents in a mythical form, the Alliance embodies as a political regime that is much closer to present-day reality, as Lackey's article, "*Serenity* and Bobby McGee," shows in considerable detail. The incarnation of a strikingly similar deprivation of freedom and exercise of mind control by an Alliance government that has sacrificed millions of its citizens for the greater good, and covered it up, forcibly reminds us that such a regime does not require the interference of the supernatural. Significantly, despite its colossal failure with Pax, the Alliance has not renounced the principle that it can, and indeed, must, use evil, consciously and deliberately, to bring forth what it considers to be the Good.

Once Mal has discovered the depth of evil in the Alliance, he, like Fred and Angel in parallel circumstances confronted by Jasmine, feels compelled to expose the truth to as many people as he can, and is even willing to sacrifice his life in order to do so. His crew, even the self-centered Jayne, accept this as a cause worth dying for, and, as a result, they achieve a kind of freedom they have never before experienced, a genuine freedom which prevents more evil from entering the world. The Alliance cannot be destroyed, but it can be, and has been, wounded.

There is also the chance that Mal's actions might inspire other, so far dutiful, citizens of the Alliance, to question and resist the regime in other (probably less dramatic) ways. That such internal resistance is a real possibility is indicated by the actions and choices of Simon Tam, who is able to overcome all the socializing imposed on him by the Alliance through its school system (seen intermittently in *Serenity*) and its other means of social control (wealth, status, etc.) and to work in a self-sacrificing way to rescue his sister. What makes Simon so dangerous to the Alliance is love, unconditional love for his sister. Whedon is using *Firefly* and *Serenity*, as he did *Buffy the Vampire Slayer* and *Angel*, to critique rationalistic systems of ethics, such as utilitarianism, and to support his alternative communitarian love ethics, built on a foundation of existential choice.

Chapter Eleven

Myth, Metaphor, and Morality: Joss Whedon as Moral Philosopher

In this study, we have argued that the entire Whedonverse, from *Buffy the Vampire Slayer* and *Angel* to the space westerns *Firefly* and *Serenity*, can be read as a sustained moral argument in which, on the one hand, various ethical theories are found wanting and, on the other hand, more acceptable alternatives are proposed and defended. This sustained moral argument cannot, we contend, be a simple rational argument since, as we have shown, reason itself is often questioned in many of the episodes. Instead, what is presented on screen is a very indirect form of argument in which difficult hypothetical cases are imagined and various ways of dealing with them considered. Television drama is, of course, an excellent and entertaining way of presenting such arguments. The use of drama in exploring ethical decision making also permits consideration of extremely exaggerated cases of moral ambiguity, such as vampires with souls for example. The examination of extreme cases is certainly a useful way of testing the viability of ethical theories, and forces us to think long and carefully about exactly how and why we make the moral judgments and practical decisions that we do. Whedon's dramas are not, of course, limited to extreme cases verging on fantasy. There are many "issue episodes" as some call them, which ostensibly deal with particular moral issues of the kind we all confront in the real world every day. For example, in our Chapter Four we discussed, among other things, Episode 3.1, "Anne" of *Buffy the Vampire Slayer*, arguing that stripped of its metaphorical content, it forces us to re-examine our usual uncaring attitude towards the homeless. Gregory Stevenson in his book, *Televised Morality: The Case of Buffy the Vampire Slayer*, confirms our reading of this episode. Noting that in the episode Buffy meets various elderly street people in LA whom she later discovers were

150

runaway teenagers captured and sent to a different temporal hell dimension where they were worked to a premature old age and spit back onto to the streets of LA in what seems like only days in our reality, Stevenson concludes, "The metaphor is clear; the despair and hardship of a life on the streets drains the life out of young people" (113).

Stevenson is the only scholar/commentator we have seen who has dealt with Whedon's exploration of metaphor and morality in anything like the depth and detail it deserves. In his thorough discussion of metaphor, Stevenson even feels it necessary to justify seeing metaphors in film and television, since metaphor is primarily a literary, and therefore a verbal rather than a visual, device. Citing George Lakoff and Mark Johnson's *Metaphors We Live By*, Stevenson argues that we are in fact justified in seeing and analyzing the metaphorical structure of a television series like *Buffy the Vampire Slayer* because "metaphors belong as much to the province of thought as to that of words" (32). Not only do metaphors help us to understand the moral perspectives of other peoples and cultures, but, as Stevenson, following *Metaphors We Live By*, points out, metaphors also "help us define reality and comprehend our world and ourselves" (33). Had Stevenson used Lakoff and Johnson's more recent book, *Philosophy in the Flesh: The Embodied Mind and its Challenge to Western Thought* (1999), he would have found an even more detailed and relevant examination of the relation between morality, metaphor, and thought. There Lakoff and Johnson distinguish between "basic experiential morality," such as "health is good," "everyone ought to be protected from physical harm," and more abstract universal moral concepts such as "justice," "rights," "nurturance," etc., all of which must be defined metaphorically. On the basis of this, they conclude, "there is no ethical system that is not metaphorical" (325). All moral metaphors, according to Lakoff and Johnson, "are inextricably tied to our embodied experience of well-being: health, strength, wealth, purity, control, nurturance, empathy, and so forth" (331). The fact that all of our experiences are embodied is of crucial importance because it avoids the problem of ethical relativism. For Lakoff and Johnson, all moral "metaphors are grounded in the nature of our bodies and social interactions, and they are thus anything but arbitrary and unconstrained" (290). This is important because, according to Stevenson, "*Buffy*'s perspective on good and evil is not a relativistic one in which the categories of good and evil are constantly redefined based on current circumstances, but neither is it an absolute one in which good and evil are always clearly defined" (73). Stevenson here recognizes Whedon's sophistication in seeing that the opposite of ethical relativism is not ethical absolutism; rather, if we may put it this way, the opposite of ethical relativism is non-relativism.

Since we are giving an existential analysis of Whedon's ethics, this point about non-relativism is extremely important. Moral philosophies based on existential choice are often accused of ethical relativism. Alvin Plantinga, for example, in his critical paper "An Existentialist's Ethics" argues, "Sartre's theory of freedom makes it impossible to draw a distinction between right and wrong, and therefore cuts off the very possibility of moral endeavor or action" (16). Bernard Wand, in his study, "Intelligibility and Free Choice," suggests just exactly what is wrong with this sense of absolute freedom: "if a criterion can never, in principle, be found for a free, and hence responsible, action the door is left wide open for wild men and lunatics" (256). However, existential moral choice need not be a criterionless choice. It can be a choice grounded in metaphorical thinking that is best presented in the form of narrative. Interestingly enough, even Lakoff and Johnson, who are fully aware of the metaphorical nature of morality, seem to suggest that existentialism leads to ethical relativism (1999, 324). They seem to forget that at least the existentialist philosopher Jean-Paul Sartre emphasizes the corporeal nature of consciousness, as we pointed out and discussed in some detail in both Chapters Three and Eight. Sartre, therefore, could use exactly the same arguments as Lakoff and Johnson for grounding his moral metaphors. In fact, in his now famous 1964 Rome Notes, "Ethics and Society," which he never published, Sartre argues that satisfying basic physical and social needs has "moral primacy" over all other goals, and is actually identical with "autonomous action," not merely a precondition of this fundamental value, without which we would not be fully human (Bowman and Stone, 280).

Joss Whedon's handling of the metaphoric dimensions of food and sex shows that he too is well aware that moral metaphors are intimately bound up with and grounded in our corporeal natures and our social interactions implied therein. An ethic that is based on a full awareness of our embodied consciousness allows for, even demands, definitive and non-relativistic moral thinking. Food and sex are linked both to our bodily and to our social contexts. Whedon explicitly links them to each other as well. We see this as early as Season Three of *Buffy the Vampire Slayer* when Faith claims that slaying makes her "hungry and horny" (3.3, "Faith, Hope, and Trick"). In this episode, Buffy coyly replies, "Well, sometimes I-I crave a nonfat yogurt afterwards," but remains silent on the sex issue. Later in Season Three, after Faith has gone bad, Buffy remarks, "I know Faith's not gonna be on the cover of *Sanity Fair*, but she had it rough. Different circumstances, that could be me" (3.16, "Doppelgängland"). By the time we reach Season Six, Buffy too has had it rough: she has been dead and buried for 147 days, with her soul in some heaven-like state in which she experiences a sense of rest and completion; then she has been forcibly torn from this blissful condition by her friends' resurrection spell, to find herself suddenly awake in a coffin six feet under. Having clawed her way out of her coffin (not unlike a vampire, in fact), she is now deeply depressed and alienated from all her friends and loved ones. Buffy is in fact coming to resemble Faith more closely than is usually recognized.

As we discuss in more detail in Chapter Three, even before the accidental killing of a human bystander pushed her over the edge, Faith was deeply disturbed and dangerously unstable. Her Watcher had been killed by the ancient vampire, Kakistos, from whom Faith had been unable to protect her. Faith fled to Sunnydale, concealing the fate of her Watcher for as long as she could, but it soon became clear that she was in a state of despair and had lost her focus and goal as a Slayer. In Season Six, Buffy is, similarly, though for quite different reasons of course, also in a state of despair. The symptoms of this despair are remarkably similar in both cases and have deep moral as well as psychological implications. The key to these similarities and their significations can be found these Slayers' attitudes toward food and sex, to being hungry and horny, as Faith so succinctly puts it. That Buffy is coming to resemble Faith is indicated in 6.10, "Wrecked," when Dawn tells Willow, "I'll leave a note for Buffy on the refrigerator. That's the first place she goes after patrolling. She's such a pig after she kills things." Buffy is not only hungry after a bout of slayage-related violence, but is also, unbeknownst to Dawn and the Scoobies, engaging in rough and violent sex with the vampire Spike.

Hunger for food and hunger for sex are fundamental, powerful bodily and social imperatives. The "normal" hunger for food serves at least three primary functions: 1) giving sustenance, nutrition, maintaining the life of oneself or of others (e.g., those who cannot for reasons of age or infirmity, etc., feed themselves); 2) giving sensual pleasure via the tastes, aromas, and textures of food; and 3) cementing social relations, establishing community, making connections, etc., especially through communal forms of eating, such as family dinners, dining on festive occasions, Native American feasts, eating with friends and colleagues, and the like, as opposed to solitary eating. Similarly, the "normal" hunger for sex serves at least three primary functions: 1) sustenance of the life of the species via procreation, creating new life; 2) sensual pleasure; and 3) cementing or establishing deep connections with another individual (at least in a monogamous system). In the cases of both Faith and Buffy, despair twists the expression or fulfillment of sexual desire in ways that are unambiguously immoral, even if it takes each character some time to recognize and deal with this immorality. The show's treatment of food is less obvious and is, of course, a symbol or symptom of other underlying problems, but is still quite revealing. Faith's approach to both food and sex shows her to be aggressive, selfish, and indiscriminate (in the sense of not discriminating). In Buffy's case, there is, perhaps, more discrimination, but in Season Six we see her being as aggressive and selfish as Faith, especially in her sexual relations.

To begin with sex, that Faith is aggressive, selfish, and indiscriminating is clear enough, both through her own testimony, which implies multiple partners that she simply uses and discards, and via what we see her do to Xander. In short, Faith's notion of a sex life involves serial partners but no attempt at either procreation or at establishing a meaningful long-term relationship or connection with anyone. Transitory sensual gratification for herself is all that Faith seeks or is prepared to deal with, at least until her connection with Principal Wood at the end of Season Seven. Buffy's Season Six affair with Spike shows her as similarly aggressive and selfish. She may stick to one partner here, but in terms of developing a normal, healthy relationship (quite apart from procreation), Spike is in many ways a decidedly wrong partner. Buffy comes to realize this, or perhaps has realized it all along at some level. The best that Buffy can get out her relationship with Spike in Season Six is fleeting sensual gratification (feeling something, anything, to reduce the numbness brought on by her despair, as she makes clear in 6.7, "Once More with Feeling"), but no true pleasure and none that outlives the moment in which it is experienced. For instance, Buffy cannot even obtain something that will give her pleasant memories; she simply feels dirty and degraded afterwards, however willingly she had participated, indeed, however much of it she had in fact initiated. When the camera shows her face as in her first sexual encounter with Spike, Buffy looks desperate, or cold and lifeless. The futility and fundamental wrongness of what Buffy is doing are registered clearly on her body here; the affair is clearly an attempt to break out of her despair, loss of focus, and loss of goal and purpose in life, but unfortunately, its main effect is to increase that very despair. It's a vicious circle, and as Buffy says when she breaks it off, "I'm using you. I can't love you. I'm just being weak, and selfish.... And it's killing me" (6.15, "As You Were"). There is only one way in which the Season Six Spike and Buffy make an appropriate couple: Spike is physically dead but thanks to his undead vampire being, he is able to go through the motions of life and thanks to his chip, he is able to imitate a human being, while Buffy is already emotionally dead and she is spiritually dead or dying. In fact, she looks almost like an object, a sex toy like the Buffybot, when she and Spike are having sex in the alley behind Doublemeat Palace. Spike keeps hoping this will somehow develop into real love, but Buffy knows that it can't, especially with her in the state she is in, and we know from Angel's experience with Darla that inappropriate sex can actually increase one's despair, as we discussed in some detail in Chapter Six.

In the Buffyverse, breaking out from the cycle of hopelessness and despair always seems to involve others. In Faith's case, as we discussed in detail in Chapter Three, her experiences when inhabiting Buffy's body are the beginning of her redemption, and then Angel guides her and helps her out. For Buffy, it is when Riley returns in Episode 6.15. Buffy then develops her old sense of self that Riley in effect reminds her of; she regains her sense of identity, goal, and focus, and thus relinquishes Spike and her mistreatment of him. The episode is significantly entitled "As You Were." In a sense, Riley's new life is a model for Buffy. Of course, Riley and his new wife, Sam, also give Buffy an image of what a healthy relationship can look like, and this too leads her to want to break things off with Spike.

Breaking up with Spike is not sufficient in and of itself to effect a complete turnaround for Buffy, which is why it is important that it is Riley who is there, since she has worked with him in demon fighting and helped him overcome his uncritical dedication to the Initiative. And the title, "As You Were," makes little sense in relation to Buffy's never-quite-successful love life (nor to anything directly related to Riley and Sam, since their relationship is new to Buffy), but does make perfect sense in terms of her vocation of fighting evil. In Season Five, Riley himself nearly went over to the dark side when he was paying vampire hookers to suck his blood. Buffy, being completely pre-occupied with her mother's health and her own efforts to gain a deeper understanding of what it means to be a Slayer, was of no help to Riley, and even contributed to his desperation. It was the opportunity provided by his military buddies (followed, one suspects, by the love and support of Sam) that saved Riley. Once again, community is the key to progress here.

Turning to food, when Joyce has Faith over for dinner in 3.3 ("Faith, Hope, and Trick"), there is a scene in which Buffy and Joyce go into the kitchen leaving Faith alone in the dining room, during which time Faith grabs food off the table aggressively, indiscriminately, and selfishly, as though she has not had a decent meal in a long time. One suspects that, at least before hooking up with the Mayor, she probably ate alone and consumed fast food and junk food in her motel room. We do know from *Angel* 1.19, "Sanctuary," that Faith does not know how to work his microwave oven, so she probably cooks little if at all. As for Buffy and food, we can note among other things that in Season Six she does not properly feed either Dawn or herself. For example, in Episode 6.5, "Life Serial," Buffy comes home with what she calls dinner, a bucket of "deep fried chicken parts." Even the Buffybot did better than this, it made gigantic stacks of sandwiches. Buffy arrives and presents her bucket of chicken, but finds that everyone else has just finished a home-cooked meal. (Giles even has a glass of wine.) The contrast between the idealized domestic dinner scene and Buffy's reliance on fast food and take-out could not be clearer or more pointed.

This contrast and its importance to themes of domestic stability and responsibilities are not confined to this one scene. The earlier seasons, those in which Joyce is still alive, have many brief references to the significance of family meals — scenes with Buffy and Joyce talking in the kitchen while doing the post-dinner cleanup; Buffy and Dawn competing for the last of the cereal; a flashback to a Christmas dinner, which suggests the importance of Joyce's nurturing matriarchal role; and Buffy's attempt to emulate her mother in staging an elaborate Thanksgiving dinner (of which, more below). When fast food, snack food, or junk food are mentioned in these earlier seasons, it is always clear that the function of such food is never to be the primary source of nutrition; it is either to keep one going temporarily until a proper meal can be had (e.g., having a doughnut while researching), to cement a bond (e.g., getting a snack for someone else as a gesture of solidarity), or to indulge oneself with a tasty, but calorie-laden and nutrition-free, guilty pleasure.

By Season Six, however, Joyce Summers has died, and Buffy, having been brought back from the dead, is now Dawn's guardian and caregiver, and is, in episode 6.11, "Gone," desperate to prove she is a suitable guardian for Dawn. While things seem to be holding together reasonably well in 6.5, they are, in reality, just about ready to fall apart: there is the problem of Buffy's depression and disconnectedness (which her friends cannot comprehend since at this point they think they saved her from an eternity in a hell dimension); Giles is both angry at the foolhardiness Willow and the others displayed in bringing Buffy back and convinced that his presence is doing Buffy more harm than good; Willow is rapidly becoming addicted to magic and the power she thinks it gives her, and this problem is generating a rift between her and Tara, the most responsible and caring of the younger characters; Dawn is a surreptitious kleptomaniac, which is related to her feeling ignored and abandoned by everyone, most especially her sister; and, finally, Anya and Xander, though engaged, both secretly have doubts about their upcoming marriage. All these submerged problems come to the surface a mere two episodes later in the musical 6.7, "Once More With Feeling," in which all the characters are forced to reveal in song the anxieties, fears, and secrets they have been concealing. In Episode 6.8, "Tabula Rasa," Giles returns to England and Tara leaves Willow. In Episode 6.9, "Smashed," Buffy begins her secretive and destructive sexual relationship with Spike.

This general moral collapse and disintegration of relationships is accompanied and underlined by an equally rapid decline in the nature and quality of food provision. For example, rather than scenes in which everyone dines and converses together, or even those in which friends bring other friends snacks to tide them over until mealtime, we have scenes in which people leave notes for each other on the fridge; food is still the center here, perhaps, but the people are not together for its preparation or its enjoyment. We also have scenes in which the food and dining norms established over the previous seasons appear in interrupted, broken, and fragmented forms. For example, early in the Episode 6.10, "Wrecked," the visiting Tara's attempts to cook breakfast for Dawn are disrupted by arrival of Amy and Willow. Later in the same episode, in the absence of Buffy, Dawn tries to make her own dinner, "peanut-butter-and-banana quesadillas." Not surprisingly, the recipe is a disaster, and Dawn jumps at Willow's offer to take her to a movie and buy her dinner (not cook one for her). That dinner turns out be a burger, which Dawn quite likes, whatever its nutritional value: "It was like a meat party in my mouth. Okay, now I'm just a kid, and even I know that came out wrong" (6.10). Willow, strung out on magic, eats nothing, saying she is saving herself for popcorn. She never has the popcorn, since she and Dawn never make it to the movie.

The burger provides at least a bit of gustatory sensual pleasure for Dawn and some social bonding. But that social bonding does not last even that one night as Willow then abandons Dawn in order to get a magic rush from her supplier, Rack. That the actions of Buffy and Willow not only fail to nourish Dawn — physically, emotionally, or morally — but potentially cause her great harm is made clear by the fact that near the end of the episode Willow crashes a car with her and Dawn in it. The dismal failures of Buffy and Willow as nurturant parents at this point is implicit in the food motif, but made absolutely plain by the car crash.

In brief, things had been much better in the past and the failure in food provision is symptomatic of the more general failures of characters to connect with and sustain each other throughout Season Six. In any case, Dawn is not being well fed or looked after. This failure in nourishment and sustenance in general is crystallized in the fact that soon after this episode (6.10), Buffy gets a job at Doublemeat Palace, a fast food joint.

In Chapter One, at the very beginning of our study, we argued that the "Doublemeat Palace" episode (6.12) is central to understanding the existential import of the entire Whedonverse. It is also important, as we can now see, for emphasizing the implied link between the metaphorical nature of morality and its grounding in our physical being, our corporeal consciousness. While Buffy is working in this fast food establishment, she frequently brings its burgers home for dinner. Just as the wrongness of Buffy's sexual exploitation of Spike is registered bodily (the deadness in her eyes is even more telling than the cuts and bruises suggestive of violent sexual practices), so is the moral stain of improperly caring for Dawn. The unwholesomeness of everything represented by the "Doublemeat experience" (6.12, "Doublemeat Palace") is manifest in the all-but-indelible odor it leaves on the body. In Episode 6.15, "As You Were," even the vampires, who are dead and smell like it, are offended by the Doublemeat stench and don't want to consume anything tainted by it. In the teaser, a vampire is about to attack Buffy, but stops himself, saying, "What's that smell? Geez, Slayer, is that you?" When Buffy informs him she has been working at Doublemeat Palace, he says, "You know what? Let's just call it a night. If it's all the same to you, and you've been eating that stuff, I'm not so sure I wanna bite you" (6.15).

Later in the episode, Riley also remarks on the smell and lumps it together with her sleeping with Spike. Just as Buffy says the Doublemeat odor, though deeply offensive, can be eradicated with effort (it "goes away after many bathings" she says), so Riley is confident that the dismal state in which he finds Buffy in this episode is not that which will ultimately define her: "Wheel never stops turning, Buffy. You're up, you're down ... it doesn't change what you are. And you are a hell of a woman" (6.15). The cleansing of Buffy's moral failings, which have been signified by and encapsulated in the Doublemeat odor, begins in this episode with Buffy's breaking off the affair with Spike and concludes in the final episode of this season.

Since Buffy has been bringing fast food home for dinner, there is nothing in the house to eat except ice cubes (6.15). There is absolutely nothing of any nutritional value in the Summers house, no food for body or soul, and all Buffy can think of to remedy this lack is junk food. This point marks the nadir in terms of the food symbolism. Although Dawn does not know it, her comment in 6.10, that Buffy is "such a pig after she kills things," clues us in to Buffy's voracious appetite for the non-sustain-ing in Season Six — the junk food of Doublemeat Palace and the junk sex with a Spike she does not love, trust, or respect. Both are fast, cheap, and "convenient" (to use Buffy's own term in 6.10, "Wrecked"), but both can spin out of control too. Buffy in 6.22, "Grave," recognizes that under the guise of protection (or over-protection) she has in effect really been neglecting Dawn, failing to give her the nurturance that Dawn needs and that Buffy as nurturant parent is morally obligated to provide. As Buffy puts it in her heartfelt apology to Dawn, "I got it so wrong. I don't want to protect you from the world. I want to show it to you" (6.22).

Buffy has been reborn twice in this season: unwillingly at the beginning, in terms of bodily resurrection as she claws her way out of her grave; and as a result of her own will at the end, as she recovers from the emotional coldness and moral lapses of the rest of the season, and emerges with Dawn from another grave, the pit into which the evil Willow has forced them. Now Buffy is finally ready to offer Dawn the sustenance she needs, both for her body and her moral development, both physically and metaphorically. It is because the metaphorical is grounded in the physical, in the corporeal, that the nurturant family morality of the Whedonverse, its existential love ethics, avoids, or at the very least sidesteps, the problem of ethical relativism.

Much of Whedon's work deals with ethical ambiguity, but this does not mean that there is not a clear distinction between good and evil. As Stevenson puts it, "*Buffy*'s worldview is absolute in its conception of good and evil in the sense that both are categories that exist unequivocally. That true evil and true goodness exist is never doubted ... the real problem is differentiating between the two" (73–74). Much of *Buffy the Vampire Slayer*, *Angel*, *Firefly* and *Serenity* is dedicated to showing how this is possible. The arguments they present are all metaphorical arguments about slaying our personal and social demons. As Stevenson quite rightly points out, such demons "can be overcome by the power of love, community, and forgiveness" (236). Stevenson also recognizes that the "metaphorical construction that governs *Buffy*'s view of family is that community is family" (150).

But as Lakoff and Johnson argue, the metaphorical construction of morality based on family can take a number of different forms depending on various different conceptions of family. They contrast, for example, "the strict father family morality" with the more caring nurturant parent family morality, recognizing that both are idealizations and that many families are a combination of both (1999, 313–316). As we have argued, the nurturant parent metaphor is much closer to the morality depicted in *Buffy the Vampire Slayer* and *Angel*. Lakoff and Johnson describe it as "a morality of caring for others out of compassion and empathy," rather than a "morality of obedience to moral laws given by divine authority" or reason (319).

Buffy the Vampire Slayer can, in fact, be seen as an attack on strict father morality as Lakoff and Johnson define it. Certainly the Watchers' Council sees itself as the moral and intellectual authority Slayers must obey. Giles, of course, recognizes the inappropriateness of this approach insofar as Buffy is concerned. We discussed in Chapter Three, in our account of Kendra, the kind of Slayers the approach of the Watchers' Council produces. Interestingly enough, Lakoff and Johnson argue that current scientific research shows "strict father family morality tends to produce children who are dependent on the authority of others, cannot chart their own moral course very well, have less of a conscience, are less respectful of others, and have no greater ability to resist temptations" (327). This, of course, is the exact opposite of the responsible, morally autonomous citizens it purports to develop. Lakoff and Johnson's point is that empirical research, particularly cognitive science, is important in helping us decide between moral systems.

Whedon's television dramas seem to reach similar conclusions using thought experiments and hypothetical cases of moral decision making. Both Lakoff and Johnson and Whedon draw attention to the important fact that the kind of moral decisions that we make and the way we make them have a tremendous influence on the kinds of persons we become. This works in both a positive and negative sense, as we showed in Chapter Three with Faith's story arc. She really did not like the person that she became and this was the first step in her redemption, which required the community, her adoptive family, to be successful.

Buffy also attacks strict father morality, patriarchy, in a number of other ways. The apparently perfect father, Ted, in Episode 2.11, is ridiculed as having a shallow binary morality, "the rules are the rules.... Right is right, wrong is wrong. Why don't people see that?" (2.11, "Ted"). Of course, Ted turns out to be a murderous automaton, which gives added meaning to his criticism of Buffy: "Do your own thing? Well, I'm not wired that way" (2.11). The criticism of strict father morality begins right in Season One, when the Big Bad of that season, the übervamp called the Master, tells his minions, who are depicted as little better than slaves, "You see how we all work together for the common good? That's how a family is supposed to function!" (1.7, "Angel"). As Rhonda Wilcox notes in *Why Buffy Matters*, "There could hardly be a nastier incarnation of the patriarchy than the ancient, ugly vampire Master" (27). As we pointed out in Chapter Five, the Initiative, like all military organizations, suffers the failings of strict father morality, and we see, through both amusing and horrifying episodes, how Buffy fails to fit into such an organization. However, in the final season of *Buffy*, when the Potential Slayers are gathered together in Sunnydale, Buffy herself succumbs briefly to a strict father morality: "Look, I wish this could be a democracy. I really do. It would be more fair, I agree. But democracies don't win battles. It's a hard truth, but there has to be a single voice. You need me to issue orders and be reckless sometimes and not take your feelings into account" (7.19, "Empty Places"). In this mindset, Buffy, in lecturing the Potentials on the importance of working together to defeat the First Evil, uses the same expression as the patriarchal übervamp of Season One, "Here endeth the lesson" (1.5, "Never Kill a Boy on the First Date"; 7.11, "Showtime").

In *Why Buffy Matters*, though Wilcox does not note Buffy's use of the expression in Season Seven, she does draw attention to the Master's use of it, in support of her observation that "most of the first season vampires are placed on the side of the adults linguistically" (27). Adults are usually represented as adhering to a strict father morality. It is a show for teenagers, after all. We contend, however, that the alternative morality usually supported by Buffy and the Scoobies is not represented as simply the morality of the idealistic young. The Potential Slayers' reaction to Buffy's brief foray into strict father morality in Season Seven is to vote her out of office and democratically replace her with Faith. The show obviously supports republicanism as opposed to absolute monarchy. It is the will of the community that is paramount, providing that it is a caring community, as Episode 3.11, "Gingerbread," negatively illustrates.

The importance of a caring community is best shown in the Thanksgiving episode, 4.8, "Pangs." This episode certainly raises the ethical issue of a caring community, particularly the care of strangers, but as Stevenson points out in some detail, it also raises the issue of cultural guilt (229). As with all so-called "issue" episodes, it also illustrates in a positive way how moral decisions are made and how ethical judgments are justified. The supposed Big Bad of this episode is the spirit of a Chumash Indian called Hus, who, once awakened, seeks vengeance for the wrongs done to his people by the early colonial settlers. For example, since the Chumash died because of many European diseases such as malaria, smallpox, and syphilis, Xander is magically inflicted with all of them at once. Since the early missionaries oppressed the Chumash, Hus seeks out and kills a priest, Father Gabriel. Hus magically creates more Chumash warriors and goes in search of the strongest European warrior he can find, who, of course, turns out to be Buffy.

Meanwhile, Buffy is just trying to have a traditional Thanksgiving dinner with her friends. They are holding the festivities at Giles's place, rather than at Buffy's, because, as Buffy explains, "Giles, if you would like to get by in American society, then you are going to have to follow our traditions. You're the patriarch. You have to host the festivities, or it's all meaningless" (4.8). The Slayer once again is just trying to lead the life of a normal girl. This can also be seen as a metaphor for all of us ignoring cultural guilt by going about our daily lives, quite ignorant of and apathetic towards the true meaning of the holidays we celebrate, being quite happy just to get the day off.

Various responses to the European occupancy of North America are considered in this episode. Willow has the most sympathy for the plight of the Native Americans. She points out that her mother refuses to "celebrate Thanksgiving or Columbus Day" because of "the destruction of the Indigenous peoples." Willow argues, "Thanksgiving isn't about blending of two cultures. It's about one culture wiping out another" (4.8). She also claims that the Chumash "were peaceful.... They were fluffy Indigenous kittens, 'til we came along" (4.8). Significantly, the episode opens with Buffy, as usual, hunting vampires. She comes across a nicely-dressed young man who does not at all look to us like a vampire. He asks politely in a quiet voice what she wants, and she in response punches him violently. His vampire face emerges and Buffy says, "Look who's home." Although we argued in Chapter Eight that, on *Buffy*, vampires in general do not represent oppressed people, in this episode it is certainly possible to argue, as Stevenson does, that this particular "vampire is a metaphorical representation of oppressed Indigenous peoples" (231). Stevenson, however, fails to point out or make anything of the fact that this vampire (representing the oppressed peoples) was peaceful before the aggression of the oppressor. On recognizing that Buffy is the Slayer, the vampire responds to her aggression by fighting back, violently defending himself, and shouting, "Why don't you just go back where you came from? Things were great before you came" (4.8). As Stevenson does rightly point out, "His comment identifies Buffy as a metaphorical representation of invading colonial forces" (231). This opening scene, the teaser, represents, then, in microcosm, the theme of the entire episode.

The very next scene confirms this interpretation. We see Buffy wearing a black cowboy hat watching, with her friends Anya and Willow, the groundbreaking ceremony for the new UC Sunnydale Cultural Partnership Center. Xander, who is now working in construction at UC Sunnydale, actually uncovers the old Sunnydale Indian Mission on, or rather under, the site of the new Cultural Partnership Center. It is because he actually falls into the cavern made by the ruins of the old Mission that Xander becomes infected with all of the diseases that decimated the Chumash. Digging into the old Mission site is also what awakens Hus, the Chumash vengeance spirit. Later that night, Hus materializes in the old anthropology department and takes a Chumash knife from their artifact display case. He then slits the throat of Dr. Gerhardt, the head of the anthropology department, and cuts off her ear, because, we learn, that's what was done to his people by the early settlers.

Many more people now know about this kind of atrocity thanks to the popularity of *Buffy the Vampire Slayer*. The episode is partially about cultural guilt, after all. Hus also attacks Buffy herself when she attempts to save Father Gabriel, whom Hus has just murdered. As they fight, Hus informs Buffy, "I am vengeance. I am my people's cry. They call for Hus, for the avenging spirit to carve out justice.... You slaughtered my people. Now you kill their spirit. This is a great day for you" (4.8, "Pangs"). Buffy holds back during the fight and Hus escapes by turning into a flock of birds. Later she tells Giles that cultural guilt got in the way of her fighting Hus: "The thing is, I like my evil like I like my men — evil. You know, 'straight up, black hat, tied to the train tracks, soon my electro-ray will destroy Metropolis' bad. Not all mixed up with guilt and the destruction of an Indigenous culture" (4.8). Buffy's reference to the black hat here, given that we have recently seen her wearing a black cowboy hat, makes her, and by extension, each of us (with British or European heritage), one of the bad guys.

The perspective of the early settlers is represented by Spike and Giles, the two most British characters on the show. Spike summarizes their stance most emphatically when he responds to Willow's "bleeding heart liberal" attitude: "You won. All right? You came in and you killed them and you took their land. That's what conquering nations do. It's what Caesar did, and he's not going around saying, 'I came, I conquered, I felt really bad about it.' The history of the world isn't people making friends. You had better weapons, and you massacred them. End of story.... You exterminated his race. What could you possibly say that would make him feel better? It's kill or be killed here. Take your bloody pick." Giles rather weakly concurs, "I made these points earlier, but fine, no one listens to me" (4.8). This is particularly interesting because Giles also agrees with Willow that the Chumash were peaceful in the beginning.

Giles' claim about peaceful Indians hearkens back to the opening teaser where the vampire is both peaceful and polite until Buffy strikes the first blow. Most of the time when Buffy patrols for vampires, they are already in vampire face and attack her first. Buffy's position in this episode is most ambiguous. She is certainly the black hat "bad guy" symbolized by her cowboy hat, but Stevenson argues that she also represents "*Buffy the Vampire Slayer*'s proposed solution to the problem of cultural guilt" (233). According to Stevenson, the episode suggests "Thanksgiving be evaluated on the basis of what this day now means and not what it may have once meant" (233). We only partially agree with Stevenson. Buffy does represent the mean between Willow's liberalism and the imperialism of Spike and Giles; however, we contend that Stevenson misses the point when he claims that Thanksgiving should be evaluated on the basis of what it means now. His evidence for this claim is to cite Buffy's conversation with Riley, who cannot join them for Thanksgiving dinner because he is going home to Iowa. Riley says, with Buffy completing the platitude, "Home's the place that, when you have to go there.... They have to take you in" (233). As Stevenson points out, it is significant that the scene immediately shifts to Spike looking for some place to stay, as his former girlfriend, the vampire Harmony, has kicked him out. Stevenson also cites Buffy's earlier conversation with Willow to the effect that they really ought to invite Anya to Thanksgiving dinner as well: "Look, pilgrims aside, isn't that the whole point of Thanksgiving — everybody has a place to go?" (233). Here too, the scene shifts to Spike, who has escaped from the Initiative's prison where, it will be remembered, a chip was implanted in his brain to neutralize his violence towards humans. Riley and his fellow commandoes had been searching for him earlier, on the grounds that, as Riley puts it, "as long as he knows about the Initiative, he's a threat" (4.8).

This raises a recurring ethical point in the Whedonverse; namely, that the representatives of evil, or at least the morally dubious, require a veil of secrecy to carry out their activities, and that once this veil is lifted, they are, if not destroyed (like the Initiative's headquarters in *Buffy* and Jasmine in *Angel*), then at least severely compromised (like the Alliance in *Firefly* and *Serenity*). However, the main point in the "Pangs" episode is that Spike is homeless and hunted. He turns to his "enemies," the Slayer and the Scooby Gang, for sanctuary, and they reluctantly take him in, once Willow confirms his claim that he has been neutered (with the chip in his brain): "It's true. He had trouble performing." Or, as only Spike could put it, "I'm saying that Spike had a little trip to the vet and now he doesn't chase the other puppies anymore. I can't bite anything. I can't even hit people" (4.8). They do, however, tie him to a chair as they still don't trust him.

According to Stevenson, "Spike here represents the Other, racially and socially. He is the homeless, the outcast, and the oppressed" (234). From the perspective of the strictly contemporary attitude towards Thanksgiving, Stevenson suggests, "If the problem has been that the early colonials killed and oppressed their perceived 'enemies' (the Chumash), here that past sin is reversed. Their enemy is not killed, but is made part of the family in a sense. On Thanksgiving Day, Buffy gives Spike a 'home'— he even sits at the table with them during their Thanksgiving meal" (234). We would point out that Spike remains firmly tied to his chair throughout this meal, suffering and complaining about pangs of hunger.

We argue that because Stevenson concentrates on the contemporary concept of Thanksgiving, rather than on its historical origins, what is missing from his argument is any understanding of the reasons for cultural guilt or the necessity of learning anything from first contact with the Indians. Near the beginning of the episode, Willow reminds us of what every American has learned in school about the original Thanksgiving: "they make animated specials about the part where, with the maize and the big, big belt buckles. They don't show you the next scene, where all the bison die and Squanto takes a musket ball in the stomach" (4.8).

It is significant that Willow mentions Squanto. He was one of the Wampanoag Indians who helped the pilgrims of the Plymouth Colony survive their first winter. The Wampanoag knew that these strange visitors were badly in need of help, because they noticed that the colonists were stealing Wampanoag corn, as James Wilson documents in his sympathetic study, *The Earth Shall Weep: A History of Native America* (79). We might even say that the Wampanoag saw themselves as "helping the helpless" (*Angel* 2.7, "Darla"). Squanto, for example, taught the English colonists how to fertilize their fields using fish, a practice still carried on today by fisherman-farmers up and down the east coast of North America. Squanto had learned English in London, having been kidnapped along with a number of other Indians and taken to Spain to be sold as slaves in 1614. By 1617, he is in London and eventually makes his way back to New England in time to help the struggling inhabitants of the Plymouth Colony survive, and celebrate with them the first Thanksgiving in 1621 (Salisbury, 606–607).

What we can learn from this is that the Wampanoag were willing to help the English colonists in spite of the fact that they stole their corn and had even kidnapped some of them, taken them to Europe and tried to sell them as slaves. Squanto himself had personally experienced such treatment and yet was still willing to be instrumental in the survival of these bar-

baric strangers. This is the example from which the Scoobies can now learn. Thanks to the interference of the Initiative, Spike, the vampire who has been their mortal enemy, is unable to feed himself, is starving, and is, in effect, in need of the assistance of a caring community. To a certain extent, his position echoes that of the early settlers who needed the help of the skeptical Native communities in order to survive in a harsh climate and an unfamiliar land.

This Thanksgiving episode of *Buffy* is not just about the Chumash or the Wampanoag. It is about learning from those our forefathers oppressed, the Indigenous peoples of North America. Squanto and the Chumash represent these peoples and what they still have to teach us. Dr. Gerhardt, the UC Sunnydale anthropologist, was not entirely wrong in her speech at the groundbreaking ceremony, when she said, "And that's why it's appropriate that the ground-breaking for the UC Sunnydale Cultural Partnership Center is taking place so soon before Thanksgiving. Because that's what the melting pot is about — Contributions from all cultures, making our culture stronger" (4.8).

The difficulty is that so few of us believe in or act on these fine, if somewhat ethnocentric, sentiments. We have been seduced by the Hollywood image of the "savage redskin" in so many cowboy and Indian movies and television shows (cf. Romesburg). The *Buffy* episode "Pangs" makes passing reference to these westerns. Giles's home is on one occasion referred to as "Fort Giles." Hus and his fellow vengeance spirits do surround and attack this homestead. Anya, Willow, and Xander, who were away when the attack started, realize that Hus, being a warrior, is probably going to go in search of their strongest warrior, who, of course, is Buffy. In order to get back to Giles's homestead and to help Buffy as quickly as possible, they each steal a bicycle. And, as the Indians are laying siege to "Fort Giles," we see Anya, Willow, and Xander riding, as a latter day cavalry, to the rescue.

This cavalry-to-the-rescue image presents a stark, though also comic, contrast to Willow's earlier, more peaceful, approach to dealing with Hus. Through much of the episode, we see Willow wearing a sweater with a large peace symbol emblazoned on the front. At one point, she arrives at Giles's front door with her arms loaded down with history books. Buffy opens the door and greets her, saying something which sounds like "Peace." Willow likewise replies, "Peace." Buffy then removes a package from the top of the pile of books Willow is carrying, and complains, "These are frozen" (4.8). We then realize that they were not greeting one another as old peaceniks, though that is certainly the way it sounds, but rather that

Willow was also bringing groceries for the Thanksgiving dinner. Buffy had requested fresh peas and Willow has brought her frozen ones. Buffy was saying, in effect, "You brought the peas?" and Willow was replying, "Yes, I brought the peas."

The discussion soon shifts from peas to war, as it were. When Buffy complains that Willow was supposed to shell fresh peas, Willow explains that she didn't have time because she was reading up on the Chumash War, hence the large pile of history books. Willow thinks that they should do something about the atrocities she has read about, at the very least, bring them to light. However, Giles responds, "If the history books are full of them, I'd say they already are" (4.8). We would suggest that a popular television program like *Buffy the Vampire Slayer* has been much more successful at drawing the public's attention to these issues than the numerous history books that nobody but intellectuals like Willow reads.

This is only one of the problems with Giles's reasoning at this point. These history books are usually written by the winners and do not tell the whole story. As Cherokee historian Jace Weaver from Yale University points out in his article, "American Indians and Native Americans: Reinhold Niebuhr, Historiography and Indigenous Peoples," "The native people in a colony are not allowed a valid interpretation of their history, because the conquered do not write their own history. They must endure a history that shames them, destroys their confidence, and causes them to reject their heritage.... A fact of imperialism is that it systematically denies native people a dignified history" (28–29). As Whedon himself puts it, through his character Mal in *Serenity*, "Half of writing history is hiding the truth."

That Indigenous people defended themselves when attacked does not mean that they were not normally peaceful and hospitable to strangers. Christopher Columbus, for example, encountered Natives in the New World who were caring, loving, and sharing both among themselves and with strangers. Even Samuel Morison's famous 1942 study *Admiral of the Sea: A Life of Christopher Columbus,* which is often criticized for being far too sympathetic to Columbus, admits as much, citing Columbus' own words: "They are so ... free with all they have, that no one would believe it who has not seen it; of anything that they possess, if it be asked of them, they never say no; on the contrary, they invite you to share it and show as much love as if their hearts went with it..." (231). Similarly, the *Jesuit Relations* depict early contact with the Hurons, expressing great surprise that they did not find the savages and barbarians they had expected: "We see shining among them some rather noble moral virtues.... Their hospitality towards all sorts of strangers is remarkable; they present to them in their feasts, the best of what they have prepared, and ... I do not know if anything similar, in this regard, is to be found anywhere. They never close the door upon a Stranger, and once having received him into their houses, they share with him the best they have; they never send him away, and when he goes away of his own accord, he repays them with a simple 'thank you'" (Mealing, 45).

There are also well documented accounts of very similar acts of hospitality from the American west of the late 1600s. Frank Waters's *Book of the Hopi*, based on reports from the Elders, contains a very revealing description of the arrival of the Navaho, often regarded as the traditional enemy of the Hopi: "At first only one stranger came, hungry and without weapons, his long hair uncombed, clothed only in the skin of a wild animal. Then little bands of men, women and children came, all dressed the same way, all hungry and homeless. The Hopi were good to these barbarians. They fed and sheltered them. They taught them to work in the fields, to weave baskets, and to spin cotton" (312). The Hopi respected and welcomed the Navaho, a people so different from themselves that they could be thought of as "barbarians." We cannot help thinking of Spike, wrapped in his raggedy blanket to shield himself from the deadly sun, arriving at Giles's door, looking far more pathetic than the Navaho ever did.

Of course the Navaho eventually outstayed their welcome, as did, incidentally, the Spanish, and hostilities did eventually break out. But as Waters also reports, even after the Hopi were victorious over the Spanish in the Pueblo Revolt of 1680, and shortly thereafter over the Navaho or Tasavuh (head bashers), as the Hopi came to call them, "the Hopi were left with a great sadness. They were a people of Peace who did not believe in war, yet they had been forced into killing both Tasavuh and the Castillas [Spanish] in order to protect their homes and their religion" (314).

However peaceful the Scoobies would like to be with respect to Hus and the Chumash spirits, Fort Giles does come under attack, and the Scoobies, not unlike the Hopi, are forced to defend themselves. When Willow arrives with the rest of the bicycle cavalry, she takes up the fight. Beating one of the spirit warriors with a handy garden shovel, Willow finds herself shouting in desperation, "Why ... don't ... you ... die?" (4.8). Buffy finally discovers that only Hus's own dagger will kill him and is at last able to end the battle. At dinner, after the fight, Willow says she feels "lousy" about the battle, and, like the Hopi, expresses her dismay and regret: "Did you see me? Two seconds of conflict with an Indigenous person, and I turned into General Custer" (4.8).

Willow is not the only one to reverse her stance as a result of Hus's attack. During the battle, Spike, still tied to the chair, finds Indian arrows flying everywhere, several of them lodging in his body. Recognizing that arrows are, like the Slayer's stakes, wooden and thus potentially lethal even to vampires, Spike cries out, "Hey! Watch the heart!" (4.8), as yet another arrow pierces his chest, rather too near the heart. Spike, who had earlier expressed the imperialist justification for conquest and colonialism, now finds himself put in the position of the threatened oppressed. Having been rendered harmless to humans by the Initiative's computer chip in his brain; then rejected by his fellow vampire, Harmony, and thus made homeless; he now finds himself tied to a chair, imprisoned and immobilized in the midst of the attack by Hus and his vengeance spirits. His imperialistic conqueror attitude changes radically under the pressure of this totally new experience: "Remember that conquering nation thing? Forget it. Apologize.... I'll do it myself. Hey, sorry. Sorry about that, Chief" (4.8).

In spite of the racist language (calling an Indian, "Chief"), it is tempting to say that Spike has almost become a "bleeding heart liberal," what with all these arrows landing near his heart and all. Of course, it is possible to question the sincerity of his moral conversion here, given that it is under extreme duress. We would, however, prefer to argue that it represents the first of a number of moral experiences which the Initiative's neutralizing computer chip makes possible for Spike. As we argued in Chapter Eight, these ethical experiences permit Spike to undergo a change of moral character which ultimately leads him to search for his soul.

In "Pangs," both Willow and Spike reassess aspects of their former attitudes to colonialism and cultural guilt by means of having a new moral experience, being actually placed in the position of the oppressed. However, one does not literally have to undergo such horrendous experiences in order to gain a new ethical insight. One can achieve it vicariously through an act of the moral imagination, putting oneself in someone else's shoes, or walking a mile in the Other's moccasins, as the saying goes. This is an area in which the artistic imagination in all of its forms (literary, visual, filmic, etc.) can be used as a form of moral thought.

Since we have been discussing learning from our Native neighbors, it is interesting to note that Ojibwa philosopher, Dennis McPherson, points out in his co-authored study, "Indigeneity in Canada: Spirituality, the Sacred and Survival," "It is a common remark that if you ask an Elder for advice you will never get a straight answer. You will often be told a story which seems to have nothing whatever to do with the question asked or the problem raised. You are given the autonomy to discover the relevance of the reply and hence to work out the problem for yourself. This is a sign of respect. It is also a method of instruction which fosters independent thinking and self reliance" (63). This, we contend, is exactly the way that the stories in the Whedonverse are intended to operate. As Rhonda Wilcox in *Why Buffy Matters* points out, comparing *Buffy the Vampire Slayer* to such shows as *Beverly Hills 90210*, *The Wonder Years*, *Seventh Heaven*, and the like, "Whedon expected more mental action from his audience.... From the earliest years it was apparent to attentive viewers that *Buffy* operated on a symbolic level" (18). Though in "Pangs" the Scooby Gang has learned something about the real meaning of Thanksgiving and how to deal with cultural guilt, it is really the viewer who has been challenged to think about how to think about these and other moral issues. The viewer has, in essence, been given an indirect lesson (really just one of a series of such lessons that constitutes the whole Whedonverse) not so much in *what* to think, but rather in *how* to think morally.

Episode 3.10 of *Buffy the Vampire Slayer*, "Amends," can also be seen as showing us how to think about cultural guilt, as well as the personal guilt of individuals. Angel is haunted not just by the memory of his past crimes, but rather by the victims themselves, who remind him that he not only murdered them, but particularly enjoyed doing so. As one of his victims says to him, "That's what makes you different than other beasts. They kill to feed, but you took more kinds of pleasure in it than any creature that walks or crawls" (3.10). Angel keeps trying to avoid taking responsibility for his past crimes, trying to explain, "It wasn't me.... A demon isn't a man. I was a man once" (3.10). In Chapter Nine, we discussed in some detail Angel's moral responsibility for crimes of Angelus. Here we want to draw a parallel between Angel's perceived guilt and the kind of cultural guilt discussed in Episode 4.8, "Pangs." As we noted in Chapter Nine, when you become a vampire your soul leaves your body and a demon moves in. This is why the re-ensouled Angel is tempted to say, "It wasn't me." However, unlike the case of cultural guilt, Angel actually remembers committing and enjoying the crimes of Angelus. There is also bodily continuity between Angel and Angelus.

In the case of cultural guilt, though we do not remember doing what our forefathers did to the Natives, we can, as Willow points out, learn from history books what it is that they did. We suggest that a growing number of properly researched historical studies, many by Indigenous scholars, as well as TV documentaries and perceptive popular cultural series like *Buffy the Vampire Slayer*, can be seen as a form of cultural memory, and thus provide some cultural continuity between our forefathers and ourselves that parallels the bodily continuity of Angelus and Angel. To the extent that we still profit from or enjoy the fruits of these past cultural crimes, we in fact do share in the guilt of our forbears and are thus obligated to respond to that guilt in some way. If we have any criticism of the Whedonian approach to cultural guilt, it is that it does not stress nearly enough the notion of how we have benefited from the actions of our predecessors. Still, there is in the Whedonverse a very real sense in which we are our culture, or at least an integral part of our community. There is certainly a deep suspicion concerning radical individualism. Catastrophe usually results when our heroes attempt to act solely on their own, whereas Buffy usually succeeds when she works closely with the Scooby Gang or with other members of her growing community such as the Potentials in Season Seven.

Interestingly enough, the close relation between the individual and the community integral to *Buffy* is shared with a Native American conception of society. As the Cherokee historian Jace Weaver argues in his book *That the People Might Live: Native American Literature and Native Community*, "Natives tend to see themselves in terms of 'self in society' rather than 'self and society'" (39). Contemporary non–Native scholars have also on occasion adopted this position, of course. For example, liberal philosopher Michael Ignatieff, in *The Rights Revolution*, argues that, although individual rights trump group rights, nevertheless, "Our very individualism is social" (138). This, we contend, is exactly the view of the individual portrayed in the Whedonverse. It is very close to the Native American conception, the "self in society" view, cited above.

In this context, the whole notion of cultural guilt takes on an entirely new significance. We find ourselves in a unique position to learn from Angel's response to the crimes of Angelus. In the relevant episode, 3.10, "Amends," we are also introduced to a concept of evil unique to the Buffyverse. It is called the "First Evil." Giles warns Buffy, "You can't fight The First, Buffy. It's not a-a physical being" (3.10). The First itself confirms this. Manifesting as the late Jenny Calendar, it threatens Buffy: "You think you can fight me? I'm not a demon, little girl. I am something that you can't even conceive. The First Evil. Beyond sin, beyond death. I am the thing the darkness fears. You'll never see me, but I am everywhere. Every being, every thought, every drop of hate" (3.10).

Though the First is incorporeal, it seems to be able to take the shape of any person who has died. These manifestations are somewhat ghost-like and cannot manipulate physical objects, and hence are still incorporeal. They can, however, manipulate people by the power of suggestion and by playing on and magnifying their insecurities and weaknesses. This is the

First's way of introducing evil into the world. For example, its appearing before Angel in the person of many of Angel's past victims accentuates his feelings of guilt. This is much more than simply remembering his past victims. He actually sees and hears them. They seem to be trying to persuade him to end these intolerable feelings of guilt by feeding on the Slayer and losing his soul again.

This is really the First's way of attempting to get Angel to kill the Slayer, since the First, being incorporeal, cannot do it itself. The First Evil really is completely powerless on its own, and requires others to commit its crimes. In Season Seven, Buffy recognizes this and speaking directly to the First, expresses this insight as only Buffy can: "Have you ever considered a cool name? I mean, since you're incorporeal and basically powerless ... how about the Taunter? Strikes fear in the hearts of..." (7.22, "Chosen"). It seems that any of us can prevent evil from entering the world by refusing to succumb to the will of the First Evil.

However, Angel illustrates how difficult resisting evil really is. He refuses to kill the Slayer, but in order to escape his unbearable feelings of guilt, he attempts to commit suicide by awaiting the sunrise in the open. Vampires in the Buffyverse, it will be remembered, burst into flame when exposed to sunlight. The First Evil admits that this was not the plan, but seems quite content with the new turn of events. Suicide is evil, after all. Buffy attempts to talk Angel out of committing suicide by pointing out that if "you die now, then all that you ever were was a monster." She reminds him that he has the "power to do real good, to make amends" (3.10). This is not an easy choice for Angel. Even he responds, "Look, I'm weak. I've never been anything else. It's not the demon in me that needs killing, Buffy. It's the man." Buffy retorts, "You're weak. Everybody is. Everybody fails. Maybe this evil did bring you back, but if it did, it's because it needs you. And that means that you can hurt it" (3.10). Angel asks Buffy to leave him alone and let him commit suicide, mistakenly believing that this is his way of being strong and resisting the temptations of the First Evil to eliminate the Slayer. Buffy, realizing that the First is now tempting Angel to commit suicide, argues, "Strong is fighting! It's hard, and it's painful, and it's every day. It's what we have to do. And we can do it together" (3.10, "Amends").

"Amends" is the famous Christmas episode. Angel's suicide attempt is made on Christmas Eve. As Christmas morning dawns, it begins to snow and the sun does not come out this day. Since this is in Southern California, and we have had various hints throughout the episode that the weather has been extraordinarily warm for this time of year, the snow on Christmas Day can certainly be seen as a miraculous intervention. Angel does not save himself through his own free choice, even with all the help that Buffy offers. Still, as Gregory Stevenson argues in *Televised Morality*, "This 'Christmas miracle' becomes a source of hope to Angel. He finds purpose for his life in making amends for the sins of his past" (228). We can apply this lesson to cultural guilt as well. Given that, in the Buffyverse at least, the individual and his or her community are interdependent in the way suggested above, it can be argued that we would not wish to be a part of a community that did not make amends for the crimes of its past. Given that in some sense we are our community, we could not live in a society that could happily think of itself as "a monster."

Buffy's statement to Angel, "if you die now, then all that you ever were was a monster," has further implications for the nature of moral thought in the Buffyverse, since ethical thinking is usually expressed through narrative in the work of Joss Whedon. The nature of narrative comes out in the aptly named *Buffy the Vampire Slayer* Episode 7.16, "Storyteller." There, Buffy reprimands Andrew for making up stories to justify his immoral behavior. He has been tempted by the First Evil in the person of the late Warren Mears to kill their friend, Jonathan, so that his blood may be used as a sacrifice to open the Hellmouth. Warren, it will be remembered, was murdered by a vengeful Willow for inadvertently killing Tara in his attempt to shoot the Slayer, Buffy. Andrew keeps trying to evade both guilt and responsibility by constructing narratives in which he is heroic. He gives contradictory stories about his killing of Jonathan, in which he either accidentally kills him in a struggle over a knife, or is tricked into killing him, having been possessed by the First Evil. In all of his versions of this story, he is struggling against the First Evil, and when he sees Jonathan's murdered body he exclaims "No!" (7.16, "Storyteller"). Buffy, in exasperation, tells him, "Stop! Stop telling stories! Life isn't a story!... You always do this. You make everything into a story so no one's responsible for anything because they're just following a script" (7.16). Jean-Paul Sartre, in *Nausea*, the most important book Joss Whedon has ever read (DVD Commentary on the *Firefly* episode "Objects in Space"), distinguishes between real existence and storytelling by drawing our attention to the importance of the conclusion for stories: "You seem to start at the beginning.... And in reality you have started at the end. It was there, invisible and present, it is the one which gives to words the pomp and value of a beginning ... the end is there, transforming everything" (39–40). According to Sartre, stories impose a structure on the chaos of living which it does not really have, "But you have to choose: live or tell.... Nothing happens while you live....

There are no beginnings. Days are tacked on to days without rhyme or reason, an interminable, monotonous addition" (39). Stories, because of their conclusions that loom over and transform all that goes before, attempt to create narratives that, in effect, supply an essence that precedes existence, and give existence a meaning that it does not, in itself, actually possess. Further, the structures stories impose are inherently selective and distorting. It can be no other way, given both our existential freedom and the nature of narrative itself.

Sartre's response to the absurd meaningless of actual existence is nausea. Our stories and mythologies, the very categories of reason and understanding, cannot capture and contain existence in itself. It seems to ooze out from between our categories like thick hot tar or sticky molasses seeping from the cracks in a damaged vessel. Whedon's response to this absurdity of existence is not the nausea of Sartre's pessimism, but is rather what Whedon calls "rapture" (DVD Commentary on the *Firefly* episode "Objects in Space"). Sartre bemoans the meaninglessness of life. Whedon celebrates the same condition as opening the possibility of creating meaning through narrative. Candace Havens in her biography of Whedon, *Joss Whedon: The Genius Behind Buffy*, suggests that he is "a 'bitter atheist' who finds meaning only in his creations" (158). She cites him as saying, "There's no meaning to life. That's kind of depressing. There's no God. That's a bummer, too. You fill your days with creating worlds that have meaning and order because ours doesn't" (158). However, these created worlds, these stories, must "tap into true emotion and reveal truth about the world" as Gregory Stevenson quite rightly points out in *Televised Morality: The Case of Buffy the Vampire Slayer* (25). Stevenson also argues that Whedon's stories allow us "to acknowledge the capacity for good and evil within ourselves and then choose who we are to become" (84). Joss Whedon has famously said that the watchword of *Buffy the Vampire Slayer* is "BYOSubtext," Bring Your Own Subtext (Bronze VIP Archive for December 3, 1998). We have argued that some subtexts fit the overall narrative rather better than others. Instead of bringing your own subtext to Whedon's narratives, we suggest that what is more important is to take away with you from these texts what you need. We would be happy if readers of our study of the communitarian existential love ethics in Whedon's narratives are able to do the same.

Bibliography

Abbott, Stacey. 2001. "A Little Less Ritual and a Little More Fun: The Modern Vampire in Buffy the Vampire Slayer." *Slayage: The Online International Journal of Buffy Studies* 3. Available: http://www.slayage.tv/essays/slayage3/sabbott.htm.

Abbott, Stacey. 2003. "Walking the Fine Line between Angel and Angelus." *Slayage: The Online International Journal of Buffy Studies* 9. Available: http://www.slayage.tv/Numbers/slayage9.htm.

Abbott, Stacey, ed. 2005a. *Reading Angel: The TV Spin-off with a Soul.* New York: I.B. Tauris.

Abbott, Stacey. 2005b. "From Madman in the Basement to Self-Sacrificing Champion: The Multiple Faces of Spike." *European Journal of Cultural Studies* 8.3: 329–344.

Aberdein, Andrew. 2003. "Balderdash and Chicanery: Science and Beyond." In South 2003a, 79–90.

Adams, Michael. 2003. *Slayer Slang: A Buffy the Vampire Slayer Lexicon.* New York: Oxford University Press.

Alderman, Naomi, and Seidel-Arpac, Annette. 2003. "Imaginary Para-Sites of the Soul: Vampires and Representations of Blackness and Jewishness in the Buffy/Angelverse." *Slayage: The Online International Journal of Buffy Studies* 10. Available: http://www.slayage.tv/Numbers/slayage10.htm.

Alessio, D. 2001. "'Things are Different Now'?: A Postcolonial Analysis of *Buffy the Vampire Slayer*." *The European Legacy* 6: 731–740.

Ali, Asim. 2000. "Community, Language, and Postmodernism at the Mouth of Hell." Available: http://www.wam.umd.edu/~aali/buffnog.html.

Aloi, Peg. 2003. "Skin Pale as Apple Blossom." In Yeffeth, 41–47.

Amy-Chinn, Dee. 2005. "Queering the Bitch: Spike, Transgression and Erotic Empowerment." *European Journal of Cultural Studies* 8.3: 313–328.

Anderson, Wendy Love. 2003. "Prophecy Girl and the Powers That Be: The Philosophy of Religion in the Buffyverse." In South 2003a, 212–226.

Bacon-Smith, Camille. 2003. "The Color of Dark." *Slayage: The Online International Journal of Buffy Studies* 8. Available: http://www.slayage.tv/essays/slayage8/Bacon-Smith.htm.

Bailey, Rachel. 2002. *Buffy—Television Fantasy and Gendered Readings.* Available: http://www.aber.ac.uk/education/Undgrad/Modsae/Ed31220diss/Rachelindex.html.

Barbaccia, Holly G. 2001. "Buffy in the 'Terrible House.'" *Slayage: The Online International Journal of Buffy Studies* 4. Available: http://www.slayage.tv/essays/slayage4/barbaccia.htm.

Bartlem, Edwina. 2003. "Coming out on a Hell Mouth." *Refractory: A Journal of Entertainment Media* 2. Available: http://www.sfca.unimelb.edu.au/refractory/journalissues/vol2/edwinabartlem.htm.

Barr, Keith. 2005. "The Phenomenon of Suicide by Cop." Available: http://www.cji.net/ CJI/CenterInfo/lemc/papers/SBC%20paper.pdf.

Bates, Margaret, Gustafson, Emily M., Porterfield, Bryan C., and Rosenfeld, Lawrence B. 2005. "'When Exactly Did Your Sister Get Unbelievably Scary?' Outsider Status and Dawn and Spike's Relationship." *Slayage: The Online International Journal of Buffy Studies* 16. Available: http://slayage.tv/essays/slayage16/Bates.htm.

Battis, Jes. 2003. "'She's Not All Grown Yet': Willow as Hybrid/Hero in Buffy the Vampire Slayer." *Slayage: The Online International Journal of Buffy Studies* 8. Available: http://www.slayage.tv/essays/slayage8/Battis.htm.

Battis, Jes. 2005. *Blood Relations: Chosen Families in Buffy the Vampire Slayer and Angel.* Jefferson, North Carolina, and London: McFarland.

Beagle, Peter S. 2004. "The Good Vampire: Angel and Spike." In Yeffeth 2004, 115–124.

Beirne, Rebecca. 2004. "Queering the Slayer-Text: Reading Possibilities in *Buffy the Vampire Slayer.*" *Refractory: A Journal of Entertainment Media* 5. Available: file:/// Cx/websites/refractory/journalissues/vol5/beirnePDF.htm.

Bem, A. 1935. "The Problem of Guilt in Dostoevsky's Fiction." Translated by Irene Verhovskoy in Dostoevsky, F. 1975, 626–629.

Bieszk, Patricia. 2005. "Vampire Hip: Style as Subcultural Expression in Buffy the Vampire Slayer." *Refractory: A Journal of Entertainment Media.* "The State of Play" website. Available: http://www.refractory.unimelb.edu.au/stateofplay/articles/PBieszk. htm.

Bloustien, Geraldine. 2002. "Fans with a Lot at Stake: Serious Play and Mimetic Excess in Buffy the Vampire Slayer." *European Journal of Cultural Studies* 5.4: 427–449.

Bodger, Gwyneth. 2003. "Buffy the Feminist Slayer? Constructions of Femininity in Buffy the Vampire Slayer." *Refractory: A Journal of Entertainment Media* 2. Available: http://www.sfca.unimelb.edu.au/refractory/journalissues/vol2/gwynbodger.htm.

Bowers, Cynthia. 2001. "Generation Lapse: The Problematic Parenting of Joyce Summers and Rupert Giles." *Slayage: The Online International Journal of Buffy Studies* 2. Available: http://www.slayage.tv/essays/slayage2/bowers.htm.

Bowman, Elizabeth A., and Stone, Robert V. 1997. "'Making the Human' in Sartre's Unpublished Dialectical Ethics." In McBride, 269–284.

Bowman, Laurel. 2002. "Buffy the Vampire Slayer: The Greek Hero Revisited." Available: http://web.uvic.ca/~lbowman/buffy/buffythehero.html.

Boyette, Michele. 2001. "The Comic Anti-Hero in Buffy the Vampire Slayer, or Silly Villain: Spike Is for Kicks." *Slayage: The Online International Journal of Buffy Studies* 4. Available: http://www.slayage.tv/essays/slayage4/boyette.htm.

Bradney, Anthony. 2003a. "Choosing Laws, Choosing Families: Images of Law, Love and Authority in Buffy the Vampire Slayer." *Web Journal of Current Legal Issues* 2.1. Available: http://webjcli.ncl.ac.uk/2003/issue2/bradney2.html.

Bradney, Anthony. 2003b. "'I Made a Promise to a Lady': Law and Love in BtVS." *Slayage: The Online International Journal of Buffy Studies* 10. Available: http://www.slayage. tv/Numbers/slayage10.htm.

Braun, Beth. 2000. "*The X-Files* and *Buffy the Vampire Slayer*: The Ambiguity of Evil in Supernatural Representation." *Journal of Popular Film and Television* 28.2, 88–94.

Breton, Rob, and McMaster, Lindsey. 2001. "Dissing the Age of Moo: Initiatives, Alternatives, and Rationality in *Buffy the Vampire Slayer.*" *Slayage: The Online International Journal of Buffy Studies* 1. Available: http://www.slayage.tv/essays/slayage1/ bretonmcmaster.htm.

Brin, David. 2003. "Buffy Vs. The Old-Fashioned 'Hero.'" In Yeffeth, 1–4.

Bronze VIP Archive for December 3, 1998. Available: http://www.cise.ufl.edu/cgi-bin/ cgiwrap/hsiao/buffy/get-archive?date=19981203.

Buffy the Vampire Slayer created by Joss Whedon 1992, 1997–2003.

Buffy the Vampire Slayer: The Script Book, Season One, Volume One. 2002. New York: Simon and Schuster.

Buffy the Vampire Slayer: The Script Book, Season One, Volume Two. 2002. New York: Simon and Schuster.

Buinicki, Martin, and Enns, Anthony. 2001. "Buffy the Vampire Disciplinarian: Institutional Excess, Spiritual Technologies, and the New Economy of Power." *Slayage: The Online International Journal of Buffy Studies* 4. Available: http://www.slayage.tv/essays/slayage4/buinickienns.htm.

Burr, Vivien. 2003a. "'It All Seems So Real': Intertextuality in the Buffyverse." *Refractory: A Journal of Entertainment Media* 2. Available: http://www.sfca.unimelb.edu.au/refractory/journalissues/vol2/vivienburr.htm.

Burr, Vivien. 2003b. "Ambiguity and Sexuality in the Buffyverse: A Sartrean Analysis." *Sexualities* 6.3–4: 343–60.

Burr, Vivien. 2003c. "Buffy Vs. The BBC: Moral Questions and How to Avoid Them." *Slayage: The Online International Journal of Buffy Studies* 8. Available: http://www.slayage.tv/essays/slayage8/Burr.htm.

Burr, Vivien. 2005. "Scholar/'Shippers and Spikeaholics: Academic and Fan Identities at the Slayage Conference on: *Buffy the Vampire Slayer.*" *European Journal of Cultural Studies* 8.3: 375–383.

Busse, Katrina. 2002. "Crossing the Final Taboo: Family, Sexuality, and Incest in Buffyverse Fan Fiction." In Wilcox and Lavery, 207–217.

Buttsworth, Sara. 2003. "*Buffy the Vampire Slayer*: The Next Generation of Television." In *Catching a Wave: Reclaiming Feminism for the 21st Century*, edited by Rory Dicker and Alison Piepmeier. Boston: Northeastern University Press.

Byers, Michele. 2000. "*Buffy the Vampire Slayer*: The Insurgence of Television as a Performance Text." University of Toronto.

Callander, Michelle. 2001. "Bram Stoker's Buffy: Traditional Gothic and Contemporary Culture." *Slayage: The Online International Journal of Buffy Studies* 3. Available: http://www.slayage.tv/essays/slayage3/callander.html.

Campbell, Richard, and Campbell, Caitlin. 2001. "Demons, 'Aliens, Teens and Television.'" *Slayage: The Online International Journal of Buffy Studies* 2. Available: http://www.slayage.tv/essays/slayage2/campbell.htm.

Cantwell, Marianne. 2004. "Collapsing the Extra/Textual: Passions and Intensities of Knowledge in Buffy the Vampire Slayer Online Fan Communities." *Refractory: A Journal of Entertainment Media* 5. Available: http://www.refractory.unimelb.edu.au/journalissues/vol5/cantwellPFV.pdf.

Carter, Margaret L. 2003. "A World without Shrimp." In Yeffeth, 176–187.

Center for Suicide Prevention. 1999. "SIEC Alert #34. Suicide by Cop." Available: http://www.suicideinfo.ca/csp/assets/alert34.pdf. Accessed Oct. 9, 2005.

Chandler, Holly. 2003. "Slaying the Patriarchy: Transfusions of the Vampire Metaphor in *BtVS*." *Slayage: The Online International Journal of Buffy Studies* 9. Available: http://www.slayage.tv/Numbers/slayage9.htm.

Chin, Vivian. 2003. "Buffy? She's Like Me, She's Not Like Me, She's *Rad*." In Early and Kennedy, 92–102.

Clark, Daniel A., and Miller, P. Andrew. 2001. "Buffy, the Scooby Gang, and Monstrous Authority: *BtVS* and the Subversion of Authority." *Slayage: The Online International Journal of Buffy Studies* 3. Available: http://www.slayage.tv/essays/slayage3/clarkmiller.html.

Clarke, Jamie. 2003. "Affective Entertainment in 'Once More with Feeling': A Manifesto for Fandom." *Refractory: A Journal of Entertainment Media* 2. Available: http://www.sfca.unimelb.edu.au/refractory/journalissues/vol2/jamieclarke.htm.

Cocca, Carolyn. 2003. "First Word 'Jail,' Second Word 'Bait': Adolescent Sexuality, Feminist Theories, and *Buffy the Vampire Slayer.*" *Slayage: The Online International Journal of Buffy Studies* 10. Available: http://www.slayage.tv/Numbers/slayage10.htm.

Coleman, Felicity. 2003. "The Sight of Your God Disturbs Me: Questioning the Post-Christian Bodies of Buffy, Lain, and George." *Refractory: A Journal of Entertainment Media* 3. Available: http://www.ahcca.unimelb.edu.au/refractory/journalissues/vol3/colman.htm.

Conner, Michael. 2003. "Suicide By Cop." Mentor Research Institute. Available: http://www.oregoncounseling.org/ArticlesPapers/Documents/SuicideByCop.htm. Accessed Oct 9, 2005.

Cordesman, Anthony H. 2001. "Biological Warfare and the 'Buffy Paradigm.'" Available: http://www.csis.org/burke/hd/reports/Buffy012902.pdf.

Cover, Rob. 2004a. "From Butler To Buffy: Notes Towards a Strategy for Identity Analysis in Contemporary Television Narrative." *Reconstruction: Studies in Contemporary Culture* 4.2. Available: http://www.reconstruction.ws/042/cover.htm.

Cover, Rob. 2004b. "'Not to Be Toyed With': Drug Addiction, Bullying and Self-Empowerment in *Buffy the Vampire Slayer.*" *Continuum: Journal of Media & Cultural Studies* 19.1: 85–101.

Crusie, Jennifer. 2003. "Dating Death." In Yeffeth, 85–96.

Curry, Agnes B. 2005. "Is Joss Becoming a Thomist?" *Slayage: The Online International Journal of Buffy Studies* 16. Available: http://slayage.tv/essays/slayage16/Curry.htm.

Dante. 1954. *The Inferno.* Translated by John Ciardi. New York: New American Library.

Daspit, Toby. 2003. "Buffy Goes to College, Adam Murders to Dissect: Education and Knowledge in Postmodernity." In South 2003a, 117–130.

Daugherty, Anne Millard. 2001. "Just a Girl: Buffy as Icon." In Kaveney 2001, 148–165.

Davidson, Joy. 2004. "'There's My Boy...'" In Yeffeth, 199–216.

Davis, Robert A. 2001. "Buffy the Vampire Slayer and the Pedagogy of Fear." *Slayage: The Online International Journal of Buffy Studies* 3. Available: http://www.slayage.tv/essays/slayage3/davis.htm.

DeKelb-Rittenhouse, Diane. 2002. "Sex and the Single Vampire: The Evolution of the Vampire Lothario and Its Representation in *Buffy.*" In Wilcox and Lavery, 143–152.

DeRosia, Margaret. 2005. "Slayers, Sluts, Vampires, Werewolves: Sexuality on Buffy the Vampire Slayer." Forthcoming in Parks and Levine.

Dechert, S. Renee. 2002. "'My Boyfriend's in the Band': Buffy and the Rhetoric of Music." In Wilcox and Lavery, 218–226.

Diehl, Laura. 2004. "Why Drusilla Is More Interesting Than Buffy." *Slayage: The Online International Journal of Buffy Studies* 13/14. Available: http://slayage.tv/essays/slayage 13_14/Diehl.htm.

Dingsdale, Paul. 1998. "'Suicide by Cop': Disturbing New Trend Revealed by USC Study of Fatal Shootings." Available: http://www.usc.edu/hsc/info/pr/1vol4/434/shootings.html. Accessed Oct. 9, 2005.

Dostoevsky, F. 1952. *The Brothers Karamazov.* Translated by Constance Garnett. Chicago: William Benton. Great Books, Volume 52.

Dostoevsky, F. 1975. *Crime and Punishment.* Translated by Jessie Coulson and edited by George Gibian. New York: W. W. Norton. Originally published serially in 1866.

Dostoevsky, F. 1972. *Notes from Underground* and *The Double.* Translated by Jessie Coulson. London: Penguin Books.

Dowling, Jennifer. 2003. "'We Are Not Demons': Homogenizing the Heroes in Buffy the Vampire Slayer and Angel." *Refractory: A Journal of Entertainment Media* 2. Available: http://www.sfca.unimelb.edu.au/refractory/journalissues/vol2/jenniferdowling.htm.

Dupey, Cora. 2003. "Is Giles Simply Another Dr. Van Helsing? Continuity and Innovation in the Figure of the Watcher in *Buffy the Vampire Slayer.*" *Refractory: A Jour-

nal of Entertainment Media 2. Available: http://www.sfca.unimelb.edu.au/refractory/journalissues/vol2/coradupey.htm.

Early, Francis H. 2001. "Staking Her Claim: Buffy the Vampire Slayer as Transgressive Woman Warrior." In *Journal of Popular Culture* 35.3: 11–28. Report in *Slayage: The Online International Journal of Buffy Studies* 6. Available: http://www.slayage.tv/essays/slayage6/Early.htm.

Early, Francis H. 2003. "The Female Just Warrior Reimagined: From Boudicca to Buffy." In Early and Kennedy, 55–65.

Early, Francis H., and Kennedy, Kathleen, eds. 2003. *Athena's Daughters: Television's New Women Warriors*. Syracuse, New York: Syracuse University Press.

Edwards, Lynne. 2002. "Slaying in Black and White: Kendra as Tragic Mulatto in Buffy the Vampire Slayer." In Wilcox and Lavery, 85–96.

Emoto, Masaru. 2005a. *The Hidden Messages in Water*. Translated by David A. Thayne. New York: Atria Books.

Emoto, Masaru. 2005b. *The True Power of Water: Healing and Discovering Ourselves*. Translated by Noriko Hosoyamada. New York: Atria Books.

Erikson, Gregory. 2002. "'Sometimes You Need a Story': American Christianity, Vampires, and Buffy." In Wilcox and Lavery, 108–119.

Erickson, Greg. 2004. "Revisiting Buffy's Theology: Religion: 'Freaky' or Just 'a Bunch of Men Who Died.'" *Slayage: The Online International Journal of Buffy Studies* 13/14. Available: http://slayage.tv/essays/slayage13_14/Erickson.htm.

Espenson, Jane. 2004. *Finding Serenity: Anti-Heroes, Lost Shepherds, and Space Hookers in Joss Whedon's "Firefly."* Dallas: BenBella Books.

Fifarek, Aimee. 2001. "'Mind and Heart with Spirit Joined': The Buffyverse as an Information System." *Slayage: The Online International Journal of Buffy Studies* 3. Available: http://www.slayage.tv/essays/slayage3/afifarek.htm.

Forster, Greg. 2003. "Faith and Plato: 'You're Nothing! Disgusting, Murderous Bitch!'" In South 2003a, 7–19.

Fossey, Claire. 2003. "'Never Hurt the Feelings of a Brutal Killer': Spike and the Underground Man." *Slayage: The Online International Journal of Buffy Studies* 8. Available: http://www.slayage.tv/essays/slayage8/Fossey.htm.

Fuchs, Cynthia. 2005. "'Looking Human Is So Overrated': Race and Displacement in Buffy and Roswell." Forthcoming in Parks and Levine.

Fudge, Rachel. 1999. "The Buffy Effect or, a Tale of Cleavage and Marketing." *Bitch* 4.1: 18–21.

Gerberth, V. 1993. "Suicide by Cop." *Law and Order*, 105–108.

Gill, Candra K. 2004. "Cuz the Black Chick Always Gets It First: Dynamics of Race in *Buffy the Vampire Slayer*." In *Girls Who Bite Back: Witches, Mutants, Slayers and Freaks*, edited by Emily Pohl-Weary. Toronto: Sumach Press.

Gilligan, Carol. 1982. *In a Different Voice: Psychological Theory and Women's Development*. Cambridge, Massachusetts: Harvard University Press.

Golden, Christie. 2003. "Where's the Religion in Willow's Wicca?" In Yeffeth, 159–166.

Graeber, David. 1998. "Rebel without a God: 'Buffy the Vampire Slayer' Is Gleefully Anti-Authoritarian(and Popular." *In These Times* 23.2. Available: http://members.tripod.com/~MikeHolt/buffy.html.

Greene, Richard, and Yuen, Wayne. 2001. "Why Can't We Spike Spike?: Moral Themes in Buffy the Vampire Slayer." *Slayage: The Online International Journal of Buffy Studies* 2. Available: http://www.slayage.tv/essays/slayage2/greeneandyuen.

Greene, Richard, and Yuen, Wayne. 2003. "Morality on Television: The Case of Buffy the Vampire Slayer." In South 2003a, 271–281.

Greenman, Jennifer. June 6, 2002. "Witch Love Spells Death." Available: http://www.newsreview.com/issues/sacto/2002-06-06/arts.asp.

Halfyard, Janet K. 2001. "Love, Death, Curses and Reverses (in F Minor): Music, Gender and Identity in Buffy the Vampire Slayer and Angel." *Slayage: The Online International Journal of Buffy Studies* 4. Available: http://www.slayage.tv/essays/slayage 4/halfyard.htm.

Halfyard, Janet K. 2003. "The Greatest Love of All: Cordelia's Journey of Self-Discovery." In the archive of talks from the Slayage conference on *Buffy the Vampire Slayer.* Available: http://www.slayage.tv/SCBtVS_Archive/Talks/Halfyard.pdf.

Hammond, Mary. 2004. "Monsters and Metaphors: Buffy the Vampire Slayer and the Old World." In *Cult Television*, edited by Sara Gwenllian-Jones and Roberta E. Pearson. Minneapolis: University of Minnesota Press, 147–164.

Harper, Steven. 2004. "Jasmine: Scariest Villain Ever." In Yeffeth 2004, 49–55.

Harris, Charlaine. 2003. "A Reflection on Ugliness." In Yeffeth, 116–120.

Harts, Kate. 2001. "Deconstructing Buffy: Buffy the Vampire Slayer's Contribution to the Discourse on Gender Construction." *Popular Culture Review* 12.1: 79–98.

Haslem, Wendy. 2003. "'I Think Every Home Should Have One of You': The Serial Killer Disguised as the Perfect Husband." *Refractory: A Journal of Entertainment Media* 2. Available: http://www.sfca.unimelb.edu.au/refractory/journalissues/vol2/wendyhas lem.htm.

Hastie, Amelie. 2005. "Buffy's Popularity, Television Criticism and Marketing Demands." Forthcoming in Parks and Levine.

Hastings, James, ed. 1963. *Dictionary of the Bible*. Revised edition by Frederick C. Grant and H. H. Rowley. New York: Charles Scribner's Sons.

Havens, Candace. 2003. *Joss Whedon: The Genius Behind Buffy*. Dallas: Benbella Books.

Heinecken, Dawn. 2003. *The Warrior Women of Television: A Feminist Cultural Analysis of the New Female Body in Popular Media*. New York: Peter Lang.

Heinecken, Dawn. 2004. "Fan Readings of Sex and Violence on Buffy the Vampire Slayer." *Slayage: The Online International Journal of Buffy Studies* 11/12. Available: http://www.slayage.tv/Numbers/slayage11_12.htm.

Held, Jacob. 2003. "Justifying the Means: Punishment in the Buffyverse." In South 2003a, 227–238.

Helford, Elyce Rae, ed. 2000. *Fantasy Girls: Gender in the New Universe of Science Fiction and Fantasy Television*. New York: Rowman and Littlefield.

Helford, Elyce Rae. 2002. "'My Emotions Give Me Power': The Containment of Girls' Anger in Buffy." In Wilcox and Lavery, 18–34.

Hibbs, Thomas. 2003a. "Buffy the Vampire Slayer as Feminist Noir." In South, 49–60.

Hill, Annette, and Calcutt, Ian. 2005. "The UK Marketing and Reception of *Buffy the Vampire Slayer* and *Angel*." Forthcoming in Parks and Levine.

Hills, Matthew. 2005. "Reading the (Teen/Star/Vampire/Cult) Romance: Buffy, Reading Formations and the Rising Stakes of Generic Hybridity." Forthcoming in Parks and Levine.

Hills, Matt, and Williams, Rebecca. 2005. "It's All My Interpretation: Reading Spike Through the Subcultural Celebrity of James Marsters." *European Journal of Cultural Studies* 8.3: 345–365.

Hinton, Sofrina. 2002. "Confluence: The Quest for Self in Buffy the Vampire Slayer." *Phase Five* 1.2. Available: http://www.bibliora.com/P5_0302/html/confluence.html.

Holder, Nancy. 2003. "Slayers of the Last Arc." In Yeffeth 2003, 195–205.

Holder, Nancy. 2004. "Death Becomes Him: Blondie Bear 5.0." In Yeffeth 2004, 153–166.

Huston, H. Range, M.D., Anglin, Diedre, M.D., et al. 1998. "Suicide by Cop." *Annals of Emergency Medicine* 32.6. American College of Emergency Physicians.

Ignatieff, M. 2000. *The Rights Revolution*. Toronto: House of Anansi Press.

Introvigne, Massimo. 2001. "God, New Religious Movements and Buffy the Vampire Slayer." Available: http://www.cesnur.org/2001/buffy_march01.htm.

Introvigne, Massimo. 2003. "Brainwashing the Working Class: Vampire Comics and Criticism from Dr. Occult to Buffy." *Slayage: The Online International Journal of Buffy Studies* 7. Available: http://www.slayage.tv/essays/slayage7/Introvigne.htm.

Jarvis, Christine. 2001. "School Is Hell: Gendered Fears in Teenage Horror." *Educational Studies* 27.3: 257–67.

Jenkins, Alice, and Stuart, Susan. 2003. "Extending Your Mind: Non-Standard Perlocutionary Acts in Hush." *Slayage: The Online International Journal of Buffy Studies* 9. Available: http://www.slayage.tv/Numbers/slayage9.htm.

Jenkins, Henry, III, and Jenkins, Henry G., IV. 2005. "The Monsters Next Door: A Father-Son Dialogue About Buffy, Moral Panic, and Generational Differences." Forthcoming in Parks and Levine. Available: http://web.mit.edu/21fms/www/faculty/henry3/buffy.html.

Jowett, Lorna. 2002. "Masculinity, Monstrosity and Behaviour Modification in Buffy the Vampire Slayer." *Foundation* 31.84: 59–73.

Jowett, Lorna. 2004. "New Men: 'Playing the Sensitive Lad.'" *Slayage: The Online International Journal of Buffy Studies* 13/14. Available: http://slayage.tv/essays/slayage13_14/Jowett.htm.

Jowett, Lorna. 2005. *Sex and the Slayer: A Gender Studies Primer for the 'Buffy' Fan*. Middletown, Connecticut: Wesleyan University Press.

Karras, Irene. 2002. "The Third Wave's Final Girl: Buffy the Vampire Slayer." *Thirdspace* 1.2. Available: http://www.thirdspace.ca/articles/karras.htm.

Kaveney, Roz, ed. 2001. *Reading the Vampire Slayer: An Unofficial Critical Companion to Buffy and Angel*. New York: Tauris Park.

Kaveney, Roz, ed. 2004. *Reading the Vampire Slayer: An Unofficial Critical Companion to Buffy and Angel*, 2nd ed. New York: Tauris.

Kaveney, Roz. 2005a. "A Sense of the Ending: Schödinger's Angel." (Excerpt from *Reading Angel: The TV Spinoff with a Soul*.) In *Slayage: The Online International Journal of Buffy Studies* 16. Available: http://slayage.tv/essays/slayage16/Kaveney.htm.

Kaveny, Cathleen. 2003. "What Women Want: 'Buffy,' the Pope & the New Feminists." *Commonweal* 7 Nov. Available: http://www.commonwealmagazine.org/article.php?id_article=801.

Kawal, Jason. 2003. "Should We Do What Buffy Would Do?" In South 2003a, 149–159.

Kaye, Sharon, and Milavec, Melissa. 2003. "Buffy in the Buff: A Slayer's Solution to Aristotle's Love Paradox." In South 2003a, 176–184.

Kearney, Mary Celeste. 2005. "The Changing Face of Youth Television, or Why We All Love Buffy." Forthcoming in Parks and Levine.

Keller, Donald. 2002. "Spirit Guides and Shadow Selves: From the Dream Life of Buffy (and Faith)." In Wilcox and Lavery, 165–177.

Kellner, Douglas. No date. "Buffy, The Vampire Slayer as Spectacular Allegory: A Diagnostic Critique." Available: http://www.gseis.ucla.edu/faculty/kellner/essays/buffy.pdf.

Kennedy, D., et al. 1998. "Suicide by Cop." *FBI Law Enforcement Bulletin*, 23–31. Available: http://www.forensiccriminology.com/Suicidebycop.pdf. Accessed Oct. 9, 2005.

Kenyon, Sherrilyn. 2003. "The Search for Spike's Balls." In Yeffeth, 25–29.

Keram, E., and Farrell, B. 2001. "Suicide by Cop: Issues in Outcome and Analysis." *Suicide and Law Enforcement*, 587–599.

Kilpatrick, Nancy. 2003. "Sex and the Single Slayer." In Yeffeth, 19–24.

King, Neal. 2003. "Brown Skirts: Fascism, Christianity, and the Eternal Demon." In South 2003a, 197–211.

Kline, George L. 1967. "Russian Philosophy." In *Encyclopedia of Philosophy*, edited by Paul Edwards. New York: MacMillan. Vol. 7: 258–268.

Korsmeyer, Carolyn. 2003. "Passion and Action: In and out of Control." In South 2003a, 160–172.

Kostova, Elizabeth. 2005. *The Historian: A Novel.* New York: Little, Brown.

Krause, Marguerite. 2003. "The Meaning of Buffy." In Yeffeth, 97–108.

Krimmer, Elizabeth, and Raval, Shilpa. 2002. "'Digging the Undead': Death and Desire in Buffy." In Wilcox and Lavery, 153–164.

Kryzywinska, Tanya. 2002. "Hubble-Bubble, Herbs and Grimoires: Magic, Manichaeanism, and Witchcraft in Buffy." In Wilcox and Lavery, 178–194.

Kryzywinska, Tanya. 2003. "Playing Buffy: Remediation, Occulted Meta-Game-Physics and the Dynamics of Agency in the Videogame Version of Buffy the Vampire Slayer." *Slayage: The Online International Journal of Buffy Studies* 8. Available: http://slayage.tv/essays/slayage8/Kryzywinska.htm.

Lackey, Mercedes. 2004. "*Serenity* and Bobby McGee: Freedom and the Illusion of Freedom in Joss Whedon's *Firefly*." In Espenson, 63–73.

Lakoff, George, and Johnson, Mark. 1980. *Metaphors We Live By.* Chicago: University of Chicago Press.

Lakoff, George, and Johnson, Mark. 1999. *Philosophy in the Flesh: The Embodied Mind and its Challenge to Western Thought.* New York: Basic Books.

Larbalestier, Justine. 2002. "*Buffy*'s Mary Sue Is Jonathan: *Buffy* Acknowledges the Fans." In Wilcox and Lavery, 227–238.

Larbalestier, Justine. 2003. "A *Buffy* Confession." In Yeffeth, 72–84.

Larbalestier, Justine. 2004. "The Only Thing Better Than Killing a Slayer: Heterosexuality and Sex in *Buffy the Vampire Slayer*." In Kaveney 2004, 195–219.

Lavery, David. 2002a. "'Emotional Resonance and Rocket Launchers': Joss Whedon's Commentaries on the *Buffy the Vampire Slayer* DVDs." *Slayage: The Online International Journal of Buffy Studies* 6. Available: http://www.slayage.tv/essays/slayage6/Lavery.htm.

Lavery, David. 2002b. "Afterward: The Genius of Joss Whedon." In Wilcox and Lavery, 251–256.

Lavery, David. 2003a. "'A Religion in Narrative': Joss Whedon and Television Creativity." *Slayage: The Online International Journal of Buffy Studies* 7. Available: http://slayage.tv/essays/slayage7/Lavery.htm.

Lavery, David. 2003b. "Apocalyptic Apocalypses: The Narrative Eschatology of *Buffy the Vampire Slayer*." *Slayage: The Online International Journal of Buffy Studies* 9. Available: http://slayage.tv/essays/slayage9/Lavery.htm.

Lavery, David. 2004. "'I Wrote My Thesis on You': Buffy Studies as an Academic Cult." *Slayage: The Online International Journal of Buffy Studies* 13/14. Available: http://slayage.tv/essays/slayage13_14/Lavery.htm.

Lawler, James. 2003a. "Between Heaven and Hells: The Multidimensional Universe in Kant and Buffy the Vampire Slayer." In South, 103–116.

Leon, Hilary M. 2001. "Why We Love the Monsters: How Anita Blake, Vampire Hunter, and Buffy the Vampire Slayer Wound up Dating the Enemy." *Slayage: The Online International Journal of Buffy Studies* 1. Available: http://www.slayage.tv/essays/slayage1/hleon.htm.

Levina, Marina. 2003. "How Vampire Got Neutered: Boundary Surveillance and Technoscientific Discourse on Buffy the Vampire Slayer." In *Vampires: Myths and Metaphors of Enduring Evil*, edited by Carla T. Kungl. Oxford, UK: Inter-Disciplinary Press, 12i–123.

Levine, Elana. 2005. "Buffy and the 'New Girl Order': Two Waves of Television and Feminism." Forthcoming in Parks and Levine.

Levine, Michael, and Schneider, Steven Jay. 2003. "Feeling for Buffy: The Girl Next Door." In South 2003a, 194–308.

Lichtenberg, Jacqueline. 2003. "Power of Becoming." In Yeffeth, 121–136.

Lindsay, Mark, and Lester, David. 2004. *Suicide by Cop: Committing Suicide by Provoking Police to Shoot You*. Amityville, New York: Baywood.

Little, Tracy. 2003. "High School Is Hell: Metaphor Made Literal in *Buffy the Vampire Slayer*." In South 2003a, 282–293.

Locklin, Reid B. 2002. "Buffy the Vampire Slayer and the Domestic Church: Revisioning Family and the Common Good." *Slayage: The Online International Journal of Buffy Studies* 6. Available: http://www.slayage.tv/essays/slayage6/Locklin.htm.

Longstreet Conrad, Roxanne. 2003. "Is That Your Final Answer...?" In Yeffeth, 5–18.

Lord, Vivian B., ed. 2004. *Suicide by Cop: Inducing Officers to Shoot*. New York: Loose Leaf Law Publications.

Lorrah, Jean. 2003. "Love Saves the World." In Yeffeth, 167–75.

Marinucci, Mimi. 2003. "Feminism and the Ethics of Violence: Why Buffy Kicks Ass." In South 2003a, 61–76.

Marlowe, Christopher. 1969. *Doctor Faustus*. Edited by Sylvan Barnet. New York: New American Library.

Marshall, C. W. 2003. "Aeneas the Vampire Slayer: A Roman Model for Why Giles Kills Ben." *Slayage: The Online International Journal of Buffy Studies* 9. Available: http://www.slayage.tv/essays/slayage9/Marshall.htm.

Martin, Bernard, ed. 1970. *A Shestov Anthology*. Athens: Ohio University Press.

McBride, William L. 1997. *Sartre and Existentialism: Philosophy, Politics, Ethics, the Psyche, Literature, and Aesthetics*. New York and London: Garland.

McClelland, Bruce. 2001. "By Whose Authority? The Magical Tradition, Violence, and the Legitimation of the Vampire Slayer." *Slayage: The Online International Journal of Buffy Studies* 1. Available: http://www.slayage.tv/essays/slayage1/bmcclelland.htm.

McCracken, Allison. 2005. "Angel's Body." Forthcoming in Parks and Levine.

McLaren, Scott. 2005. "The Evolution of Joss Whedon's Vampire Mythology and the Ontology of the Soul." *Slayage: The Online International Journal of Buffy Studies* 18. Available: http://www.slayage.tv/essays/slayage18/McLaren.htm.

McNeilly, Kevin, Fisher, Sue, and Sylka, Christina. 2001. "Kiss the Librarian, but Close the Hellmouth: 'It's Like a Whole Big Sucking Thing.'" *Slayage: The Online International Journal of Buffy Studies* 2. Available: http://www.slayage.tv/essays/slayage2/mcneilly.htm.

McPherson, Dennis H., and Rabb, J. Douglas. 2001. "Indigeneity in Canada: Spirituality, the Sacred and Survival." *International Journal of Canadian Studies/Revue internationale d'études canadiennes* 23: 57–79.

Mealing, S. R., ed. 1990. *The Jesuit Relations and Allied Documents: A Selection*. Ottawa: Carleton University Press.

Melton, J. Gordon. 2001. "Words from the Hellmouth: A Bibliography of Books on Buffy the Vampire Slayer." *Slayage: The Online International Journal of Buffy Studies* 4. Available: http://www.slayage.tv/essays/slayage4/meltonbooks.htm.

Mendelsohn, Farah. 2002. "Surpassing the Love of Vampires; or Why (and How) a Queer Reading of Buffy/Willow Is Denied." In Wilcox and Lavery, 45–60.

Middleton, Jason. 2005. "Buffy as Femme Fatale: The Female Heroine and the Male Cult Fan." Forthcoming in Parks and Levine.

Mikosz, Philip, and Och, Dana. 2002. "Previously on Buffy the Vampire Slayer..." *Slayage: The Online International Journal of Buffy Studies* 5. Available: http://www.slayage.tv/essays/slayage5/mikosz%20and%20och.htm.

Miller, Jessica Prata. 2003. "'The I in Team': Buffy and Feminist Ethics." In South 2003a, 35–48.

Miller, Laura. 2003. "Bye-Bye, Buffy!" Salon.com May 20, 2003. Available: http://www.salon.com/ent/tv/feature/2003/05/20/buffy/index.html.

Molloy, Patricia. 2003. "Demon Diasporas: Confronting the Other and the Other Worldly in *Buffy the Vampire Slayer* and *Angel*." In *To Seek out New Worlds: Exploring Links between Science Fiction and World Politics*, edited by Jutta Weldes. New York: Palgrave Macmillan.

Money, Mary Alice. 2002. "The Undemonization of Supporting Characters in *Buffy*." In Wilcox and Lavery, 98–107.

Montgomery, Carla. 2003. "Innocence." In Yeffeth, 152–158.

Moore, Dene. 2005. "Harry Now Required Reading." *Toronto Star*. November 19, L11.

Morison, Samuel Eliot. 1942. *Admiral of the Sea: A Life of Christopher Columbus*. Boston: Little Brown.

Morris, Phyllis Sutton. 1976. *Sartre's Concept of a Person: An Analytic Approach*. Amherst: University of Massachusetts Press.

Moss, Gabrielle. 2001. "From the Valley to the Hellmouth: Buffy's Transition from Film to Television." *Slayage: The Online International Journal of Buffy Studies* 2. Available: http://www.slayage.tv/essays/slayage2/moss.htm.

Muntersbjorn, Madeline M. 2003. "Pluralism, Pragmatism, and Pals: The Slayer Subverts the Science Wars." In South 2003a, 91–102.

Murphy, Kevin Andrew. 2003. "Unseen Horrors & Shadowy Manipulations." In Yeffeth, 137–151.

Murray, Susan. 2005. "I Know What You Did Last Summer: Sarah Michelle Gellar and Cross-over Teen Stardom." Forthcoming in Parks and Levine.

Ndalianis, Angela, and Colman, Felicity, eds. 2003. "Special Issue on Buffy the Vampire Slayer." *Refractory: A Journal of Entertainment Media* 2. Available: http://www.ahcca.unimelb.edu.au/refractory/journalissues/vol2/vol2.htm.

Nevitt, Lucy, and Smith, Andy William. 2003. "'Family Blood Is Always the Sweetest': The Gothic Transgressions of Angel/Angelus." *Refractory: A Journal of Entertainment Media* 2. Available: http://pandora.nla.gov.au/pan/30981/20030512/www.sfca.unimelb.edu.au/refractory/journalissues/index.htm#lnas1.

Ono, Kent A. 2000. "To Be a Vampire on *Buffy the Vampire Slayer*: Race and ('Other') Socially Marginalizing Positions on Horror TV." In Helford, ed. 163–186.

Overbey, Karen Eileen, and Preston-Matto, Lahney. 2002. "Staking in Tongues: Speech Act as Weapon in Buffy." In Wilcox and Lavery, 73–84.

Owen, A. Susan. 1999. "Buffy the Vampire Slayer: Vampires, Postmodernity, and Postfeminism." *Journal of Popular Film and Television* 27.2: 24–31.

Parent, R. 1998. "Victim-Precipitated Homicide: Police Use of Deadly Force in British Columbia." *Policing: An International Journal of Police Strategies and Management* 21: 432–448.

Parent, R. 2004. "*Aspects of Police Use of Deadly Force In North America: The Phenomenon of Victim-Precipitated Homicide*." Ph.D. Dissertation, Simon Fraser University.

Parks, Lisa. 2005. "Behind Buffyspeak: An Interview with Writer/Producer Jane Espenson." Forthcoming in Parks and Levine.

Parks, Lisa, and Levine, Elana, eds. 2005. *Red Noise: Critical Writings on Buffy the Vampire Slayer*. Durham: Duke University Press. Forthcoming.

Parpart, Lee. 2003. "'Action, Chicks, Everything': On-Line Interviews with Male Fans of *Buffy the Vampire Slayer*." In Early and Kennedy, 78–91.

Pasley, Jeffrey L. 2003. "Old Familiar Vampires: The Politics of the Buffyverse." In South 2003a, 254–268.

Pateman, Matthew. 2006. *The Aesthetics of Culture in "Buffy the Vampire Slayer."* Jefferson, North Carolina, and London: McFarland.

Paule, Michele, and Davison, Laura. No date. "Superheroes and Superlearning: Enriching the Lower School Curriculum with Buffy the Vampire Slayer." A project from the Westminster Institute of Education, Oxford Brookes University. Available: http://www.brookes.ac.uk/schools/education/rescon/Buffy%20Brookes.pdf.

Pender, Patricia. 2002. "'I'm Buffy and You're History': The Postmodern Politics of *Buffy the Vampire Slayer*." In Wilcox and Lavery, 35–44.

Petrova, Erma. 2003. "'You Cannot Run from Your Darkness.' 'Who Says I'm Running?' Buffy and the Ownership of Evil." *Refractory: A Journal of Entertainment Media* 2. Available: http://pandora.nla.gov.au/pan/30981/20030512/www.sfca.unimelb.edu. au/refractory/journalissues/index.htm#ep.

Plantinga, Alvin. 1997. "An Existentialist's Ethics." In McBride, 1–22.

Playdon, Zoe-Jane. 2001. "'What Are You, What's to Come': Feminisms, Citizenship and the Divine." In Kaveney 2001, 120–147.

Playdon, Zoe-Jane. 2002. "'The Outsiders' Society': Religious Imagery in Buffy the Vampire Slayer." *Slayage: The Online International Journal of Buffy Studies* 5. Available: http://www.slayage.tv/essays/slayage5/playdon.htm.

Porfirio, Robert. 1996. "No Way Out: Existential Motifs in the *Film Noir*." In *Film Noir Reader*, edited by Alain Silver and James Ursini. New York: Limelight Editions, 77–93.

Postrel, Virginia. 2003. "Why Buffy Kicked Ass: The Deep Meaning of TV's Favorite Vampire Slayer." *Reason* Online Aug/Sep 2003. Available: http://www.reason.com/0308/cr.vp.why.shtml.

Potts, Donna L. 2003. "Convents, Claddagh Rings, and Even the Book of Kells: Representing the Irish in Buffy the Vampire Slayer." *Simile: Studies in Media and Information Literacy Education* 3.2. Available: http://www.utpjournals.com/simile/issue 10/pottsfulltext.html.

Pyers, Louise C. 2001. "Suicide by Cop — Results of Current Empirical Studies." Available: http://www.cableweb.org/Information/SBC/sbcstudy.pdf. Accessed Oct. 9, 2005.

Quinn, Daniel. 1996. *The Story of B: An Adventure of the Mind and Spirit*, New York: Bantam.

R, Skippy. 2002. "The Door Theologian of the Year." Available: http://www.thedoor magazine.com/archives/buffy.html.

Rabb, J. Douglas. 1983. "Reason and Revelation Revisited." In *Religion and Reason: A Symposium*, edited by J. Douglas Rabb. Winnipeg: Frye Publishing, 2–19. *Religie si ratiune — o perspectiva canadiana (de J.D. Rabb)*— English to Romanian. Available: www.geocities.com/aga_10/religiesiratiune.htm).

Rabb, J. Douglas, and Richardson, J. Michael. 2003. "Russian Existentialism and Vampire Slayage: A Shestovian Key to the Power and Popularity of *Buffy the Vampire Slayer*." In the archive of talks from the Slayage conference on *Buffy the Vampire Slayer*. Available: http://www.slayage.tv/SCBtVS_Archive/Talks/Rabb-Richardson. pdf.

Rambo, Elizabeth. 2004. "'Lessons' for Season Seven of *Buffy the Vampire Slayer*." *Slayage: The Online International Journal of Buffy Studies* 11/12. Available: http://slayage. tv/essays/slayage11_12/Rambo.htm.

Reed, Joseph W. 2003. "For a Newer Rite Is Here: *Buffy the Vampire Slayer*." *Refractory: A Journal of Entertainment Media* 2. Available: http://pandora.nla.gov.au/pan/30981/ 20030512/www.sfca.unimelb.edu.au/refractory/journalissues/index.htm#jrl.

Resnick, Laura. 2003. "The Good, the Bad, and the Ambivalent." In Yeffeth, 54–64.

Riess, Jana. 2004. "The Monster Inside: Taming the Darkness within Ourselves." *Slayage: The Online International Journal of Buffy Studies* 11/12. Available: http://slayage.tv/ essays/slayage11_12/Riess.htm.

Riess, Jana. 2004. *What Would Buffy Do?: The Vampire Slayer as Spiritual Guide*. San Francisco: John Wiley & Sons.

Rogers, Brett, and Scheidel, Walter. 2004. "Driving Stakes, Driving Cars: California Car Culture, Sex, and Identity in *BtVS*." *Slayage: The Online International Journal of*

Buffy Studies 13/14. Available: http://slayage.tv/essays/slayage13_14/Rogers_Schei del.htm.

Romesburg, Rod. 2006. "Regeneration through Vampirism: *Buffy the Vampire Slayer*'s New Frontier." *Slayage: The Online International Journal of Buffy Studies* 19. Available: http://slayage.tv.

Ros, Giada Da. 2004. "When, Where, and How Much Is *Buffy* a Soap Opera?" *Slayage: The Online International Journal of Buffy Studies* 13/14. Available: http://slayage.tv/essays/slayage13_14/Da_Ros.htm.

Rose, Anita. 2002. "Of Creatures and Creators: Buffy Does Frankenstein." In Wilcox and Lavery, 133–142.

Rosenfeld, Lawrence B., and Wynns, Scarlet L. 2003. "Perceived Values and Social Support in *Buffy the Vampire Slayer*." *Slayage: The Online International Journal of Buffy Studies* 10. Available: http://slayage.tv/essays/slayage10/Rosenfeld_&_Wynns.htm.

Rust, Linda. 2003. "Welcome to the House of Fun: Buffy Fanfiction as a Hall of Mirrors." *Refractory: A Journal of Entertainment Media* 2. Available: http://pandora.nla. gov.au/pan/30981/20030512/www.sfca.unimelb.edu.au/refractory/journalissues/index.htm#lr.

Sakal, Gregory J. 2003. "No Big Win: Themes of Sacrifice, Salvation, and Redemption." In South 2003a, 239–253.

Salisbury, Neal. 1996. "Squanto (Tisquantum)." In *Encyclopedia of North American Indians*, edited by E. E. Hoxie. Boston and New York: Houghton Mifflin, 605–607.

Sartre, Jean-Paul. 1943. *L'Être et le Néant: Essai d'Ontologie Phénoménologique*. Paris: Librarie Gallimard.

Sartre, Jean-Paul. 1946. *No Exit*. Translated by Stuart Gilbert in *No Exit and Three Other Plays*. New York: Random House.

Sartre, Jean-Paul. 1947. "The Republic of Silence." Translated by R. Guthrie in *The Republic of Silence*, edited by A.J. Liebling. New York: Harcourt, Brace.

Sartre, Jean-Paul. 1949. *The Emotions: Outline of a Theory*. Translated by Bernard Frechtman. New York: Philosophical Library.

Sartre, Jean-Paul. 1961. *The Psychology of the Imagination*. Translated by anon. New York: Citadel Press.

Sartre, Jean-Paul. 1963. *Saint Genet: Actor and Martyr*. Translated by Bernard Frechtman. New York: New American Library.

Sartre, Jean-Paul. 1964. *Nausea*. Translated by Lloyd Alexander. New York: New Directions.

Sartre, Jean-Paul. 1972. *Being and Nothingness: A Phenomenological Essay on Ontology*. Translated by Hazel E. Barnes. New York: Washington Square Press.

Sartre, Jean-Paul. 1976. *Les Mains Sales*. Paris: Gallimard.

Sartre, Jean-Paul. 1989. *No Exit and Three Other Plays*. New York: Vintage International Edition.

Sartre, Jean-Paul. 1989. *No Exit*. Translated by Stuart Gilbert. In Jean-Paul Sartre, *No Exit and Three Other Plays*, 1–46.

Sartre, Jean-Paul. 1989. *Dirty Hands*. Translated by Lionel Abel. In Jean-Paul Sartre, *No Exit and Three Other Plays*, 125–241.

Sartre, Jean-Paul. 2001. "Existentialism and Humanism." In *Jean-Paul Satrre: Basic Writings*, edited by Stephen Prince. New York: Routledge, 27–38.

Saxey, Esther. 2001. "Staking a Claim: The Series and Its Slash Fan-Fiction." In Kaveney 2001, 187–210.

Sayer, Karen. 2001. "'It Wasn't Our World Anymore. They Made It Theirs': Reading Space and Place." In Kaveney 2001, 98–119.

Schlosser, Eric. 2002. *Fast Food Nation: The Dark Side of the All-American Meal*. New York: Harper Collins.

Schlozman, Steven C. 2000. "Vampires and Those Who Slay Them: Using the Television Program *Buffy the Vampire Slayer* in Adolescent Therapy and Psychodynamic Education." *Academic Psychology* 24.1: 49–54.

Schudt, Karl. 2003. "Also Sprach Faith: The Problem of the Happy Rogue Vampire Slayer." In South 2003a, 20–34.

Scott, Suzanne. 2003. "All Bark and No Bite: Siring the Neutered Vampire on Buffy the Vampire Slayer." In *Vampires: Myths and Metaphors of Enduring Evil,* edited by Carla T. Kungl. Oxford, UK: Inter-Disciplinary Press, 125–28.

Shakespeare, William. 1997a. *Macbeth.* In *The Riverside Shakespeare,* 2nd ed., edited by G. Blakemore Evans, et al.

Shakespeare, William. 1997b. *The Tempest.* In *The Riverside Shakespeare,* 2nd ed., edited by G. Blakemore Evans, et al.

Sharpe, Matthew. 2003. "Is Buffy a Lacanian? Or, What Is Enlightenment?" *Refractory: A Journal of Entertainment Media* 2. Available: http://pandora.nla.gov.au/pan/30981/20030512/www.sfca.unimelb.edu.au/refractory/journalissues/index.htm#ms.

Shestov, Lev. 1975. *In Job's Balances: On the Sources of the Eternal Truths.* Translated by Camilla Coventry and C.A. Macartney. Athens: Ohio University Press.

Shestov, Lev. 1977. *All Things are Possible and Penultimate Words and Other Essays,* edited by Bernard Martin. Athens: Ohio University Press.

Shestov, Lev. 1968a. *Athens and Jerusalem.* Translated by Bernard Martin. New York: Simon and Schuster.

Shestov, Lev. 1968b. *Potestas Clavium.* Translated by Bernard Martin. Athens: Ohio University Press.

Shuttleworth, Ian. 2001. "'They Always Mistake Me for the Character I Play!': Transformation, Identity and Role-Playing in the Buffyverse (and a Defence of Fine Acting)." In Kaveney 2001, 211–236.

Siemann, Catherine. 2002. "Darkness Falls on the Endless Summer: Buffy as Gidget for the Fin De SiÈcle." In Wilcox and Lavery, 120–129.

Simkin, Stevie. 2004a. "'Who Died and Made You John Wayne?': Anxious Masculinity in *Buffy the Vampire Slayer.*" *Slayage: The Online International Journal of Buffy Studies* 11/12. Available: http://slayage.tv/essays/slayage11_12/Simkin_Wayne.htm.

Simkin, Stevie. 2004b. "'You Hold Your Gun Like a Sissy Girl': Firearms and Anxious Masculinity in *Buffy the Vampire Slayer.*" *Slayage: The Online International Journal of Buffy Studies* 11/12. Available: http://slayage.tv/essays/slayage11_12/Simkin_Gun.htm.

Skwire, Sarah E. 2002. "Whose Side Are You on, Anyway? Children, Adults, and the Use of Fairy Tales in *Buffy.*" In Wilcox and Lavery, 195–204.

Slayage: The Online International Journal of Buffy Studies. Edited by David Lavery and Rhonda Wilcox. Available: http://www.slayage.tv.

South, James B. 2001. "'All Torment, Trouble, Wonder, and Amazement Inhabits Here': The Vicissitudes of Technology in *Buffy the Vampire Slayer.*" *Journal of American and Comparative Cultures* 24.1/2: 93–102.

South, James B., ed. 2003a. *"Buffy the Vampire Slayer" and Philosophy: Fear and Trembling in Sunnydale.* Chicago: Open Court.

South, James B. 2003b. "'My God, It's Like a Greek Tragedy': Willow Rosenberg and Human Irrationality." In South 2003a, 131–146.

South, James. 2004. "On the Philosophical Consistency of Season 7." *Slayage: The Online International Journal of Buffy Studies* 13/14. Available: http://slayage.tv/essays/slayage13_14/South.htm.

Spah, Victoria. 2002. "Ain't Love Grand: Spike & Courtly Love." *Slayage: The Online International Journal of Buffy Studies* 5. Available: http://www.slayage.tv/essays/slayage5/spah.htm.

Spicer, Arwen. 2002. "'Love's Bitch but Man Enough to Admit It': Spike's Hybridized Gender." *Slayage: The Online International Journal of Buffy Studies* 7. Available: http://www.slayage.tv/essays/slayage7/Spicer.htm. Dec. 2, 2003.

Stafford, Nikki. 2004. *Once Bitten: An Unofficial Guide to the World of Angel.* Toronto: ECW Press.

Stengel, Wendy A.F.G. 2001. "Synergy and Smut: The Brand in Official and Unofficial *Buffy the Vampire Slayer* Communities of Interest." *Slayage: The Online International Journal of Buffy Studies* 4. Available: http://www.slayage.tv/essays/slayage4/stengel. htm.

Stern, Alfred. 1967. *Sartre: His Philosophy and Existential Psychoanalysis.* New York: Dell.

Stevens, Katy. 2002. "Inside the Buffyverse 01: Hum of the Box." Dec 8. Available: http: //www.vibewire.net/articles.php?id=1318.

Stevens, Katy. 2003a. "Inside the Buffyverse 02: Spike as Spectacle." Jan 12. Available: http://www.vibewire.net/articles.php?id=1412.

Stevens, Katy. 2003b. "Inside the Buffyverse 03: Buffy's Spectatorial Dilemma." Apr 7. Available: http://www.vibewire.net/articles.php?id=1524.

Stevens, Katy. 2003c. "Inside the Buffyverse 04a: Defending Season 6 (Pt 1)." Aug 7. Available: http://vibewire.net/articles.php?id=1700.

Stevens, Katy. 2003d. "Inside the Buffyverse 04b: Defending Season 6 (Pt 2)." Nov 16. Available: http://vibewire.net/articles.php?id=2167.

Stevens, Katy. 2004. "Bronzers, Breakaway Pop Hits and Karaoke: Popular Music in the Whedonverse." Jossology website. Available: http://www.sushipop.net/buffyverse/ popmusic.htm.

Stevenson, Gregory. 2003. *Televised Morality: The Case of Buffy the Vampire Slayer.* Lanham: Hampton Books.

Stincelli, Rebecca. 2004. *Suicide By Cop: Victims from Both Sides of the Badge.* Folsom, California: Interviews & Interrogations Institute.

Stowell, Louie. 2004. "I've Died Twice: Absurdity, Death and the Body in Buffy the Vampire Slayer." *Stimulus Respond* 1. Available: http:/www.stimulusrespond.com.

Stroud, Scott R. 2003. "A Kantian Analysis of Moral Judgment in Buffy the Vampire Slayer." In South 2003a, 185–194.

"Suicide by Cop" Websites:
Justice Institute of BC. Available: http://www.jibc.bc.ca/police/main/PIIMIC/2_Sui cide/police_inflicted.htm. Accessed Oct. 9, 2005.

http://www.suicidebycop.com. Accessed Oct. 9, 2005.

http://suicideandmentalhealthassociationinternational.org/libsuibycop.html. Accessed Oct. 9, 2005.

Police Stressline. 2003. Available: http://www.geocities.com/~halbrown/suicide_by_ cop_1.html. Accessed Oct. 9, 2005.

http://www.policeone.com/suicide-by-cop. Accessed Oct. 9, 2005.

Symonds, Gwyn. 2003. "'Bollocks!': Spike Fans and Reception of Buffy the Vampire Slayer." *Refractory: A Journal of Entertainment Media* 2. Available: http://pandora.nla.gov.au/ pan/30981/20030512/www.sfca.unimelb.edu.au/refractory/journalissues/index. htm#gs1.

Symonds, Gwyn. 2004. "'Solving Problems with Sharp Objects': Female Empowerment, Sex and Violence in Buffy the Vampire Slayer." *Slayage: The Online International Journal of Buffy Studies* 11/12. Available: http://www.slayage.tv/essays/slayage11_12.Symonds. htm.

Symonds, Gwyn. 2005. "'A Little More Soul Than is Written': James Marsters' Performance of Spike and the Ambiguity of Evil in Sunnydale." *Slayage: The Online International Journal of Buffy Studies* 16. Available: http://slayage.tv/essays/slayage16/ Symonds.htm.

Tabron, Judith. 2004. "Girl on Girl Politics: Willow/Tara and New Approaches to Media Fandom." *Slayage: The Online International Journal of Buffy Studies* 13/14. Available: http://slayage.tv/essays/slayage13_14/Tabron.htm.

Tassone, Janelle. 2003. "Buffy: The Evolution of a Valley Girl." *Refractory: A Journal of Entertainment Media* 2. Available: http://pandora.nla.gov.au/pan/30981/20030512/www.sfca.unimelb.edu.au/refractory/journalissues/index.htm#jt.

Taylor, Charles. 1999. "The WB's Big Daddy Condescension." Salon.com 26 May. Available: http://www.salon.com/ent/log/1999/05/26/buffy_rant/index.html.

Thompson, Jim. 2003. "'Just a Girl': Feminism, Postmodernism and Buffy the Vampire Slayer." *Refractory: A Journal of Entertainment Media* 2. Available: http://pandora.nla.gov.au/pan/30981/20030512/www.sfca.unimelb.edu.au/refractory/journalissues/index.htm#jtla.

Tjardes, Sue. 2003. "'If You're Not Doing Something Wrong': Textual and Viewer Constructions of Faith, the Vampire Slayer." In Early and Kennedy, 66–77.

Tomlinson, Martin. 2004. "A Question of Faith: Responsibility, Murder, and Redemption in *Buffy the Vampire Slayer*." *Chrestomathy* 3. Available: http://www.cofc.edu/chrestomathy/vol3/tomlinson.pdf.

Tonkin, Boyd. 2001. "Entropy as Demon: Buffy in Southern California." In Kaveney 2001, 37–52.

Topping, Keith. 2004. *The Complete Slayer: An Unofficial and Unauthorised Guide to Every Episode of "Buffy the Vampire Slayer."* London: Virgin Books.

Treatment Advocacy Center. 2005. "Briefing Paper: Law Enforcement and People with Severe Mental Illnesses." Available: http://www.psychlaws.org/BriefingPapers/BP16.htm. Accessed Oct. 9, 2005.

Turnbull, Sue. 2003. "Teaching Buffy: The Curriculum and the Text in Media Studies." *Continuum: Journal of Media and Cultural Studies* 17.1: 19–31.

Turnbull, Sue. 2004. "'Not Just Another Buffy Paper': Towards an Aesthetics of Television." *Slayage: The Online International Journal of Buffy Studies* 13/14. Available: http://slayage.tv/essays/slayage13_14/Turnbull.htm.

Turnbull, Sue. 2005. "Moments of Inspiration: Performing Spike." *European Journal of Cultural Studies* 8.3: 367–373.

VanZandt, Clinton. No date. "Suicide by Cop." Available: http://www.threatlink.com/pr/publications/Suicide%20by%20Cop-VZA.pdf. Accessed Oct. 9, 2005.

Vint, Sherryl. 2002. "'Killing Us Softly'? A Feminist Search for the 'Real' Buffy." *Slayage: The Online International Journal of Buffy Studies* 5. Available: http://www.slayage.tv/essays/slayage4/stengel.htm.

Wall, Brian, and Zryd, Michael. 2001. "Vampire Dialectics: Knowledge, Institutions and Labour." In Kaveney 2001, 53–77.

Wand, Bernard. 1962/1963. "Intelligibility and Free Choice." *Dialogue* 1: 239–358.

Wandless, William. 2001. "Undead Letters: Searches and Researches in Buffy the Vampire Slayer." *Slayage: The Online International Journal of Buffy Studies* 1. Available: http://www.slayage.tv/essays/slayage1/wandless.htm.

Warnock, Mary. 1966. *The Philosphy of Sartre.* London: Hutchinson University Library.

Waters, Frank. 1963. *Book of the Hopi.* New York: Ballantine Books.

Watt-Evans, Lawrence. 2003. "Matchmaking on the Hellmouth." In Yeffeth, 188–194.

Weaver, Jace. 1996. "American Indians and Native Americans: Reinhold Niebuhr, Historiography and Indigenous Peoples." In *From Our Eyes: Learning from Indigenous Peoples,* edited by Sylvia O'Meara et al. Toronto: Garamond Press.

Weaver, Jace. 1997. *That the People Might Live: Native American Literature and Native Community.* New York: Oxford University Press.

Wernham, James C. S. 1968. *Two Russian Thinkers: Berdyaev and Shestov.* Toronto: University of Toronto Press.

West, Dave. 2001. "'Concentrate on the Kicking Movie': Buffy and East Asian Cinema." In Kaveney 2001, 166–186.

West, Michelle Segara. 2003. "For the Love of Riley." In Yeffeth, 65–71.

Westerfeld, Scott. 2003. "A Slayer Comes to Town." In Yeffeth, 30–40.

Wilcox, Rhonda V. 2001. "'There Will Never Be a Very Special Buffy": Buffy and the Monsters of Teen Life." *Slayage: The Online International Journal of Buffy Studies* 2. Available: http://www.slayage.tv/essays/slayage2/wilcox.htm.

Wilcox, Rhonda V. 2002a. "'Every Night I Save You': Buffy, Spike, Sex and Redemption." *Slayage: The Online International Journal of Buffy Studies* 5. Available: http://www.slayage.tv/essays/slayage5/wilcox.htm.

Wilcox, Rhonda V. 2002b. "'Who Died and Made Her the Boss?': Patterns of Mortality in Buffy the Vampire Slayer." In Wilcox and Lavery, 3–17.

Wilcox, Rhonda V. 2002c. "T.S. Eliot Comes to Television: Buffy's 'Restless.'" *Slayage: The Online International Journal of Buffy Studies* 7. Available: http://www.slayage.tv/essays/slayage7/Wilcox.htm.

Wilcox, Rhonda. 2005. *Why Buffy Matters: The Art of "Buffy the Vampire Slayer."* London and New York: I.B. Tauris.

Wilcox, Rhonda V., and Lavery, David, eds. 2002. *Fighting the Forces: What's at Stake in Buffy the Vampire Slayer.* Lanham, Maryland: Rowman Littlefield.

Williams, J. P. 2002. "Choosing Your Own Mother: Mother-Daughter Conflicts in *Buffy*." In Wilcox and Lavery, 61–72.

Williams, Rebecca. 2004. "'It's About Power': Spoilers and Fan Hierarchy in On-Line Buffy Fandom." *Slayage: The Online International Journal of Buffy Studies* 11/12. Available: http://www.slayage.tv/Numbers/slayage11_12.htm.

Williamson, Milly. 2005a. "Spike, Sex and Subtext: Intertextual Portrayals of the Sympathetic Vampire on Television." *European Journal of Cultural Studies* 8.3: 289–311.

Williamson, Milly. 2005b. *The Lure of the Vampire: Gender, Fiction and Fandom from Bram Stoker to Buffy.* London and New York: Wallflower Press.

Williamson, Milly, and Amy-Chinn, Dee, eds. 2005. "The Vampire Spike in Text and Fandom: Unsettling Oppositions in Buffy the Vampire Slayer." *European Journal of Cultural Studies* 8.3: 275–288.

Wilson, Edward F., et al. 1998. "Homicide or Suicide: The Killing of Suicidal Persons by Law Enforcement Officers," *Journal of Forensic Sciences,* 43.1. American Academy of Forensic Sciences.

Wilson, James. 1999. *The Earth Shall Weep: A History of Native America.* New York: Atlantic Monthly Press.

Wilson, Steve. 2001. "'Laugh, Spawn of Hell, Laugh.'" In Kaveney 2001, 78–97.

Winslade, J. Lawton. 2001. "Teen Witches, Wiccans, and 'Wanna-Blessed-Be's': Pop-Culture Magic in Buffy the Vampire Slayer." *Slayage: The Online International Journal of Buffy Studies* 1. Available: http://www.slayage.tv/essays/slayage1/winslade.htm.

Wisker, Gina. 2001. "Vampires and School Girls: High School Highjinks on the Hellmouth in Buffy the Vampire Slayer." *Slayage: The Online International Journal of Buffy Studies* 2. Available: http://www.slayage.tv/essays/slayage2/wisker.htm.

Wisniewski, Christopher. 2003. "The (Un)Bearable Darkness of Buffy." Available: http://www.poppolitics.com/articles/2003-05-20-buffydark.shtml.

Wright, John C. 2004. "Just Shove Him in the Engine, or The Role of Chivalry in *Firefly*." In Espenson, 155–167.

Yarbro, Chelsea Quinn 2003. "Lions, Gazelles and Buffy." In Yeffeth, 48–53.

Yeffeth, Glenn, ed. 2003. *Seven Seasons of Buffy: Science Fiction and Fantasy Writers Discuss Their Favorite Television Show.* Dallas: BenBella.

Yeffeth, Glenn, ed. 2004. *Five Seasons of Angel: Science Fiction and Fantasy Writers Discuss Their Favorite Vampire.* Dallas: BenBella.

Zacharek, Stephanie. 2001a. "The Hills Are Alive with the Sound Of... Vampire Slaying!" Salon.com 7 Nov. Available: http://dir.salon.com/ent/tv/feature/2001/11/07/buffy_musical/index.html.

Zacharek, Stephanie. 2001b. "Buffy's Will-to-Power." Salon.com 28 Nov. Available: http://dir.salon.com/sex/feature/2001/11/28/buffy/index.html.

Zacharek, Stephanie. 2002a. "Willow, Destroyer of Worlds." Salon.com 22 May. Available: http://archive.salon.com/ent/tv/feature/2002/05/22/buffy.

Zacharek, Stephanie. 2002b. "Modern and Mythical Sexuality in *Buffy the Vampire Slayer*." Salon.com 9 Nov. Available: http://archive.salon.com/ent/tv/feature/2002/11/09/buffy_paper/index_np.html.

Zettel, Sarah. 2003. "When Did the Scoobies Become Insiders?" In Yeffeth, 109–115.

Zweerink, Amanda, and Gatson, Sarah N. 2002. "www.Buffy.Com: Cliques, Boundaries, and Hierarchies in an Internet Community." In Wilcox and Lavery, 239–250.

Zynda, Lyle. 2004. "We're All Just Floating in Space." In Espenson, 85–95.

Index